W9-BSH-333

Defending Their
Own in the Cold

· ·

Latinos in Chicago and the Midwest

Series Editors
Frances R. Aparicio, University of Illinois at Chicago
Pedro Cabán, State University of New York
Juan Mora-Torres, De Paul University
Maria de los Angeles Torres, University of Illinois at Chicago

*A list of books in the series appears
at the end of this book.*

Defending Their Own in the Cold

The Cultural Turns
of U.S. Puerto Ricans

Marc Zimmerman

University of Illinois Press
Urbana, Chicago, and Springfield

First Illinois paperback, 2020
© 2011 by the Board of Trustees
of the University of Illinois
All rights reserved
Manufactured in the United States of America
1 2 3 4 5 C P 5 4 3 2 1
∞ This book is printed on acid-free paper.

A project of the Latin American and Latino/a Activities and Studies
Arena—LACASA (Director, Marc Zimmerman) of the program of World
Cultures and Literature, Department of Modern and Classical Language,
University of Houston.

The author wishes to acknowledge the financial support from the Small
Grants Program of the University of Houston's Division of Research.
Thanks to Elías Carmona, Elizam Escobar, Ramón Flores, Adal Maldonado,
Juan Sánchez, and Gamaliel Ramírez for their permission to produce their
images. They retain their copyrights for any reproduction of the images
herein.

The Library of Congress cataloged the cloth edition as follows:
Zimmerman, Marc, 1939–
Defending their own in the cold : the cultural turns of
U.S. Puerto Ricans / Marc Zimmerman.
    p.   cm. — (Latinos in Chicago and the Midwest)
Includes bibliographical references and index.
ISBN 978-0-252-03646-0 (cloth)
1. Puerto Ricans—United States—Intellectual life. 2. Puerto Ricans—
United States—Ethnic identity. 3. Puerto Ricans—United States—
Attitudes. 4. Arts, Puerto Rican—Social aspects—United States.
5. Puerto Ricans—Illinois—Chicago—Intellectual life. 6. Puerto Ricans—
Illinois—Chicago—Ethnic identity. 7. Puerto Ricans—Illinois—Chicago—
Attitudes. 8. Arts, Puerto Rican—Social asepcts—Illinois—Chicago.
I. Title.
E184.P85Z56   2011
305.868'7295073—dc22   2011014506

Paperback ISBN 978-0-252-08558-1
E-Book ISBN 978-0-252-09349-4

. . . .

Thanks to my many Puerto Rican guides—among them:

Ramón Luis Acevedo	Elizam Escobar	Héctor Nieves
Frances Aparicio	Jorge Félix	Luis and Raúl Ortiz
Eduardo Arocho	Juan Flores	Miguel Palacios
Sonia Báez Hernández	Migdalia Galarza	Emilio Pantojas y Luz Acevedo
Efraín Barradas	Margarita González	Ángel Quintero Rivera
Inés Bocanegra	David Hernández	Gamaliel Ramírez
Juanita Camacho	Nicolás Kanellos	Maricarmen Ramírez
Sheila Candelario	Ada López	Sara María Rivas
Ralph Cintrón	José López	Juan Carlos Rodríguez
Luis Felipe Díaz	Ramón López	Gini y Meca Sorrentini
Virgilio Díaz	Enrique Marcano	Diana Vélez
Juan Duchesne Winter	Madie and Roberto Márquez	Iris Zavala

To my many Puerto Rican students (who were also teachers of mine) at the University of Illinois at Chicago and Puerto Rico–Río Piedras.

Of course, thanks to Esther and Samuel Soler—Nancy, Jeannette, and María del Pilar. Alex and Eddie, Jackie and Tiffany, Sammy and Sammyra (nietos) Eulalia, Daisy and Leo Ramos, Ángel, Angelica, Lucy, Luisa, Salvador, Cindo, Migdalia y Raúl, Danny, Saúl, and the entire Soler-Ramos clan.

Above all, to the memory of Michael Piazza, Otto Pikaza, and other Puerto Rican–related friends and family members now gone:

Rane Arroyo	Pedro Pietri
James Blaut	Fito Ramos
Frank Bonilla	Silvia Ramos
Emilio Díaz González	Salima Rivera
Milagros López	Frank Sánchez
Samuel Medina	Lorenzo Soler
Carmelo Muñiz	

Finally, to those *muchos* I have forgotten to include (forgive me if you can and add your names here).

Contents

Preface

This book brings together a group of texts drafted at different moments over the past several years that constitute much of what I have come to understand about U.S. Puerto Rican culture and literature in the twenty-some-odd years I have been privileged to live among Puerto Ricans both in Chicago and on the island, with some excursions to New York and elsewhere. As the introduction to this volume indicates, I am a secularized "left-leaning" North American Jewish student of Latin American and Latino culture who has had several unique opportunities to experience U.S. Puerto Rican life, letters, and culture, though always from outside, always as a beginning student, as a non–Puerto Rican—always with a certain sense of humility.

Married to a Puerto Rican woman and part of a Puerto Rican family for years, I have had that privileged inside/outside place that has enabled me to observe and, hopefully, understand at least some aspects of Puerto Rican life; I have experienced family tragedies that are very much part of the Puerto Rican diasporic experience and its effects; I have had abiding friendships and commitments. What I present here modestly is a group of essays (two of them written for specific occasions, the others representing efforts to come to grips with a field others have developed) that, taken together, give some sense of a range of understandings and that, over time, have come to constitute a book.

In the introduction, I explain something of the occasions that brought forth different texts. Here in this preface, I simply wish to indicate the sources for the essays that are here reedited, updated, and published. I include the following list, with thanks to the diverse publishing outlets:

Chapter 1: "Erasure, Imposition and Crossover of Puerto Ricans and Chicanos in U.S. Film and Music Culture," *Latino Studies* 1, no. 1 (March 2003): 115–23.

Chapter 2: "Puerto Rico 98: One Hundred Years and Three Artists," *Que Ondee Sola* 26, nos. 4–5 (1998): 14–32—with some extrapolations from Marc Zimmerman. *Sueños de los pueblos/Village Dreams and Dreamers* (Chicago: LACASA/Collage de las Américas, 1998). A translation of my contribution to the section on Ramón López also appeared as "Ramón López: Tejiendo una plenitud/Trazando una invasión," Catalog supplement for the artist's one-man show at Galería de las Américas, San Juan, Puerto Rico, April 1998. Part 1 of the essay also involves some extrapolations from MZ, "Isla más isla: Puerto Rico, Vieques, y la descolonización cultural: Un collage montado con la ayuda de Elías Adasme, Arcadio Díaz Quiñones, y Agustín Laó-Montes," a paper presented at a panel on Puerto Rican Art and Decolonization at the Viequethon, Vieques, Puerto Rico, May 2002.

Chapter 3: "U.S. Puerto Rican Literature in Evolution," Puerto Rican Studies Association Conference, Chicago, 2003—updated and with extrapolations of the Puerto Rican materials from my book, *U.S. Latino Literature: An Essay and Annotated Bibliography* (Chicago: MARCH/Abrazo Press, 1992).

Chapter 4: "Poetas puertorriqueños en Chicago," *Puerto Rico Caribe: Zonas poéticas del trauma,* ed. Juan Duchesne Winter, in *Revista Iberoamericana* 5, no. 229 (Oct.–Dic. 2009): 1003–36. Updated/revised Spanish-language version of "Defending their Own in the Cold: Puerto Rican Poets in Chicago," *Latino Studies Journal* 1, no. 3 (DePaul University) (September 1990): 39-58.

Chapter 5: "Dancing from Puerto Rican New York to Anglo Illinois: The Poetry of Carmen Pursifull," an expanded version of "Carmen Pursifull" in Kanellos, ed., 2008, 940–42.

Chapter 6: "Miguel Barnet and *La vida real."* Paper presented at a panel on Miguel Barnet chaired by Elzbieta Sklodowska, Latin American Studies Association conference, Washington, D.C., September 1995.

Acknowledgments

I wish to thank Esther Soler, her daughters Nancy, Jeannette, and Pilar, and her brother Samuel, as well as other relatives and friends, for showing me how to at least begin understanding Puerto Rican representation, and for putting up with my efforts. My thanks to the Latin American and Latino Studies program of the University of Illinois at Chicago for helping me get started, and offering me the opportunity to teach Puerto Rican texts and themes to Chicago Puerto Rican and Latino students; and of course to the students, who taught me so much. Thanks also to the Department of Modern and Classical Languages and our World Cultures and Literatures program, as well as to the Small Grants committee of the Division of Research of the University of Houston for providing the funding that made the completion of this book possible.

Nicolás Kanellos made fierce commentaries about the penultimate versions of the first four chapters of this book—commentaries that changed many things and, in several cases, are incorporated in the book version set forth herein (designated as "NK"). Kanellos's unsparing read clearly helped to enrich this effort—though I failed to follow all his advice and I am fully responsible for any errors, failures of understanding, and false or questionable steps taken. Thanks are due to two of Kanellos's students: María Teresa Rojas and Luziris Turi helped by providing names and a bibliography about several writers during the period from 1920 to the 1960s (see chapter 3, note 3). I wish finally to thank the anonymous readers of my original text, as well as another reader, Ben Pacheco (all three raised issues leading to several changes in my introduction and the book as a whole). I also wish to thank my indexer, Jenni Wiggins, as well as Joan Catapano, Tad Ringo, and the entire staff at the University of Illinois Press.

Thanks to Elizam Escobar, Ramón López, Juan Sánchez, and Gamaliel Ramírez for granting me permission to produce their art work—and thanks to Elías Carmona as well as Eduardo Arocho and the *Que Ondee Sola* journal editor Xavier L. Burgos for their help with the image and caption credits for chapter 2. Finally, my thanks to the Puerto Rican people in Chicago and New York, in San Juan and Quebradillas, including the artists and critics among them, who taught me so much. The dedicatory page of this book mentions several friends and relatives living and dead (please forgive me for omissions!). But above all this book is dedicated to the memory of my former director and friend, Otto Pikaza, who more than anyone helped secure my professional life and who always fought the good fight for Puerto Ricans, Latinos, and others he saw as oppressed. With Michael Piazza's sudden death, this book is also dedicated to him as one of my closest non–Puerto Rican friends and collaborators orienting me to Puerto Rican art and especially to the life and work of Elizam Escobar. I miss Otto and Michael very much, and I include several of Michael's fine comments about key images from an article he wrote (Piazza 1998), accompanying mine in the original *Que Ondee Sola* issue from which chapter 2 is drawn.

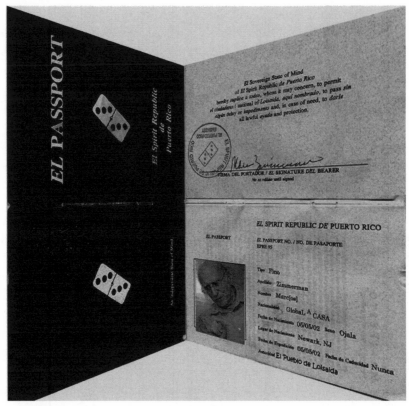

Copy of El Puerto Rican Passport issued to Marc Zimmerman by Rev. Pedro Pietri
during the Viequethon, April 2002—a three-day festival of poetry and music
to protest the U.S. Navy's occupation of the island of Vieques, Puerto Rico,
coordinated by El Puerto Rican Embassy. For more on El Puerto Rican Passport—
a concept of Adal Maldonado, Eduardo Figueroa, and Rev. Pietri, designed by
Adal Maldonado (1994)—see Acosta Belén and Santiago 2006, 215; also see
www.elpuertoricanembassy.org.

Introduction

Puerto Rican Erasures

Just a few years ago, after three decades of relating to Latin American and Latino worlds, and after having been married to a Soler-Ramos from Puerto Rico,
I remembered a Ramos in my high school class in Elizabeth, New Jersey. Check-
ing our yearbook, I saw a young man who looked very much like my Nuyorican
nephew, Danny.

Puerto Ricans had been working in cigar manufactories and on the docks for
decades; ever-growing numbers had been settling in New York and New Jersey for
some years—*Manos a la obra* was well in march. Puerto Ricans and Mexicans had
been working in New Jersey zinc mines since the 1940s; they mixed with Mexicans
in the tomato and cranberry fields near Camden;[1] many were working with or for
Jews in New York's garment industry, and even in my hometown of Elizabeth, New
Jersey. But the growing "Latino thing" was not on my radar screen, which was centered on my Jewish world and expanding toward Italians and African Americans.
I do not sense it made much of a dent on my parents' world beyond the rumbas,
mambos, and cha-chas they loved to dance so much.

I was not alone in my epistemological blockage, this systematic and constant
erasure of the Puerto Rican and Latino world around me. Only years later would I
ask about that Carlos between William and Williams; only years later would I realize that my Puerto Rican wife could not relate to Woody Allen's movies, because
the great film poet and jazz lover of New York only presents African Americans
as waiters and hookers. At a time of the growing Puerto-Ricanization and Latinization of New York, at a time when Puerto Ricans by the thousands, and then
Dominicans, Colombians, and Mexicans were arriving, transforming New York and
the United States, so very few Latinos had entered his representation of the city
he so Gershwinly loved.

How can we explain this absence, or almost total erasure? Well, not quite total: There was of course that great stereotyping machine, *Bananas,* with most of the Cuban scenes actually filmed in Puerto Rico and with several Puerto Rican actors, including a young Jacobo Morales as a revolutionary. A blind Puerto Rican ventriloquist appears briefly in *Broadway Danny Rose,* and Tito Puente conducts a Latino band for a second in *Radio Days,* but otherwise there's hardly a Puerto Rican to be found in Allen's opus. Indeed, I would argue that the Great Woody's representational amnesia, though clearly part of a U.S. Jewish imaginary, is indicative of a more general syndrome involving the U.S. erasure of Latinos that only demographic pressure and consumer potential have gradually and only selectively eroded.

Of course, Puerto Ricans might be justified in forgetting Woody, but not all Puerto Ricans have done so. I believe there is not a film by Jacobo Morales that does not reveal Allen's post-*Bananas* influence. And in 1974 a young, apparently now failed, Nuyorican comic, Luis Caballero, tried explicitly to present himself as a Boricua Woody in a very negative and painful film, *The Puerto Rican Mambo: Not a Love Song,* specifically about the constant social erasure of himself and other Puerto Ricans—even by other Latinos. Why is it that of all Latinos, Caballero asks at one point, we, the Puerto Ricans, are the ones who are least respected and have achieved the least? How is it possible, we might ask, that the racialization and stigmatization of Nuyoricans could reach such a level that Caballero could feel this way and project it throughout his film?

Clearly this negativity, this psychological state that Rene Marqués and others inaccurately dubbed as docility, is not part of any Jewish conspiracy, but rather a matter of internalized colonial and racial stigmatism that results in paralysis and explosive violence but also, in reaction, a certain creative verve we recognize in so many island- and U.S.-based writers and artists—in Miguel Piñero and Pedro Pietri, as well as José Luis González, Luis Rafael Sánchez, and Mayra Santos; in Antonio Martorell, Arnaldo Aroché, or Juan Sánchez; in Hector Lavoe and—why not?—Chayenne, Ricky Martin, Marc Anthony, India, and Jennifer Lopez. And how is it that other Latinos participate in the stigmatizing exercise—that Linda Chavez notes how excluding the dismal diaspora from Puerto Rico, most Latinos have fared well in their pursuit of the American dream; that such a "progressive" Latino popularizer like Earl Shorris (1992) provides such negative accounts of the U.S. Puerto Rican experience; that such a keen Latino critic like the late Juan Bruce-Navoa (1990) could see U.S. Puerto Rican literature and culture as superficial compared with Chicano profundities?

All this to say that my reference to Woody Allen is far from being an example of

"Jewish self hatred." Married into a Puerto Rican family that comes and goes from Chicago, New York, and Houston to the island, this secular and leftist American Jewish professor, critic, and sometime writer grew aware of Puerto Rican erasures, and ironically found when New York Puerto Ricans erased Chicanos (see chapter 1) and even Chicago Puerto Ricans (see chapter 4) and when U.S. Cubans erased U.S. Puerto Ricans (chapter 6).

This Book and the Particular Essays

This book is an effort at dis-erasure, focusing on what some U.S. Puerto Ricans have done in cultural, artistic, and literary work as an expression of lives lived and people attempting to create. It is not a thorough, systematic treatment of the themes evoked here, but rather a collection of essays and articles that somehow nevertheless end up constituting what I believe is a coherent, if sometimes oblique, look at key dimensions of U.S. Puerto Rican culture.

The various occasions and some of the themes connecting the different chapters deserve some special reference here. In effect, since my late-life introduction to things Puerto Rican, I have felt the wish to give some expression to what I have seen and at least partially understood. Weaned on Jewish perspectives found in Oscar Lewis's *La Vida* and Leonard Bernstein's *West Side Story* and then negative images of Puerto Rican migration from René Marqués, Pedro Juan Soto, José Luis González, and other writers of the Puerto Rican generation of 1940, I sought to understand Puerto Rican problems and join others in projecting a richer, and indeed more positive, image of U.S. Puerto Rican life—a vision that is critical and yet somehow redemptive. These chapters represent various points along the continuum of my projected effort.

Chapter 1 was written as a response to an essay by Frances Aparicio (2003) questioning the implications of Puerto Rican pop artists becoming marketed as Latinos. The paper and my commentary, along with a highly polemical response by Chicana critic and writer Alicia Gaspar de Alba, were presented at the conference inaugurating the journal *Latino Studies* and later appeared in the journal's first issue. I remember reading Aparicio's paper and thinking, "but Puerto Ricans have always portrayed Mexicans and Chicanos." So Jennifer Lopez doing Selena was not such a special thing after all. Or was it? Of course, uncovering the African dimension and the erased but still existent connections in Mexican/Chicano as well as U.S. Puerto Rican literature was inevitably a crucial theme in my understanding of things Latino and Puerto Rican. And so this would be one of the themes I would trace in my article. The response indeed constitutes an article of its own, however indebted to Aparicio's original. It was one of the most pleasurable articles I had written in years, causing me to recall so many films, so many moments, that are now part of my U.S. Puerto Rican and broader Latino repertory. However, the chapter is also the one that most directly enunciates the theme of U.S. Puerto Rican performativity in a world of Latinos and others.

Chapter 2 is an essay written to serve as a guide in relation to an art exhibit, Puerto Rico: 98, at Chicago's Puerto Rican Cultural Center and then at the Chicago Art Institute commemorating one hundred years of U.S. control over Puerto Rico and featuring visual meditations with respect to the Puerto Rican flag and the island's problematic nationhood. The published essay excluded the first section—a perhaps overly melodramatic reflection on Puerto Rican identity, which I later adapted and expanded to serve as part of a collage of reflections drafted for the Viequethon, a cultural/artistic "marathon" (April 2002) bringing Nuyorican poets and musicians together in solidarity with the eventually successful struggle to pressure the U.S. Navy off the island. One day I received a letter from Professor Sheila Candelario inviting me to participate as one of the intellectuals of the Viequethon, during some of the most charged days of the Vieques effort. Accompanying the letter was a list of outstanding Puerto Rican intellectuals invited to attend—and seeing that I was one of the few "Americanos" on that list, I knew I had to put aside all my plans and cares to make my participation possible. When my wife and I arrived at the Nuyorican Café in el Viejo San Juan to meet the group, I found the place crowded with young Nuyorican musicians and poets, many of them visiting their family's homeland for the first time. As I gave her a hug, I just could not resist. "Sheila," I asked, "where are the other intellectuals?" "Oh Marc, they couldn't make it," she told me. "What's more, most of the local ones will be celebrating the anniversary of *Claridad*,[2] so you're our intellectual." I virtually trembled and asked my wife how I might beg off. But she kicked me in the leg, to let me know that I could not back out. I felt a little better when Elizam Escobar, a Puerto Rican POW who served more than twenty years in prison as a convicted "terrorist," and Jan Sussler, his lawyer and friend, arrived, and then Ángel Quitero Rivera and his wife Margarita González came by. Then I was introduced to the famed Nuyorican poet Pedro Pietri, dressed in black as usual and tripping out poems as the night went on. The next day, on the road to Fajardo, the kids were shocked when I pointed to a corner, indicating that a granddaughter of mine lived down the street.

On Vieques they played music all night, and introduced me all around as "our intellectual." They seemed to like my talk well enough (Sheila helped me present it in as a semi-rap collage), shouting and shaking their hands. And then Jesús Papoleto Meléndez joined *el reverendo/poeta* Pietri in honoring me with a passport for Loisaida—the Lower East Side—a passport I carry to this day, even though the reverend/poet is no longer with us.[3] Because of the Vieques trip, I have restored the first part of the essay on the art exhibit, but in the more complex version I developed for my Viequethon presentation. As a son of the New Jersey extension of Gershwin's Jewish world, I felt the need to relive the Lower East Side connection, and it is clear to me that Vieques only intensified the issues evident in my background article of the Chicago Puerto Rican exhibit of 1998.

The third, largest, and most systematic chapter of the volume, on U.S. Puerto Rican literature, represents an elaboration and updating of a brief essay and many annotations I prepared for my book *U.S. Latino Literature* (1992). While attempting to cover many dimensions of Nuyorican literature (but also leaving out much), the original book had the virtue of including writers from Chicago and elsewhere. The version for this volume includes much updating in terms of books written from 1991 on, but its other, important new dimension is an effort to at least mention a number of the many Puerto Rican writers living in New York during the first half of the twentieth century. This pre-fifties turf has been primarily treated in function of progressive, working-class-related writers (Bernardo Vega, Jesús Colón, and Luisa Capetillo) as part of a search, initiated by Frank Bonilla,

Poet Pedro Pietri in the Viequethon. Vieques, Puerto Rico, April 2002. Photo by Esther Soler.

Juan Flores, and others in the Centro de Estudios Puertorriqueños of New York, to plot a history of Puerto Rican resistance in opposition to a vision of Puerto Rican docility and submission to some trumped-up culture of poverty.

One of the virtues of Nicolás Kanellos's Recovering the Hispanic Literary Heritage Project is to present us with as many voices as possible from a given community. At least in a couple of extended notes, this current version of my essay mentions several of the project's discoveries, and especially of Kanellos's students, Edwín Padilla and Maria Teresa Rojas-Vera, whose research on several, virtually forgotten and unknown writers gives us a fuller sense of the New York Puerto Rican community and its textual representations in the years prior to the emergence of the Nuyorican generation.

Drafted and published earlier than my more general "U.S. Puerto Rican" essay, chapter 4, on Chicago Rican poetry, was a pioneer effort in part inspired by Félix Padilla's important publications (1985 and 1987) on Chicago Latino and Rican experience (the essay was published in Padilla's *Latino Studies Journal*), to illuminate the work of writers who became more generally known among Latino literature students through a special issue of Kanellos's and Luis Davila's pioneering *Revista Chicano-Riqueña* (1977). Entitled *Nosotros,* this issue featured the visual as well as literary art of a group of cultural workers, mainly Puerto Ricans, involved in a city-funded project known as Taller and led by visual artist Gamaliel Ramírez and poet David Hernández. While my article surveys more recent Chicago Rican writing, it has the virtue of focusing on what must be considered the core group of Chicago Rican writers, including Hernández, Julio Naboa, Salima Rivera, and others.

Following up on this Chicago essay is one on an Illinois-based New York transplant, Carmen Pursifull, whose poetry includes unconscious or coincidental echoes of Julia Burgos, Nicolasa Mohr, Lorena Santos, and others and who, like many of the writers of the first half of the twentieth century, were distanced from the radical politics of community ideologues and dreamers. I seek to explore Pursifull's work in an effort to grasp her conceptual universe and its ties to Puerto Rican political and social themes, and also because I believe she may indeed represent significant sectors whose voices should be heard to understand the Puerto Rican community. I can remember when I presented an earlier draft of this essay as part of a larger paper on Illinois Latino writers, at a library conference in Urbana, Illinois. I had never met Carmen, but assumed she might very well show up at this conference in what had become her town. And when I began to read about her, she called out joyously from the audience, "That's me you're talking about!" And, at my invitation, she proceeded to read the poems cited in my text, proving, I would argue, some of the points in my essay and this book about questions of Puerto Rican performance.

In a final essay for this volume, I trace the portrayal of Puerto Ricans and Puerto Rican/Cuban relations in Miguel Barnet's attempted answer to Oscar Lewis's *La vida real,* and show that in spite of his good intentions the Cuban Barnet is as guilty of denigrating Puerto Ricans as are Cuban American writers like Cristina García, Oscar Hijuelos, and Achy Obejas. In this essay, as in the others, I show that we can't view U.S. Puerto Rican life and literature without considering its ties to Chicano, Cuban, and other Latino as well as other lives and literatures. I can still remember the surprise and unhappiness that met my presentation of this paper at a Latin American Studies Association session on Barnet chaired by Elzbieta Sklodowska and attended by many leading Cubanistas, including Barnet himself. Was I not attacking Barnet as I lashed out at the uncritical treatment of Puerto Ricans in his text? Was I attacking Barnet or his testimonial hero? Was I not attacking *Cubanidad?* All I had to have done to make matters worse at that session was to have said that salsa was at least as Puerto Rican as it was Cuban, in spite of the Yuruba beat. (And that is the truth—long live Willie Colón's trombone.)

In this sense our concluding comments return us to the question of one of the most important representations of the Puerto Rican community, Lewis's *La Vida,* dealing with one of the most telling and ultimately pernicious critiques of Puerto Rican life (a Jewish one, taking us back to this introduction, as well as, I understand, a forthcoming study by Ilan Stavins) and also to the representation of Puerto Ricans even by supposedly sympathetic and progressive Cubans like Oscar Hijuelos, Cristina Garcia, and so forth.

Some Framing Words on Books, Authors, and Ideas That Guide this Study

U.S. Puerto Rican cultural expression has generally been studied as a minority ethnic product. However, a specific characteristic of this minority culture (in literature but also in music and art) is that the question of colonial and national status has continued to be a central, though clearly not the only, theme—and this, in spite of differences, is also a characteristic of much Puerto Rican island culture, which is not an ethnic minority culture except as it has been influenced by U.S. minority thematics. Even when unemployment, poor housing, drug dependency, the welfare system, gang life, school dropouts, prostitution, petty and not-so-petty crime, become endemic themes in U.S. Puerto Rican life and literature, these problems have generally been seen as legitimate only in function of the situation of Puerto Ricans as a colonized people.

Let me be perfectly clear on this point. Puerto Ricans standing between other Latinos and ethnic Americans (Italian Americans, Jewish Americans, and so forth) is a central theme of my book, and an effort to contest Oscar Lewis's views on the culture of poverty haunts every chapter. However, Puerto Rican experience can't be readily subsumed to comparative immigration or U.S. minority studies because of the colonial question—what Aníbal Quijano (1992) and Walter Mignolo (2000) have called "the coloniality of power"—which affects the way Puerto Ricans relate to their U.S. experience, and also the relative facility of Puerto Rican departure and return, so that they are more readily transnational subjects partaking of a postmodern and nomadic fluidity beyond immigrants from other nations in transnational times. It is the failure to grasp Puerto Rican coloniality that has made it difficult for some very astute critics to portray Puerto Rican life, which in turn has been seen as just a particular version of "Latino" life in general. It is perhaps this "colonial difference" that has enabled at least some U.S. Puerto Rican writers, directors, and performers to more successfully portray other Latinos not marked by the particular Boricua colonial privilege and cross.

It is further noteworthy that the process of migration, seen from the perspective of the creole intelligentsia as a struggle to preserve and affirm a fragile and threatened national identity, has generally been seen as a matter of loss. And this sense of loss has led to a full-scale romanticism with respect to the island or a rejection of the island and a look for other worlds. In the two cases, we confront the sense of negativity described in the first section of this introduction. Because of their colonial status, their vulnerability in postindustrial capitalism, and a series of cultural imperatives stemming from their circumstances, Puerto Ricans were so positioned in the United States as well as on the island to fall into many negative situations and develop attitudes that were often contrary to their own best interests resulting from their dual status. However, it is also true that the negative circumstances faced by Puerto Ricans heightened their drive for cultural assertion, expressivity, and performance—a matter embodied in the title of Tato Laviera's well-known collection, *La Carreta Made a U-Turn*. As performers on and off stages, playing fields, and arenas, some Puerto Ricans could compensate for their situations and achieve wonders in sports, the arts, and other fields.

This book does not present an elaborate thematization of Puerto Rican performativity. But there are instances on every page of this text. Let it suffice here to indicate the coordinates of my own position on this question. No doubt, in thinking about matters of Puerto Rican performativity, I was initially influenced by Lowell Fiet and Janette Becerra's provocative collection (1997); more recently, Diana Taylor offered a more comprehensive theorization in *The Archive and the Repetoire* (2003), especially in her introduction and the chapters on Walter Mercado and 9/11; and I have also drawn on the work of Arturo Sandoval on his own (1997) and with Nancy Saporta Sternbach (2000–2001).[4]

In my own efforts to understand U.S. Puerto Rican cultural life, probably the first text I read was Lewis's *La Vida,* with its lurid reductions of poverty life in San Juan and New York to one model based upon the author's advanced formulation of his culture of poverty thesis. Subsequently, I read many other texts that took up Lewis's work as either a positive or negative model. Aside from the essays by René Marqués on the New York Puerto Rican experience (1993), the first important work I read attempting to interpret emergent U.S. Puerto Rican identity by a Puerto Rican and attempting to counter the Lewis model was Jaime Carrero's book with Robert F. Muckley, *Notes on a Neorican Seminar* (1972). Works by Virginia Sánchez-Korrol, Clara Rodríguez, Frank Bonilla, Ricardo Campos, Juan Flores, and others were among the first texts I read by Puerto Ricans dedicated to the New York and U.S. Latino contexts of Puerto Rican life.

Over the years many other books and essays became central to my overall understanding. With regard to historical perspective, José Luis González's *El país de cuatro pisos* and the recent volume by César Ayala and Rafael Bernabe, *Puerto Rico in the American Century,* have been crucial historical guides that have now joined with the work of Picó, Scarano, Pabón, and others to displace Manuel Maldonado-Denis and other earlier historians in providing a richer and more contradictory view of the Puerto Rican past and present than was available a generation ago. The first book simplifies the complexities of Puerto Rican history through a spatial metaphor that emphasizes African and also Mediterranean dimensions and their impact on racial and political attitudes in the wake of U.S. impositions. It also includes González's important essay on Puerto Rican exile writing. The second book recomplicates the historical interpretations relating stages of Puerto Rican to world capitalist development but also emphasizing the varied responses to Puerto Rico's standing as a colony in a postcolonial universe and giving great emphasis to distinctions between independence and autonomy, as well as to cultural and literary questions both on the island and in the diasporic communities.

In addition, as I have sought to cancel Oscar Lewis's culture of poverty prism imposed on Puerto Rican and U.S. Puerto Rican problematics, I have often drawn on Arcadio Díaz Quiñones's *La memoria rota*. I find his more recent book, *El arte de bregar,* to be an extremely valuable if indirect answer to Lewis as well as to René Marqués and others who have misread Puerto Rican reactions to colonial power as acquiescence, docility, or passivity and fail to see the processes of everyday resistance practiced by thousands of Puerto Ricans in their relations to each other and the wider world. Díaz Quiñones's two volumes are important portrayals of key dimensions of Puerto Rican survival tactics. These works are not only important studies of the diaspora, but they indicate the reemergence of the cultural essay as a key dimension of Puerto Rican literature, representing the more recent generation of intellectuals formed by transnational dimensions of the Puerto Rican experience.[5]

In seeking to elaborate a more nuanced analysis, I have been drawn to the questions recently posed in Arturo Torrecilla's *La ansiedad de ser puertorriqueño* (2004), especially his views of *gestualidad, etnospectáculo,* and *virtuosismo* in a Puerto Rican version of what he calls, after Zygmunt Bauman (2000), *la modernidad líquida.* In this regard, I also find much to learn about Puerto Rican ironies and extrapolations in the writings of Rubén Ríos Ávila, Juan Duchesne, Ramón Grosfoguel, and several other Puerto Rican postmodernists, some of whom appear or are discussed in my collection with Luis Felipe Díaz, *Globalización, Nación, Postmodernidad* (2001). However, crucial for my own understanding of several of the questions of colonial mind/body split and *cimaronaje,* including camouflage, as central to Caribbean and specifically Puerto Rican identities, themes that emerge in the writings of Edgardo Rodríguez Juliá (see *Una noche con Iris Chacón* and *El entierro de Cortijo* among other texts) but are most theorized and linked to questions of popular culture and performativity in the opus of Ángel Quintero Rivera. His *Salsa, Sabor y Control* (1998) traces transcultural processes in the creation and development of a predominant Puerto Rican form of resistance and expression, and Quintero Rivera's latest book, *Cuerpo y Cultura* (2009), directly links these questions to the notion of the coloniality of power mentioned above. In effect, because colonialism has been a power exerted over the body, over sexualized and racialized identities, it is no surprise that creativity, simultaneously colonial and postcolonial, in the case of Puerto Rico should be directed toward creative embodiment in sports, acting, and (above all) music but, by extension, also in art, literature, analytical writing, and everyday life. In Quintero Rivera's vision, the primacy of Sidney's Mintz's plantation America is constantly offset and undermined by the counter-plantation of *cimmarons* who come to represent not only escaped Tainos and blacks but all those social sectors who have found means for real, psychic, and cultural expression in music and other cultural forms.

Taking up U.S. Puerto Rican concerns in relation to these thematics, no recent study could replace the book by Edna Acosta-Belén and Carlos E. Santiago, *Puerto Ricans in the United States* (2006), which is remarkable for combining perspectives from history, sociology, and cultural studies (see "Voices and Images from the Diaspora," 169–218, much cited in chapters 1 and 3, following).

For my purposes, the important contemporary work on U.S. Puerto Rican culture begins with Juan Flores's *Divided Borders* (1993), in which Flores, the key U.S. Puerto Rican cultural studies critic of his generation, brings together a collection of his essays in a volume that has provided the basis for the development of a more coherent approach to U.S. Puerto Rican culture and literature in recent years. Included are Flores's fine overview article with George Yúdice, "Living Borders/Buscando América: Languages of Latino Self Formation," as well as some works that set forth a framework for Puerto Rican literary studies. Many other articles join to make *Divided Borders* a major statement and an antidote to those who underplay and misconceive dimensions of U.S. Puerto Rican culture and literature. Following up on this text, Flores's *From Bomba to Hip-Hop* (2000) represents a more recent take on the ways in which Puerto Ricans appropriate and transform dimensions of dominant Anglo and African American culture. In addition to Flores's work, I might just mention Frances Aparicio's *Listening to Salsa* and Raquel Z. Rivera's *New York Ricans from the Hip Hop Zone* (2003), as well as Rivera's coedited volume with Wayne Marshall and Deborah Pacini, *Reggaeton* (2009).

Other works worth mentioning include *Puerto Rican Jam* (1997), a collection edited by Frances Negrón-Muntaner and Ramón Grosfoguel, of a new Puerto Rican generation presenting postmodern interpretations of Puerto Rican life on the island and in the United States; and *Migration, Transnationalization, and Race in a Changing New York,* edited by Héctor R. Cordero-Guzmán, Robert C. Smith, and Ramón Grosfoguel (2001). More rounded statements in this direction have recently appeared, including Grosfoguel's *Colonial Subjects* (2003) and Jorge Duany's *The Puerto Rican Nation on the Move* (2004). Arlene Dávila's *Sponsored Identities* (1997) pointed to top-down processes in the articulation of Latino and Puerto Rican cultural elements; and her subsequent volumes like *Barrio Dreams* (2004) have provided a rich, ever more complex vision of New York Puerto Rican life. Of recent interest also are Dávila's excellent collection edited with Agustin Laó-Montes, *Mambo Montage* (2001) and Gabriel Haslip-Viera, Félix V. Matos Rodríguez, and Angelo Falcón's *Boricuas in Gotham: Puerto Ricans in the Making of New York City* (2004).

Finally, like several other students of U.S. Puerto Rican culture, I'm drawn to the controversial and sometimes questionable perspectives of Frances Negrón-Muntaner in her *Boricua Pop* (2004). Negrón poses Puerto Rican culture as one based on psychological and corporeal shame imposed by colonial controls; she views performativity as a means of representing and at times resisting that shame and the forces that gave it power in relation to sexual, racial, and national identifications. While this view seems exaggerated and extremist, it corresponds to some of my own observations on Puerto Rican literature, arts, music, and cinema, always with the caveat that shame seems one dimension of a culture that adds counterweights of spontaneity, resistance, *cimarronaje,* and *"el arte de bregar."*

On the basis of these and other books (see the recent ones by artist Ramón López and other Chicago-centered works mentioned in chapter 4) we may anticipate the next phase of mapping U.S. urban culture and its corresponding literary production.

For U.S. Puerto Rican literary studies per se, my main initial sources were the books by Eugene Mohr (1982) and Faythe Turner (1978 and 1991) and the essays of Edna Acosta-Belén, Juan Flores, and others published in the MLA's ADE Bulletin (1988). Asela Rodríguez de Laguna's edited volume, *Imágenes e identidades: el puertorriqueño en la literatura* (1985), was another important find, especially for the perspectives it provided for understanding U.S Puerto Rican questions. Margarite Fernández Olmos's *Sobre la literatura puertorriqueña de aquí y de allá* (1989), a feminist study of island and New York women's writing, including the question of New York influences on Etnairis Rivera and a comparative analysis of Nicholasa Mohr and Magali García Ramis, is a text that makes valuable contributions and points to commonalities (for example, the attack on patriarchal norms) but tends to underplay differences and tensions. A more recent effort of tracing feminist perspectives is Carmen Rivera's *Kissing the Mango Tree* (2002), with close looks at Nicholasa Mohr, Sandra María Esteves, Judith Ortiz Cofer, Aurora Levins Morales, Rosario Morales, Luz María Umpierre-Herrera, and Esmeralda Santiago. Interesting perspectives emerge in Lyn Di Iorio Sandin's *Killing Spanish* (1998), which stresses the role of language in literary identity formation. Clearly, William Luis's *Dance Between Two Cultures* (1997) and Lisa Sánchez González' *Boricua Literature* (2001) have impacted my most considered literary perspectives. Luis's effort is one of the first to theorize U.S. Puerto Rican literature in relation to Cuban and Dominican cases, drawing upon postmodern and postcolonial perspectives. Sánchez González continues in these directions, polemicizing with the early efforts of Mohr, Flores, and others to map out the space and historical development of U.S. Puerto Rican literature in relation to a perspective that elides the nation-centered agendas generally imposed on Rican literary interpretation. *Boricua Literature* provides the fullest version of U.S. Puerto Rican writing we have to date, with considerable research on the decades prior to *Manos a la obra,* and involving a highly critical perspective on the overall U.S. Puerto Rican literary field. Based on wide-ranging research, and drawing perspectives from cultural, subaltern, critical race, and gender studies, this book presents a series of chapters focusing on a given writer and writer group, seen as representative of a given generation's struggle for social change. Covering Schomburg and W. C. Williams, and even including a treatment of salsa, *Boricua Literature* is sometimes dogmatic and rigid but it provides the basis for the further development of U.S. Puerto Rican literary and cultural studies.

Most recently, the collections *Writing off the Hyphen,* edited by Jose L. Torres-Padilla and Carmen Haydée Rivera (2008), and *Puerto Rico Caribe,* edited by Juan Duchesne (2009), exerted considerable influence in my final draft of chapter 3. In the introduction to their volume, Torres-Padilla and Rivera seek to rethink the stages of U.S. Puerto Rican literature in relation to efforts by Clara Rodriguez (1997) and Jorge Duany (2002) to chart the characteristics of different stages of Puerto Rican migration to the United States, with a special emphasis on transnational questions. The authors then review Rican literature and literary interpretation by drawing on Sánchez González and recent work by Acosta-Belén and Flores to emphasize diasporic "inbetweenness" and a conception of Rican writing as a rejection of the hyphenated identity central, for example, to the perspective of Cuban-American critic Gustavo Pérez-Firmat. Meanwhile, Duchesne's recent collection charts a Deleuzian nomadicity of island and U.S. Puerto Rican literatures in relation to questions of historical trauma, shame, and resistance connected with 1898, Operation Bootstrap, and the many wars in foreign lands and urban U.S. barrios, as well as the postmodern ambience emerging in relation to contemporary globalization and transnationalization processes. Finally, I should mention Roberto Márquez's *Puerto Rican Poetry* (2007), which helped me rethink my view of U.S. Puerto Rican poetry and its relation to the island's canonic production.

I wish to note here also that although I'm influenced by all the books, writers, and perspectives mentioned above (and many others not mentioned!), I do not always address or cite them in the text, as one might expect in a standard academic volume on the book's overall subject. This is so because my book is posed explicitly as primarily based on my own particular perceptions as a Jewish American semi-insider/outsider, and so I only drew on those aspects of past and present critique that seemed related to those perceptions. For example, the best writing I know of on Jewish-U.S. Puerto Rican relations is that found in Negrón's chapter on *West Side Story;* I cite the text and refer the reader to it, without analyzing Negrón's viewpoint but merely going on with my own.[6] That procedure, typical of much in the volume, may not be what a reader seeking a state of the art, comprehensive volume on U.S. Puerto Rican cultural studies will want. We all need and someday may have such a comprehensive volume, but we do not have it yet—and this book can't fill that bill, though it sometimes points in that direction.

Concluding Thoughts

In spite of whatever limitations I could point to with respect to this book, I wish to conclude this introduction by meeting the demand of one of my outside readers for the University of Illinois Press' review process, that I put aside my mantle of modesty and epistemic insecurity stemming from my outsider/insider status (see my remarks in the preface) and instead state what I believe "are the specific contributions" that my book may make to "the analysis of various manifestations of cultural expression, and to the process of rectifying the 'Puerto Rican erasures' that [have] for a long time dominated the scholarship on U.S. Puerto Ricans."

In this regard I can do no better than cite that reader's own assessment—that I provide "a detailed . . . attempt 'to dis-erase' Puerto Rican presence and cultural contributions to U.S. society"; that I give "centrality to the colonial experience of Puerto Ricans and to their subaltern condition as colonial trans-migrants [which constitute] unifying strategies that are key to understanding cultural production, resulting in persuasive arguments about how these experiences differ from those of other Latinos (as well as other minority groups), and about the ways in which the intersectionalities of ethnicity, race, class, and gender shape their various forms of Puerto Rican cultural expression." The reader also notes how I engage "in a more detailed . . . and . . . panoramic review of the scholarly efforts" [including my own] "that have taken place in the process of rescuing U.S. Puerto Rican contributions from cultural 'oblivion'"; how I incorporate some of the most relevant literature, including recent scholarship "to contextualize my selected examples in U.S. Puerto Rican literature, film, and art," and how I provide "some compelling illustrations of cultural and political resistance, negotiation and adaptation to U.S. society, and of the reconstitution of cultural identities by those who live in conditions of marginality and oppression." In sum, this reader notes how I introduce "insightful and provocative arguments about U.S. Puerto Rican cultural experiences, and underscore some noteworthy, but neglected aspects of Puerto Rican cultural production that will undoubtedly stimulate further research."

If I have accomplished half of what my reader indicates, my efforts in constructing this book will have succeeded. I believe I may rightly say that I have approached the materials presented with a certain affection but also humility. As an intellectual who came to Puerto Rican themes in the final stages as a late-blooming Latino and Latin American studies scholar, I do not consider myself an "expert" on the themes I explore.

Now, as I complete this introduction, I'm mindful of the Cuban *són* that has as its refrain, *Castellano, que bueno baila usted, Castellano que bueno baila usted*. I understand that these words are generally interpreted as an affirmative expression of the white Cuban's ability to integrate himself into Afro-Cuban culture—or what some call *cubanidad*. Literally, the phrase says, "Castillian man, how good you dance." But perhaps the grammatical problem (*bueno* instead of *bién*, good instead of well) points to other problems as well. I believe that the repetition of the phrase points to parody and mocking, as if to say, "look, white man, you think you can make it in our world and even move our women to admiration. But, look, you sexual predator, you condescending bastard, you're a colonialist and imperialist, you can't really do our dance (you even got the basic form [equivalent to the grammar] wrong), and you don't even know it when we tell you." This is one of my problems with Antonio Benítez-Rojo's wonderful *The Repeating Island*, in that he can't seem to distinguish between genuine Afro-Caribbean expression and efforts that are conscious or unconscious imitations. From a U.S. jazz point of view, we might ask if, as great a virtuoso as Arturo Sandoval might be, is he really *with it?* And, while admiring much that he wrote, we might ask to what degree was Benítez-Rojo himself *with it* in an Afro-Caribbean "kind of way"?

Of course, I feel in a similar, vulnerable position with respect to Puerto Rican cultural matters. And here I can't help but recall another Jewish–Puerto Rican anecdote that may be valuable to the reader thinking about the implications and value of this text. One afternoon, sitting on my mother-in-law's porch in Quebradillas, Puerto Rico (a virtual center of return diasporic encounters), I met still another of the many family members visiting their old hometown from the New York/New Jersey area of my own youth. As often happened, I found myself talking in Spanish while my newly found U.S. Puerto Rican relative spoke to me in English. "De donde vienes?—Where are you from?" I asked. "From New Jersey," he answered. "Elizabeth." "Elizabeth!" I exclaimed. "I grew up there," I said, remembering my youth and Bar Mitzvah, wondering at the now-resident of a space I had thought somewhat mine. "Really," he said, apparently not very impressed or surprised—he had apparently been through similar interchanges before. "Sí! I still have family there," I explained. "And you like living there?" I asked in Spanish after a long silence. "Oy gavalt!" he shot back in perfect Yiddish (no "Ay bendito" on his lips), eyeing me, perhaps cueing and clueing me to a refrain not unlike that mocking one of the Cuban *són*, answering my question oh so Jewishly with a question based on a translation of Yiddish: "What's not to like?"

Just recently, after hearing me speak about one Puerto Rican issue or another, my brother-in-law turned to me to say, "My god, Marc, more than twenty years among us y no sabes nada—you just don't know anything about us." Of course, this may be true and not true—perhaps the result of my deep-rooted inabilities in combination with the quixotic, mercurial liquidity of "diasporican" being. This is the fear that haunts my every word and observation in this book. The truth will come out in what follows, and perhaps the result will not be as unfavorable as I imagine in my most pessimistic moments. I leave such matters to the opinion of those who will read the published work.

**Defending Their
Own in the Cold**

Chapter 1

Puerto Rican and Chicano Crossovers in Latino Film and Music Culture

....

To the memory of Sammy Medina (RIP)

Selena, Lopez, and Latino Identifications

In a fascinating essay on Selena (2003), Frances Aparicio seeks to trace the history of Latino/a as opposed to specific national identifications. Interestingly, she notes how the publicity mill has taken not just one but three Puerto Ricans and sought to constitute them as Latino as opposed to Boricua figures for a Latino-centered market. This essay, originally drafted as a response to Aparicio's, will show, among other things, that in spite of the U.S. Puerto Rican erasure in the very epistemology of Anglo America, and in spite of the negligible and negative representation of Puerto Ricans in film, Puerto Ricans, ironically enough, have participated significantly in subsuming Mexican and Chicano spaces in the configuration of Latino identities in U.S. and mainly Hollywood cinema. In this sense, the case of Jennifer Lopez's representation of Selena is simply the most famous and crucial example of a rather unexceptional phenomenon. I've also tried to understand why Puerto Ricans have been able to play Mexicans, but—with the possible exception of the Mexico City–based movie biopic of composer Rafael Hernández and a recent television effort I'll mention below—I can't think of a single instance of Mexicans playing Puerto Ricans. A rather odd turn of thought, perhaps, but it may well have something important to tell us about the social construction of Puerto Rican, Mexican, and Latino identities.[1]

The context for this examination is the evolution of Latino/a identity and its theorization in Suzanne Oboler, Félix Padilla, and others. Oboler's critique constitutes a view of the emergence of the term as a top-down process aimed at labeling and homogenizing the various Latin Americans present in the United States. A similar slant is implicit in Arlene Dávila's view of the effect of marketing in the creation of sponsored Latino identities (1997). Along with Aparicio, I agree with Agustín Laó-Montes, who argues that the particular groups that have extended beyond their national roots to consider themselves not only in nationalist but Latino terms have themselves played a significant role in the emergence of their sense of identity. Unlike Padilla (1985), who sought that identification in the political calculation of community leaders that each particular national group is too weak to achieve its rights on its own and seeks to adapt and win group acceptance for the broader label, I believe that the Latino base, the subaltern subject of Latinidad or Latinismo, the people in their barrios and their everyday life interactions, participate in the creation of Latino as opposed or complementary to specific national identities—and this in spite of their sometime resentment toward one group or another or toward the effects of the generalizing process on their sense of specificity.

My own view is that all the manipulations and appropriations labeled Hispanic or Latino are not simply imposed or created but are based on certain commonalities or affinities of identity that result not from some racial or otherwise essentialist base, but rather from the imposition, however uneven, of similar, Iberian-based cultural patterns emanating from the colonial and postcolonial periods. In effect, the Conquest broke down the initial heterogeneity of the Americas, imposing a series of patterns that, however varied, constituted an Iberianization or, taking the Church dimension most seriously, a Latinization of the Amerindian populations and the African and other populations that came to inhabit the Latin American world.

The term we call "Latino" designates that fragment of the Latin American world that, through conquest, treaty, or immigration, in territories that came, legally or formally, to belong to the United States. The Latino population has been subject to colonization, racialization, and stigmatization as well as the formation as a particular minority in the United States. Those who have arrived in successive waves in the twentieth century are Latin Americans who gradually, in varying degrees, have become Latinos. Recent patterns of transnational migration and the transnational cultural processes involved in the recent transformation of labor, media, information, and so forth have led to mixed, hybrid identifications that resist easy classifications; but in general I would say that being Latino as opposed to Latin American in the United States means having passed through the processes of stigmatization and racialization that occur in every aspect of everyday life but most acutely in school, work, and neighborhood settings.

To be sure, in this sense, Chicanos and U.S. Ricans are distinct groups, but so are those from different parts of the United States or Mexico who identify primarily as either Chicano or U.S. Mexicano. Eventually, all these groups have had interactions that have led to their self-identification as Latinos as well as Mexicans, Puerto Ricans, or some other Latin American identity. Part of this process is also an identification as Latin Americans—as if they had all read Bolívar and Martí. And I think there is much truth to the view that at least until Che Guevara and Hugo Chávez, pan–Latin American and Caribbean identifications are more rooted in exile and migration than in Latin America and the Caribbean as such. Indeed, a sense of Latinidad, Latinismo, or whatever has more to do with the sense of common cultural traditions and other dimensions that make for commonalities and affinities. Since Martí, Pachín Marín, and other early Latin Caribbean exiles in New York, Latinos have seen themselves simultaneously as having pan-national, Latino, as well as national identifications. Naturally, this process is not even and involves multiple contradictions and strategies. Though very far from constituting a heterogeneous group in terms of class, regional background, or U.S. experience, U.S.-based Mexicans, sometimes resenting the impact or entitlement claims of smaller Latino groups, frequently see the Latino label as an attempt to blot out their particular concerns. Puerto Ricans and others resist being homogenized in function of predominantly Mexican norms and stereotypes. And Puerto Ricans have a special set of concerns and characteristics related to their colonial status and sense of nationhood that lead to discomfort with being "Latinized."

The identification processes I'm invoking are perhaps best explained with the theories of Michel de Certeau (1984), but given their specifically Boricua rendition by Arcadio Díaz-Quiñones in his book *El arte de bregar* (2000). Here, I should also note that before the terms Hispanic or Latino came to the fore, there was the term Latin that was used sometimes quite broadly to include Italians and even French as well as Iberians. The term "Latin lover" was applied to Valentino; the notorious *Esquire* article, "Latins are Lousy Lovers," refers to Italians, even though recently amnesia has led people to think otherwise. In New York and other eastern cities, Puerto Ricans have entered Spanish, Italian, Cuban, Irish, and other, mainly Catholic, spaces. But their racialized, stigmatized identities drew in part from their similarities with Italians and their complicated but even more important relation with African Americans. The Italian connection probably starts with Italian workers on the docks and in the factories, as Bernardo Vega and Jesús Colón tell it; then, as Piri Thomas, Nicholasa Mohr, and Edward Rivera continue, the relation extends to gangs and politics. Indeed the portrayal of Communist-identified Vito Marcantonio's popularity among Ricans in the 1940s and 50s in Nicholasa Mohr's *Nilda* is probably an unexplored link with Vega and Colón, extending perhaps to more recent political configurations, and probably (here's another secret), in spite of the questionable claim by his parents that he was named after the Mexican singer Marco Antonio Muñíz, the conscious or unconscious source of Marc Anthony's anglicized—seemingly Shakespeareanized—name.[2]

Italians and Sicilians were involved in the New York Latino club scene of the fifties. Carmen Padilla, later the Illinois Puerto Rican poet Carmen Pursifull, partnered with Italian Killer Joe Piri at the Palladium; Italians, and not only Jews, were involved in Fania's salsa revolution; Al Pacino made the move from the Marielito of *Scarface* to the sad ex-con of *Carlito's Way*. But the most recent important Italian connection was made by Madonna before her Evita imitation and Cuban parenting experiment when, during an island appearance, she rubbed the Puerto Rican flag across her genital zone.

In Chicago, more so than in New York or Los Angeles and other southwest cities, we know of the crossover from Puerto Rican to Mexican and from Puerto Rican or Mexican to Latino because of the more than half-century proximity of the two groups, and also because of the many interrelationships and experiences the two groups have shared. In the Windy City, the notion of Hispanic and Latino identity emerges early and independent indeed of Félix Padilla's myth of a Latino consciousness stemming from the decisions of community workers in the 1970s. The journal *Vida Latina* dates in Chicago from the 1950s; in Gary, Indiana, Greek–Puerto Rican professor Nick Kanellos cofounded *Revista Chicana Riqueña* in 1972 and then went on to *Americas Review*, Arte Público Press, and his Recovering the Hispanic Literary Heritage project, all aimed at finding, researching, presenting, and promoting Latino literary and cultural production. Chicago Rican Victor Rivera was a major mariachi player in Chicago's Mexican clubs during the 1970s and after. Chicago Rican poet Salima Rivera always emphasized her Mexican ties, from her Mexican foster parents to her Mexican husband and friends. Chicago Rican painter Gamaliel Ramírez joined Mexican artists in several mural projects and identified with Chicago's Mexican Southside. Nuyorican news analyst Ray Suárez learned to both Latinize and also stand outside his national identity in Chicago. Chicago Mexican *timbalista* Victor Parra came to prominence with his Mambo Express radio programs (cohosted with U.S. Puerto Rican Billy Zayas) and then his mambo band (though he preferred Cuban to Puerto Rican sounds, mambo to salsa). Chicago Cuban Achy Obejas and Chicago Chicana Sandra Cisneros have telling Puerto Rican pages, as did Chicano Luis Rodríguez during his Chicago days. Ana Castillo, who has a few of her sharpest Chicago poems about Mexican and Italian schoolgirls in *My Father Was a Toltec*, has more than once portrayed Chicago's multiple Latino relations, especially in *Sapagonia, Peel My Love like an Onion,* and *Bad Boys.*

The number of Mexican–Puerto Rican marriages has long been high in Chicago, and now New York follows the Chicago lead by the new relational patterns achieved by the Mexirican children of Mexican–Puerto Rican marriages, most generally, I'd venture, between Puerto Rican men and Mexican women.[3] To be sure, Mexican–Puerto Rican relations are often tense and difficult, involving resentments over entitlements, in clashing levels of body proximity, formality, and so forth.[4] But in all of this I would argue that many Latinos, while recognizing and smarting from the problems generated by their Latino labels, actually enjoy crossing the border from their specific national identity to other national possibilities and identifications within their Latino/a Latin American universe. Crossing borders is something many enjoy in spite of the problems such crossings involve. Chicago Puerto Ricans and Mexicans have clearly recognized the importance of funding that goes to all Latinos, of a film festival that seeks to cover all Latinos, of a politician like Luis Gutiérrez, congressman and *independentista*, who is supposed to represent all Latinos even as he represents Puerto Ricans like himself. The most recent example of pride in the Latino extension is the case of U.S. Supreme Court Justice Sonia Sotomayor, who, in spite of her "wise Latina" remarks, tried to maintain her Puerto Rican connection even as she was touted as Latina or even Hispanic.

Latinos know that the land of opportunity is the land of hybridized, manipulated identities. As subalterns, they live the benefits of relative exploitation. They know that each group has a relative range of possibilities and advantages. Aparicio is disturbed by the Boricua involvement with the Selena story as instances of Puerto Ricans surrendering their national identity in function of a manipulated and outward (and Mexicanized) sense of Latinness. But one might in fact see the moves of Lopez as instances of relative Puerto Rican hegemony in the spread and articulation of Latinness.

As "Latinos," Puerto Ricans surely lose some of their exclusive identity, and they have a special resentment against being considered as a minority because of the special circumstances of migration and settlement as second-class citizens. But insofar as they take on the Latino label, they extend and deepen their hold on one of the few areas of achievement historically open to them. That area is, since slavery, one of command performance: do what the master says, do it with your body, and use your commanded performance to create some space of opportunity, maybe some space of freedom and even power. Perform, entertain. And of course, outperform the other Puerto Ricans and Latinos. And while it's mainly Afro-Ricans who excel in baseball, basketball, and *boxeo*, it's also the others, because after all: their grandmothers, where are they? With *manos a la obra,* the Puerto Rican diaspora fully launched, Puerto Ricans were lumped with African Americans and learned they were more black than Italian; late to New York's waning industrialization, subject to post–World War II layoff and welfarization, they learned they had to perform in their informal economy barrio worlds or die, even as they contended with African American and Italian as well as other Latino and Boricua performers. The performance syndrome extends the immigrant take (the Sinatra doing it or anything "my way"); and this sense of independence, which remains central to diasporic success, is in almost direct, defiant proportion to political and economic dependence—and in like proportion also to even that phenomenon Laó-Montes characterizes as the "Diasporican" version of Aníbal Quijano's "coloniality of power."[5]

With the palpable exception of *Mambo Café* (1999), featuring Thalía, Paul Gonzalez and Rosanna de Soto as (I believe) not very believable U.S. Ricans (there's nothing specifically Puerto Rican about them), I can't think of a single instance of Mexicans playing Puerto Ricans.[6] Perhaps Woody Allen would have written about U.S. Puerto Ricans had he realized how *Zelig*-like they've had to become to survive and have a chance to thrive; how clear it is to me that many Puerto Rican actors have learned *el arte de bregar*.

U.S. Puerto Rican and Chicano Performances

Many of us know the painful side of the U.S. Puerto Rican story; I only have to touch on some of the details to place things in context. We can invoke a famous Mexican American woman, Linda Chavez, and her assertion (1991) that if we left out the clearly depressing statistics referring to U.S. Puerto Ricans, we would see that Latinos as a group have done well in the United States relative to their years of U.S. residence. Let's be clear. In Chavez's view, the Puerto Rican performance is so low that it falsifies the true happy story of other Latinos and, of course, Mexicans, that would emerge if we would (as we should) eliminate the U.S. Puerto Rican numbers, and perhaps the U.S. Puerto Ricans themselves. And the explanation for the dismal showing is welfarism, post-Rooseveltian liberalism, and probably the inherent laziness and recalcitrance of a population whose roots are tied to an early plantation system, and of course the African roots that that system failed to obliterate.

That is, of course, the reactionary and indeed racist version. But even look at the one told about Puerto Ricans by the supposedly liberal Oscar Lewis or the supposedly progressive Earl Shorris in his book *Latinos* (1992). We need not even think of the diminishment of Puerto Rican cultural and literature accomplishment in Juan Bruce-Novoa's *RetroSpace* (1990) or, to a degree, Ilan Stavans's *The Hispanic Condition* (2001). It has taken people like Juan Flores, Nick Kanellos, Edna Acosta-Belén, and a whole generation of Puerto Rican writing to call attention to Francisco Gonzalo "Pachín" Marín, Bernardo Vega, Luisa Capetillo, Jesús Colón, Nicholasa Mohr, Judith Ortiz Cofer, Abraham Rodríguez, and so many other important Puerto Ricans developing or growing in U.S. turf. At the level of high literary culture, of course, island-rooted but not U.S. poverty community Puerto Rican writing is heralded. And even given the demographic difference, the number of recognized U.S. Rican writers is miserably small in relation to the Chicano/Mexican or Cuban numbers; and, for the most dismal figure of all, consider the U.S. Puerto Rican women writers—and this at a time when we have a large list of island Rican women writers producing significant bodies of work.

In fact, if we want to understand Nuyorican and U.S. Rican literary production, we would best consider Tato Laviera, Miguel Piñero, Miguel Algarín and the rest in the same breath we consider countless Boricua boxers and baseball players. Now we're getting to it. Nuyorican writers have the same relative space in U.S. and even U.S. Latino letters that Afro and other Puerto Ricans from the island have in baseball and boxing.

But, glory of glories, Puerto Ricans have had a somewhat happier story in the film and music industries. And there, their success has been proportionately greater in recent years, I believe, than Chicanos and even Cuban Americans. Of course, relative success can mean very limited results, after all. There has been only the smallest number of Hollywood films focusing on U.S. Puerto Ricans—much fewer films, I'd say, than ones focused on Chicanos or Cubans. *West Side Story, Trash, Popi, Show of Force, Carlito's Way, I Like It Like That,* the notorious *Fort Apache, the Bronx, Short Eyes, Piñero, El Cantante, Nothing like the Holidays,* plus, as Acosta-Belén and Santiago remind (2006, 205), such dance-centered films as *Salsa* (featuring ex-Menudo singer Robby "Draco" Rosa), *Dance with Me* (featuring Chayanne—but playing a Cuban!)—doesn't this almost exhaust the list? But how does a small national population with a small potential market share achieve a special status without generalizing its identity, as Caribbean, tropical, or even North American Latino? This is what the new Puerto Rican Latinos have done. As transnationalized Puerto Ricans adept in English, and somewhat adept in crossovers to Anglo, African American, and other Latino worlds, they've taken their demeaned cultural capital and used it in ways that most Chicanos with a potentially greater national and cross-border audience have not felt inclined or been able to do.

We can think back to the thirties and forties and realize the role of Puerto Ricans in the development of boleros and trio music—we can think of Rafael Hernández roaming between New York, Puerto Rico, Mexico, Havana; of Johnny Albino, Bobby Capó, and we can think of—why not?—*La importancia de llamarse Daniel Santos.* In jazz, Juan Tizol played valve trombone in several of Duke Ellington's bands, while writing some songs (for example, "Perdido"—virtually the theme song for Luis Valdez's *Zoot Suit*—and "Caravan"—a Puerto Rican dessert fantasy). While Dizzy Gillespie clearly favored a large array of Cuban musicians, still, in his last years, he opened the door to the young David Sánchez. In between, Puerto Ricans gradually asserted their role in the formation of salsa, and through Tito Puente, Ray Barreto, Eddie Palmieri, and company came to equal and sometimes surpass the Cubans in the formation of Latinized jazz. In all of this, hardly a Mexican appears—hardly a Chicano in jazz, and hardly a Mexican in salsa or other dominant Latino forms.

Of course things have been somewhat different in the pop field. Carlos Santana has probably been more successful than the great Puerto Rican crossover phenomenon of the 1960s and 70s, José Feliciano. Then one might mention Trini López, Ritchie Valens, and Los Lobos. As for the women, there were Vickie Carr and Linda Ronstadt. Meanwhile, Mexicans suffered from horrendous parody and stereotyping in film after film. Stars like Dolores del Rio, Emilio Fernández, and Gilbert Roland played out rather depressing Hollywood careers. Of course there were the Latin lovers Valentino style, and the hot tamales like Lupe Vélez and Katy Jurado had their limited success. Even the most successful early figure, Rita Hayworth, a Spanish performer discovered in Tijuana, ended miserably; and the most famous Mexican actors of the period were Wallace Beery as Pancho Villa, Paul Muni as Benito Juárez, J. Carroll Nash as the Cisco Kid, and Tyrone Power as Zorro. Later, in the 60s, we'd have Marlon Brando as Zapata, Rod Steiger as a Mexican Revolution general, and Ringo Starr as a Chicano gardener whose besmirched honor is defended by his motorcycling *chola* sisters in the 60s cult film, *Candy*. Here perhaps we should mention the most striking instance of all: Orson Welles, after describing 1898 in strictly U.S.-Spanish-Cuban terms (in *Citizen Kane*), married Rita Hayworth and attempted to make a major film in Brazil, then gave the role of Vargas, the honest Mexican cop, to a young Charlton Heston, brown-faced for his performance in what is probably to this day (and this in spite of *Born in East L.A.*, *The Border, Traffic,* and other efforts) the most powerful border movie made in the United States or anywhere, *Touch of Evil*.

It would be impossible to rehearse all the Latin American and Latino stereotypes generated by Hollywood—one just has to look at the documentary *Gringo in Bananaland* for a limited but useful catalog. The emergent television industry would generally follow suit. Again and again, we see non-Latinos in Latino roles, or sometimes Latinos having the honor of stereotyping themselves. By the late '40s and early '50s, the most successful Latinos were supporting actors, like José Martí's illegitimate son, César Romero—later known for his exploitation of Asian workers; Xavier Cugat, a Spaniard playing at being Cuban; and of course that icon of icons, Carmen Miranda, whose headdress and comic sensuality were a white, Portuguese caricature of Bahia Afro-Brazilian culture. In the fifties, television brought a run-of-the-mill white Cuban singer, Desi Arnaz, to acting prominence, while Bill Dana, drawing on material developed by a writing team that included the young Woody Allen, played his comic José Jiménez Latino stereotype to the hilt—was it inoffensive good fun?—week after week on *Your Show of Shows,* one of the most watched television variety shows of the 1950s.

In the 1960s, Anthony Quinn and Ricardo Montalbán emerged, the first hardly ever playing a Latino, let alone a Mexican or an Irishman (though he did play the father in *Los hijos de Sánchez* and Marlon Brando's brother in *Zapata,* and did play Italian, Irish, Greek, and Arab others over the course of his long career), and the second, almost always playing out one generalized Latin American identity after another, ending his career on *Fantasy Island.* In the 1970s, Al Pacino got to play *Scarface,* just as he would play a Puerto Rican underworld ex-con in *Carlito's Way;* non-Cubans played the *Mambo King* brothers; and Andy Garcia frequently got billing in films that paid little attention to his Latino roots. Then we can think of Natalie Wood as María.

Where indeed were the Puerto Ricans in all this? While there were few films on Puerto Rican subjects, there were some actors. The first Puerto Rican film star, probably, was José Ferrer, who played Toulouse Lautrec (as John Leguizamo was to do a generation later), but also Cyrano de Bergerac, and who never if ever, to my knowledge, played a Latino, and didn't name names to the House Un-American Activities Committee (some rumored he made a deal—a claim his nephew by marriage George Clooney recently and emphatically denied).[7] Meanwhile, Lolita Lebrón, Rafael Cancel Miranda, and company were in the early stages of their time in prison. Not only did Ferrer play Frenchmen, but swarthy outsiders of every kind, from a Jewish lawyer (*The Caine Mutiny*) to a sadistic Turkish military man (*Lawrence of Arabia*), as well as those French figures with great corporal or extremity problems: What should we make of that, or the fact that in the Australian *Moulin Rouge,* Leguizamo has produced a grotesque parody of Ferrer's Toulouse performance? Should we see all this in light of the Puerto Rican diaspora characterized by Albizu Campos as *la patria enfermiza?* Are Diasporicans apt subjects of disability as well as performance studies? The question of Ángel Quintero-Rivera's nexus of *cuerpo y cultura* in his book of 2009 takes on the oddest turns in the film industry.

After Ferrer, there is of course the great phenomenon, the first lady of Puerto Rican/Latina film identity: Rita Moreno. Puerto Ricans complained bitterly when Natalie Wood won the part of Maria, just as many complained when Moreno won out over her only Puerto Rican rival, Chita Rivera, for the film version of the musical (some years ago, Rita teased Chita that she would play the great Broadway star in the film version of *Chita Rivera: The Dancer's Life*). Alan Arkin was to play the Puerto Rican father in *Popi*—quite successfully, my Puerto Rican friends grudgingly admit. Moreno had become the Puerto Rican/Latina leading lady in film from the '60s throughout the rest of the twentieth century and into the new millennium. She always complained of stereotyping, of her limited role possibilities, but on she went.

In the meantime, there were very few possibilities for others. There was the eager Puerto Rican worker admiring and trying to learn from the embittered Holocaust survivor Rod Steiger in *The Pawn Broker,* only to be killed in the store robbery; there were the stereotyped figures in *Twelve Angry Men; Fort Apache, the Bronx;* and other films. There's a fine Puerto Rican/Cuban confrontation in Iván Acosta's *El Super;* there are probably countless moments I can't remember. But the key phenomenon of the 1990s was the emergence of Raúl Juliá, though, to my knowledge, he never played a U.S. Rican or Latino (perhaps he came closest as bug-eyed Gómez in the Adams family), but almost always, the Latin American—as a macho South American revolutionary, as Monseñor Romero, and as Chico Mendes, and whoever—except in Marcos Zurinaga's island film efforts, *La gran fiesta* and *Tango Bar* (best to forget Zurinaga's subsequent, disastrous Puertorricanization of García-Lorca's life, with Cuban Andy García in *Lorca*). Still before Jennifer Lopez came Rosie Perez, a Nuyorican who crosses over between African American and Nuyorican worlds, but whose film career has seemed limited perhaps because of her borderline identity. Miriam Colón played Pacino's Cuban mother. More recently there has been Leguizamo, Benicio del Toro, Luis Guzmán, and a few others who have made their marks. In the 2001 release of *The Blue Diner,* we could see a whole new array of Latino and specifically Puerto Rican actors, playing alongside Miriam Colón once again. Finally, we may note the presence of a Mexi-Rican protagonist in the rather lame film, *Bella.*

But what we may forget in that little litany is how, many years ago, Puerto Ricans began to supplant Anglos and others playing Mexicans. Yes, again we have to remember that Jennifer Lopez was not the first. Perhaps that honor falls to Freddie Prinz in *Chico and the Man,* but that was to be followed by Esai Morales in his film-stealing performance as Ritchie Valens's brother, and in other Chicano roles culminating with his role in the PBS telenovela, *Familia.* And of course there is Jimmy Smits, of Puerto Rican mother and Surinamese father, who has played so many Chicano and Mexican roles (for example, his parts in *Mi familia, The Old Gringo,* and *The West Wing*) that most people are shocked to find out that he identifies not only with his Brooklyn birthplace but with his mother's hometown, Ponce. We can even extend this story if we think of Ruben Blades as a Panamanian nevertheless rooted in the Nuyorican salsa scene, because the only films I can think of place him as a Chicano cop in *Milagro Beanfield War,* a Chicano gardener in a made-for-TV movie, and, of course, as Diego Rivera in *The Cradle Will Rock.* Then of course there's del Toro's breakthrough role as a Mexican cop in *Traffic* and his more recent role as the Argentine Che Guevara.

This is the immediate context, perhaps, for seeing Jennifer Lopez as Selena, but the context also includes that broader history of U.S. Mexican exclusionism. Even when the Hollywood Left made the wonderful *Salt of the Earth,* they chose their Chicano players mainly from the people who participated in the original events portrayed, but they imported the fine left-elite Mexican actress Rosaura Revueltas to play the protagonist. When Luis Valdez brought *La Bamba* to the screen, he not only brought in Morales, but gave the part of Ritchie to the wooden Lou Diamond Phillips, a big mistake which damages that film (as does the casting of Phillips, who identifies as Filipino) as a Puerto Rican in *Show of Force,* the Hollywood take on Puerto Rico's Cerro Maravilla encounter involving government attacks on *independentista* rebels). Robert Redford strained his otherwise engaging, if overly quaint, film adaptation of John Nichols's *The Milagro Beanfield War* by casting the Brazilian Sonia Braga and Blades in key roles, and giving the central role to a rather weak Italian American actor no one has heard of since—this when there were countless Chicano actors unemployed and standing in casting lines in Hollywood.

The Mexican question is, let's face it, scandalous. Thousands of Chicanos and Mexicans reside in the Los Angeles area, a struggling population with its great share of struggling actors. In all these years, there seems to have been no significant harnessing of this great energy, no formation of schools to give special training to this group as actors and directors, to say nothing of film performers and filmmakers. The only recent exception I can think of is the case of Robert Rodriguez. But the development of U.S. Mexican film representation is outrageously thin, outrageously unacceptable—even as film from Mexico is going through a renaissance and, led by *Como agua para chocolate (Like Water for Chocolate)*, *Amores perros*, and *Y tu mamá también,* has been attracting crossover audiences in the United States, culminating most richly, perhaps, with *Babel.* And meantime, Mexicanos and other Latinos are all over U.S. film credits—as painters, plumbers, catering staff, and at best (or is it worst?), walk-on drug addicts, *gangueros*, or the like.

It would seem that we could almost develop the thesis that people in the industry believe that only non-Mexicans can convincingly play Mexicans or Chicanos—or at least the stereotypes that people in the industry assume the grand

U.S. and world public will accept. But of course, even as Danny Valdez and other *Teatro campesino* regulars, who performed key roles in *Zoot Suit,* failed to establish themselves as actors, still, Edward James Olmos did, emerging as the Chicano and indeed Latino actor of his generation, playing the *pachuco* in Luis Valdez's classic play, and then almost every Chicano leading role the film studios could cook up for the next twenty years. And of course there's Cheech Marin and Paul Rodríguez, but not much more for male Chicano comics in the U.S. film world of the last century. (Now we have George Lopez.) And as far as women are concerned, until the recent arrival of Salma Hayek, the only consistent Chicana actress has been Rosanna DeSoto, who played the mother in *La Bamba,* the wife in *Stand and Deliver,* and so forth. Of course the Mexican female actress engaged in Hollywood Latina presentation after presentation is Lupe Ontiveras, who stars in *Zoot Suit* and, of course, plays every comic overweight, middle-aged Mexican woman one could imagine (in *El Norte,* in *Mi Familia,* in *Y no se tragó la tierra*—though here with a new sinister note), until she reappears, once again, with Olmos, but this time in another register, in the *Selena* film itself, as the infamous Yolanda Saldívar.

Ontiveras had cornered the mature Mexican women's market through her deft comic and sinister performances (consider her performance in *Babel,* for example). But who, in the pre-Hayek period, could play a female Chicana lead? It is at this point that Lopez, pursuing a rather mediocre career as a New York Latina in Hollywood, goes beyond her Chicana impersonation in *Mi Familia* and succeeds in generalizing her identity by winning a nationwide competition for the role of the Tex-Mex Selena. Was it a question of sheer talent and professional skills triumphing over rigid ethnic correctness? Was it a question of a good agent or some favor owed? Once again a Puerto Rican takes the Chicano or in this case Chicana role, and crosses over to achieve a kind of pan-Latinness that weaves Mexican and Puerto Rican identifications and seems to lead to some kind of generalized Anglo-American acceptance. And meanwhile, all those Chicana girls who tried out for the part cried when Lopez and not they were chosen.

Selena: The Movie

The film by Gregory Nava has one of its most telling moments when Selena succeeds with an initially hostile Monterrey, Mexico, audience even as the stage collapses around her. Parallel to this is Lopez's own success as a Puerto Rican who is accepted in her portrayal of a Chicana. This kind of crossover underlines the sense that the Latina is in effect a U.S.—or as it's called—American figure. That is, Lopez succeeds as Selena because as a Nuyorican she shows that she, like

Chita Rivera and Rita Moreno before her, is an American Latina (at this level, U.S. Puerto Rican and Mexican differences become trivial) rather than a Latin American. Selena is not accepted as a Mexican but an Americanized Chicana singing U.S. rock but also traditional Mexican music with passion and *sabor*. But the Latina audience that watched the film primarily identified with Lopez's enactment of Selena-ized Chicana stereotypes, and willingly crossed over with Lopez into a broader identificational context. For U.S. Puerto Ricans, this was in fact crucial that they could be accepted by the great U.S. Mexican population group even in relation to a music structure and hierarchical/patriarchal power structure generally foreign to and unaccepted by Puerto Ricans.

All this was negotiated in an atmosphere of patriarchal schizophrenia. With the hit-and-miss careers of Luis Valdez, Moctezuma Esparza, Silvia Morales, and Jesús Treviño (the latter two "resurrected" with *Resurrection Boulevard*), the heavy hand of Gregory Nava has taken over the production of Latino images for a mass audience. First, *El Norte,* then *Mi Familia,* then *Selena* marked his ascendency. Soon after, his *American Family* television series did it again. Nava both distinguishes—between Guatemalan, Mexican, and Chicano in *El Norte*—and homogenizes by casting Latinas removed from their nation and ethnic specific backgrounds. He is the patriarchal god who gives and takes away. He made a *vato* of Jimmy Smits, now he has made a Chicana out of Raquel Welch—so why not a *chola* or a Selena out of Jennifer Lopez?

But the *Selena* film suffered from multiple patriarchy—Nava, the studio, but also Selena's father, who insisted the story had to be told one way and not another, who dominated the production, dominated Olmos and even Nava himself. The story seems too self-serving, too caught up in Quintanilla's imperatives and prohibitions. And I believe this may have affected the film's impact even for those who did not know the behind-the-scenes dirt. As far as I can make out, *Selena* was no blockbuster with a mass U.S. audience, while thousands of Mexicans and Chicanos and some Puerto Ricans flocked to the theater. The Puerto Rican-Chicana crossover paralleled Selena's own Chicana-Mexican one, but her Mexican-U.S. crossover, well in progress at the time of her death (through her songs, but also through her evocative appearance in *Don Juan DeMarco*), was not immediately paralleled by any mass Anglo interest in Jennifer Lopez as the film *Selena*.

Perhaps one of the problems rooted in the events of Selena's death, and inevitably enacted, though left murky in the film version, was the fact that her tragedy could be seen as a result of her Chicano-Mexican success, and only possibly a product of her growing Anglo-American crossover drive. The other problem was that her fan club manager and assassin turned out to be another Chicana. This made the whole business too much an internal affair to constitute a crossover trag-edy with which Latinos and non-Latinos could readily identify. Even the rumored "secret of Selena," so much the part of the postmurder publicity mill, had to do in most people's minds with another potential crossover—a sexual one with juicy, lurid undertones—suggesting that Saldívar's crime stemmed from an unrequited (or was it requited and then spurned?) lesbian passion. But, as I remember, this secret is not at all made explicit in the intervention of still another U.S. Puerto Rican, María Celeste Arraras, in her *El Secreto de Selena* (1997).

Of course *Selena*, like *La Bamba* before it, was a film about crossing over; and it dramatized the process. It showed Lopez's crossover capacity and made her a star. I believe that many Mexicanos, Latinos, and non-Latinos kept looking for some tell-tale Boricua touch that would weaken the presentation. You do not just become a Mexican crossover, you learn how to be one. As Selena had learned from her father, so Lopez learned from hers—that is, from Nava himself. Study-ing all the clips she could find, she learned how to walk and talk, look sexy-cute without becoming too sexy, learned how to tease, please, and placate her Chicano audience. There is a kind of voyeurism involved, something of a transvestite ef-fect too, as some people commented that Lopez played Selena more convincingly than Selena herself. I would argue that it was the African American dimension, the possible slide into some overtly African American stereotype, that would ne-gate her (supposedly non–African American) Mexicanness, which is the element most crucial to the crossover and its unconscious fascination.

Frances Aparicio is right to note that Lopez's Mexican crossover abilities stem not only from her great performance skills, but also from the fact that she could translate her hip-hop and also her salsa cultural capital into Mexican capital, through the medium of the most African-marked dimension of Mexican border culture, the *cumbia*. The *cumbia* is clearly the heart of Selena's own crossover style; it enables her to get beyond a narrow Chicana border identity to a larger Chicana/Mexicana crossover; it also enables a minimal and controlled sexualiza-tion of her body and movements and a slide from narrowly colonized Mexicana and Chicana identification to more Caribbeanized, Africanized ones. To be sure, the suppressed African, or third root, of Mexican culture is one not readily taken on by a people already stigmatized but seeking to rise. Nevertheless, taking on such an identity, challenging rather than internalizing dominant forms of racism that are also part of Mexican as well as U.S. colonial and postcolonial history, may well be construed as something decisively positive—a genuine victory. By adapt-ing her own Afro-Caribbean New York cultural base to African American affirma-tion through *cumbia*, Lopez is able to enact the crossover that creates a fantasy of sexual and more generally colonial and human liberation. In this sense the African base of Lopez's cultural capital enables her to embody Chicano liberation perhaps more fully than might a Chicana more specifically rooted and bound by her restricted identity bounds.

Nava has made a career of exposing inter-Latino tensions and dispelling most normative claims to unity. So we have the Guatemalan/Mexican, Chicano/Mexican/Guatemalan conflicts of *El Norte*. So, in *Mi familia,* Elpidia Carrillo, the Central American paper-bride of Jimmy Smits, wins him over by teaching him to overcome his hardened East L.A. barrio mask and dance with her in broad daylight on an East L.A. neighborhood street. It's almost science fiction to watch a Central American teach a Puerto Rican how to dance. But of course, Smits is playing a Chicano, so the scene isn't totally unreal. In *Selena,* however, the tensions are more severe, because what's set up is an Oedipal rivalry for Selena's soul that involves Quintanilla against her guitar-playing boyfriend and Saldívar. Selena dies because she has drifted from her father's authority. In spite of his reconciliation with his daughter after her marriage, Quintanilla kills off his rival but sacrifices his rebellious daughter in the process. And in some way the picture is sacrificed as well, because Quintanilla's control of Nava, I would argue, prevents the director from exploring the Selena/Saldívar relationship fully enough to make the necessary end filmically believable or effective. What does emerge, however, is that the tragedy of Selena stems from the illusion, confirmed by her victory in Mexico, that in her efforts to cross over, she can count on her own people. If she had been more wary of Saldívar in the first place, if she had not been forced to distance herself from daddy, she might have survived. In effect, the Latino identity projected by Selena's crossover is negated by the killing itself, which gives the rebellious crossover Chicana and, again, her Puerto Rican imposter, their comeuppance. I would argue finally that the Chicano crossover failure, the theme of *Zoot Suit, La Bamba,* and *Selena* may be rooted in U.S. racism, but also in a rejection of that process that has grown in the Mexican and Chicano imaginary—a rejection not paralleled in the Puerto Rican case. The ultimate irony of *Selena* is that if the film portrays the failure of crossover, it does so while achieving the triumph of crossover (from Nuyorican to Chicana) in Lopez's career move.

Lopez after Selena

After *Selena,* her remarkable recent career fully launched, Lopez would improve her Spanish but play havoc with her potential for African American crossover, making mistakes in her public persona, in her assumption that having had an African

American boyfriend would give her the crossover license to use the "n" word in her hip-hop forays. Other mistakes and successes, her new films, CDs, tear-away dresses, and poses for photo-essay hymns to that remarkably flexible and very much socially constructed Lopez body made her top gun just at a moment when Marc Anthony and Ricky Martin were surging above a whole group of Latino singers and making the crossover most of them could not make to constitute the Boricua triumvirate that was rather exaggeratedly heralded as the Latin explosion.

It would be worthwhile to reflect briefly on that explosion and its historical conjuncture, so easy to forget in the wake of more recent events. Nevertheless, I remember walking down Broadway in Los Angeles' annual Cinco de Mayo celebration soon after Selena was murdered but before Jennifer Lopez won the part. I remember all the Selena paraphernalia on sale at the many stalls that lined the long street down to the main performance area. I remember the Selena T-shirts, the Selena caps and halters, even a Selena *ofrenda* seemingly so out of place in this event. But in the context of it all, I remember a very small group of women who carried placards and passed out information protesting Proposition 187 and the overall anti-Mexican backlash, which was all so powerful in the Los Angeles area at that time. I remember interviewing these women with my video camera, asking them why they were protesting, why there were not more Mexicans protesting. And they spoke to me of community apathy, and one even complained that there was more interest in Selena and in the recent happy discovery that a Latina (or at least a Salvadoran woman—wasn't she undocumented like Linda Chavez's maid?) gave at least some Latino dimension (though not much) to the O.J. Simpson case.

Of course, the Latino explosion of Boricuas identified as Latinos occurs as Mexicans are being subjected to the largest wave of racist resentment since the heyday of César Chávez. I believe this is indeed the context. It may have been a U.S. psychological compensatory act, attempting to counter anti-Mexican racism by indicating that the real problem was undocumented workers because, after all, we love our legal Latinos and admire their wonderful talents. But surely it was no coincidence that the explosion was rather limited to our three Boricua figures, that none of these figures was Mexican, that the super-super was identified as white and maybe gay, that the secondary male figure was touted as the Puerto Rican Frank Sinatra; and that the one woman figure was showing herself capable of Mexican and African American crossovers, even as she pursued and was pursued by very white lovers in at least some of her post-Selena film work and in her personal life.

So the Puerto Rican explosion is interpolated as Latina as part of a compensatory tactic and is in no clear way an antidote for the Chicano, and soon, the Latino backlash. The explosion was an East Coast projection in relation to a syndrome diagnosed on the West Coast and now spreading east. Selena was the Tex-Mex connection in all this, but I believe she was a figure rooted in long-term Tex-Mex traditions and not, like Los Tigres del Norte, for example, directly linked to undocumented Mexicans, no matter how many undocumented workers might have taken up her music.

Several years have passed since the backlash and explosion began. On one hand, the backlash produced a new Chicano renaissance in which thousands of Mexicans who never identified as Chicanos and never even knew who César Chávez was have come to participate. U.S. Mexicans have indeed struggled for political entitlement, and this has produced a new cultural wave, with new musical groups, new videos, new Chicano forms—and this includes the comeback of a figure like Santana. But in all this, no Chicano superstar has fully crossed over toward the larger U.S. consumer world—only Mexicans such as Salma Hayek and perhaps Gael Bernal have been able to break through.

The Big 3 have held on, making some key adjustments along the way. Martin came out of the closet even as he had previously reasserted island identifications with his "Peace in Vieques" call, and Anthony made a super-explicit affirmation of his Puerto Ricanness with his version of "Preciosa"; Lopez has survived her "n-word" gaffe, but after her Ben Affleck fling (including her gender crossover in *Gigli*), she has recuperated from her sins in her crossover reversal—by marrying her brother Nuyorican and then stealing his major movie attempt by seeing to it (or was it the Cuban American director?) that the film more than often seemed to merit the title, *La mujer del Cantante*).[8] But while the fame and success of the Big 3 continue, it is like the three tenors—it does not seem to extend much beyond them, no matter how many people try. Chayanne simply hasn't crossed over (his playing a Cuban opposite Vanessa Williams brought him neither Latino/African American or non-Latino U.S. attention)—although his romantic songs and his dancing have made him very popular throughout the Latin American/Latino world. Olga Tañón's baseball player romances haven't led to any crossover success—maybe she doesn't care; maybe, too, la India has come closest to succeeding, mainly with the help of Marc Anthony. In effect, no other Puerto Rican or Latin American figure has been able to participate much in the so-called explosion or its generalization. Christina Aguilera started in English, but perhaps her failure to remember the words of the U.S. national anthem (was it a Bolivarian or Freudian slip?) will help her to cross over to the Latino/Latin American world. Shakira has had the greatest success, even though at first she seemed too exotic, too Latin American/Lebanese, so that it was difficult to project the kind of impact she has had in recent years.

In the same period, Dominican meringue and Nuyorican hip-hop moved ahead in Puerto Rican island music, so much so that Juan Luis Guerra even acknowledged the growing Puerto Rican hegemony of meringue in Elvis Crespo and others. Now we live the world of *reggaetón*—in which New York Afro-hip-hop, Jamaican reggae, and salsa rhythms come together in a new mode that begins to absorb and transform earlier musical forms. And meanwhile, island Puerto Ricans complain bitterly about those from outside, and especially the "Africanization" coming from Hispaniola and the rap and hip-hop Harlemized U.S. Puerto Ricans have brought to Borinken—and this even as Afro–Puerto Ricans continue rivaling Dominicans and Venezuelans in producing most of the boxers and baseball players who keep up the colonial/racialization pattern of body performance.

Meanwhile, as if to counter or supplement all this, the island is producing a significant number of intellectuals who study at major U.S. institutions and are then dispersed across the United States and even international academic turf, and who now have crossed over from Puerto Rican studies to virtually every field the academy has to offer—although they are mainly "blanquitos" whose main function remains that of producing intellectual work related to Puerto Rican bodies and their transnationalizing/latinizing/diasporic identifications. The mind/body split persists (see Quintero-Rivera 2009).

In the United States, Dominicans and now Mexicans have penetrated the Nuyorican universe, and diasporican identity has spread more fully to Boston, Philadelphia, Orlando, Chicago, and the West Coast. Rican educational failures and informal economy participation continue, even as a significant and apparently growing proportion of the U.S. population begins to defy Linda Chavez, goes into higher education, and achieves successes at every level.[9] Ironically, however, to this day, it's almost exclusively the relatively privileged island creoles or "blanquitos" located on the island or in the United States who have virtually monopolized knowledge production not only about Puerto Rico but about U.S. Puerto Ricans as well. The development of the contemporary Puerto Rican intelligentsia has been remarkable; and now even U.S. Puerto Rican communities in the midst of poverty and stigmatization have indeed produced barrio-based intellectuals that give better or richer autochthonous representations of their own world.[10] This question of Latino identity from below has always been a problematic one in U.S. reality; but it seems to me essential for Latino and human survival in our hemisphere. In the face of homogenizing globalization patterns, the forging of Latino unities in the midst of conflicts has been part of the history of Latinos in the United States. It requires another generation, I think, for a more adequate articulation of this unity, but its even partial achievement—the articulation of a unity that does not erase specific national identities—would, I believe, be very important for a more human future in the American hemisphere.

To conclude this essay, I would just like to mention the massive tribute to Selena that took place in Houston's Reliant Stadium in the spring of 2005—a concert in the grand style in which Gloria Estefan, Christina Aguilera, and Don Francisco paid homage to the rising Chicana star and thereby incorporated Texmexland into their vision of Latinidad. How elated Houston Mexicans and Central Americans felt to be finally, fully accepted by the grace of Selena. How sad it was too, however, that Marc Anthony and his Selena-blessed Boricua wife were not there to join the party, pay due tribute, and confirm what the Cuban and other Latino others were saying—that Selena had to die tragically to accomplish in death and now resurrection the greatest Chicana crossover of all time. But how wonderful that she too was, however dead, now more alive than ever (at least so she seemed, as contemporary greats joined in singing along with her filmed images—so alive she seemed on the screen that Abraham Quintanilla cried), now most fully projected and consecrated as a Latina star, with all the honors, tears, and commercials Miami Latino hegemons could bestow. If Jennifer Lopez played a Tex-Mex star from Corpus Christi, Selena in death had become what Linda Chavez most abhorred: a Puerto Rican. She and Lopez were sister Latinas, after all.

The Splendid Little War, Elizam Escobar. "Escobar overlays a transparent image of a Puerto Rican flag on top of torn pages [out of] a text [from] which the title of the work derives. The text contains printed images of U.S. expansionism at the end of the 19th century. The images of the text depict U.S. President McKinley, General Miles, battle scenes, black U.S. troops fighting in Cuba, and other atrocities in the name of Manifest Destiny. The text becomes the ground that cannot be covered up or erased. The images appear to bleed through the red stripes of the flag. Betances' portrait is placed on the star which like the island of Puerto Rico itself is surrounded by the soft oceanic blue." Michael Piazza, 1998, 7.

Chapter 2

The Flag and
Three Rican Artists

....

To the memory of Michael Piazza (RIP)

A Meditation on Puerto Rico
and its Artistic Production

What is Puerto Rico? Or, as Boricuas ask of the grandmother so loved (but so hidden), where is she? First an indigenous—*Arawak-Boricua-Taino*—world; then a colony of plantations and small farms, of slaves, freed slaves, artisans, store-keepers, struggling, with the mother country and its own social sectors. Then it became the site of a second colonization—a special status, a unique situation, a remarkable, problematic diaspora.

What is Puerto Rico? A space in the Caribbean or wherever Puerto Ricans make their home. An island but also more—*Isla-plus,* including those other islands: Culebra, Vieques . . . A Caribbean space so far from itself and the other islands of its sea, neighbor of South America tied to the Bronx and even Chicago: In the Bayamón Blockbuster, you have to look for Jacobo Morales's movies of is-land life in the section on foreign films. What is Puerto Rico? An island clinging to its Caribbean and Latin American identities, to what it has been and can be, while dealing, *bregando,* with McDonaldization, Miamization, Disneyfication, postmodernity, liquidity. A hyper-version of what globalization has been doing throughout the world . . .

Who are the Puerto Ricans? To what degree is their history tied to sugar and slavery, their culture to its indigenous and African strains? To what degree is its European side Andalucian, Gypsy, Sephardic, Catalunian, Italian—from Mallorca, Corsica, the Canary Islands, or from distinct points in the Caribbean? And what of its other populations—from China, the Middle East, or New Jersey? To what de-gree has its U.S.-projected modernization and its accommodations and resistances made it different from or deeply representative of other parts of the Caribbean? And what has been the history and character of Puerto Rican arts? In literature and painting? What has been their expressive character or dynamism with respect

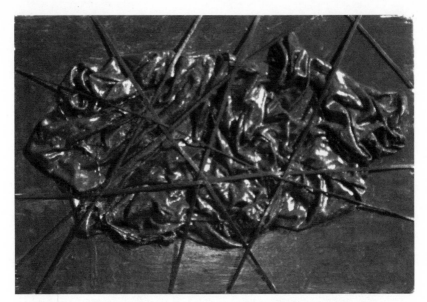

Isla Cautiva, Elizam Escobar. "A discarded cloth (a flag?) in the shape of the island is painted over in dark brown and bound by leather (boot) straps. Here is the act of imposition, as though everything is already wrapped-up bound and determined." Piazza 1998, 9–10.

to other Puerto Rican spaces—as the *guagua aerea* extends the island traffic jam of *La guaracha* to Manhattan, the Heights or the barrio that's now Manhatitlán, and the Lower East Side, to the Bronx and out toward Hartford and Boston, to New Jersey and Philadelphia, to Chicago and Orlando—and then moves on to Los Angeles, Hawaii, Vietnam, to Bosnia, Afghanistan, Iraq, wherever . . .

With answers that are ever couched and complicated, with a sense of collective self so deeply intense and at the same time so fragile, defensive, and fragmented, most Puerto Ricans, regardless of their political ideologies, have lived for decades torn over and yet centered on the question of their racial, geographical, and political identities, ever vigilant of slight or wound, ever defiant against perceived insult and injury. Add to this their sense of entitlement and rancor with their position in U.S. life. They have rarely been docile (as René Marqués 1993 would have it); but in one way or another, they have been involved in using "the weapons of the weak," in that complex, defensive, postcolonial process of cultural struggle Arcadio Díaz Quiñones has characterized as "el arte de bregar," by means of which they have always defended what they have considered theirs—their customs, their myths, and icons of identity—even their *"Pollo*

Picu"(their local-brand chicken), so much fresher than foreign competitors', even if the chicken costs more.

So many problems of imposition, and of adjustment, of occupation, of colonialization, of unequal struggle and negotiation of spaces; and with and beyond the anniversary of one hundred years of special colonial status, so many family ruptures for political, economic, and religious reasons, for reasons of immigration and alienation. So many struggles and rivalries, so many failed projects and dreams. And now, when far more than one hundred years have come and gone, at the beginning of a new millennium, and without a change in Puerto Rico's not very postcolonial status, now as many Puerto Ricans live abroad as they do on the island, now the *guagua aerea* is more than ever a round trip, in the great commuter transnation in which citizenship, while second class, involves borders that extend from one homeland to another as so many Puerto Ricans continue participating and dying in the struggles and wars of the Empire. And now, after more than one hundred years of solitude under the ever and always democratic and honest custody of the United States, now, after the problems of narco-capitalism and criminalization, after the fall of Law 936, which had provided tax incentives to investing companies, after the fights over the super-tube water supply system, the privatization of the telephone company, after one plebiscite after another, and the famous "no a lo anterior," or "none of the above"—after all the crises caused by globalization, neoliberalism, and transnational processes, after the decades of controversy, the military occupation of Vieques came forward once again to front page, intensifying the struggles over national identity, revealing ever more decisively that Puerto Rico is not just one island.

In the first years after January 1, 2000, Puerto Rican ex-POWs awoke from their twenty-plus-year nightmare to find they had struggled and sacrificed for a land under the thumb of McBurger and Wal-Mart. The controversy over Vieques intensified Puerto Rican identity struggles even while showing all-to-clearly that Puerto Rico was not just an island. David Sanes killed, and even the pro-statehood governor obliged to argue before the U.S. Congress that the military should leave the island, receives the same treatment as do the majority of Latinos in the great country of perfect democracy. Welcome to statehood. After Madonna rubbed the Puerto Rican flag against her genitalia (or *zona deshonrada,* as one critic dared to phrase it) in 1992, after the postmodern defense of Madonna by presenting Albizu in scandalous attire,[1] after the flag scandal of Seinfeld, Marc Anthony sings his affirmation of nationhood in a special hyped rendition of *Preciosa,* and in 2001, Ricky Martin affirms his commitment to *Peace for Vieques.* And now after the relative victory in Vieques, now with 9/11, as the war in Afghanistan rages, Puerto Ricans continue on their precarious path, the death toll mounting, the price of their "colonial advantage" ever thrown in their faces and mounting in their hearts.

As the Castilian saying puts it, better alone than poorly accompanied. But in the case of Puerto Rico, its accompaniment has constituted now more than one hundred years that serve as the basis of its culture and art. Its accompaniment has led to an isolation and solitude in relation to its Caribbean and Latin American being. It is an ensemble of spaces that constitute a land, so far from itself and the other islands of its sea, neighbor to Venezuela and South America, but tied to Bronx and Chicago—and so many other spaces . . . And in all its ensemble, in each space during its now more than one hundred years of special status, cultural resistance has been the history of Puerto Rico in its daily doings and its artistic work.

Whether on the island, in the barrios of the massive Puerto Rican diaspora, or in the prisons of the state or state of mind, contemporary Puerto Rican artistic expression is structured and articulated between the pressures of national history and cosmopolitan influence, between desires for "authentic expression" and the overt or internalized imperatives of the market. From the conquest to the end of the nineteenth century, the struggle of artists was to maintain and develop modes of expression within the frame of Spanish colonial power and norms. After the invasion of 1898, artists worked in the midst of the intense influences of the United States. Increasingly the struggle has been to maintain dimensions of identity but also to escape or elude them in relation to postmodern questions of gender feminism, antipatriarchal critique, queer theory, and so forth—and an overall "nomadicity" in the midst of those influences and the processes of economic globalization.[2]

In this context, every horned mask, every *vejigante* carnival costume[3] flirts with kitsch and commercialism even as it expresses a potential, imagined, or real victory over cultural erasure, an affirmation of a Puerto Rican will to live and thrive in spite of military invasions, linguistic incursions, cruise ship excursions, and Burger King/Pizza Hut immersions. No wonder that for so many Puerto Rican artists on the island and in the vast Puerto Rican Diaspora, the icons and symbols come and go, like the Puerto Ricans themselves, between subjective and social themes, between political and even spiritual nuances. No wonder the face of nationalist leader Pedro Albizu Campos stares out from so many places in Puerto Rican art; no wonder the Puerto Rican flag is a constant obsession and center of play in the images of so much fabricated or handmade kitsch—and even the finest handicraft, and yes, its finest art.

With José Campeche as its brightest light, Puerto Rico was an important center of colonial art; at the end of the nineteenth century, Oller, Pau, and others etched the crisis of their times; subsequently Carlos Raquel Rivera, Julio Tomás Martínez, Myrna Baez, Lorenzo Homar, Rafael Tufiño, Carlos Osorio, José Antonio Torres-Martínez, and others simultaneously related Puerto Rican art to the world while expressing national concerns and, some among them, participating in a movement of social protest art. In recent years, nostalgia and politics have dominated the scene, while young college-bred artists, trained (like Arnaldo Roche Rabell) at the School of the Art Institute of Chicago and like places, have entered international/cosmopolitan art worlds. At the same time, Puerto Rican visual works by artists academically trained or not flourished in New York, Chicago, and, for more than a few years, even a prison in Oklahoma.

Speaking of the spaces for Puerto Rican visual art, Díaz Quiñones notes that:

> The map of the Puerto Rican territory is, simultaneously precise and unreachable, very local and very changeable, with mythic and other more exact geographies. It is in these new frontiers where they have extracted from the constant struggle known as "the *brega*," the force that has permitted them to continue affirming themselves in spite of the difficulties. . . . The artist Antonio Martorell has gone over this new Puerto Rican archipelago, struggling and negotiating—that is, *bregando*—with the deterritorialized practices which have renewed images of the culture. Martorell emerges from the encounter of prejudices derived from the static and commercialized concepts of culture, opposing to them his "installations" and his multiple and portable "casas." . . . A dual passion moves him: on the one hand, the real and imaginary voyage, the detours and the flights to unforeseen places, and on the other hand, the more stable interiors . . . the places of memory. His installations point to fundamental questions: What constitutes the unity of "place?" And how do we struggle and negotiate with abrupt changes of place? These are the same questions that have been formulated in contemporary debates about the cultural relations between identity, place and communities. These interrogations have brought him to fix his gaze on old histories and create other flights in Cayey, Ponce, New York or Chicago. (Díaz-Quiñones 2000, 79)

It is to the artistic production of three U.S.-based Puerto Ricans[4] dealing with Puerto Rican maps, memories, and related themes—above all, the flag—that we must now turn.

Clandestine Cries, 1998–99, Juan Sánchez. This work and others in the series by Juan Sánchez show "his continued exploration of collaged and painted surfaces. [Here,] Sánchez joins two rectangular canvas panels in a T formation as an alternative to completely obliterating the traditional Western picture plane. Sánchez decided to establish a consistent format in which to confront issues of Puerto Rican identity during the 100th year since Spain left the island from his vantage point growing up in Brooklyn, New York. Sánchez puts a different twist on . . . the Puerto Rican flag, turning it on end as in a banner display. But . . . the image which is turned vertical is squashed to fit the confines of the horizontal rectangle. The stripes of the flag appear squat or truncated. The flag should be longer but looks as though it is conforming to some absurd rule of distortion. The lower panel attached to the Puerto Rican flag consists of an upside down image of a palm tree, an image identified with Puerto Rico as well as the statehood movement" (Piazza 1998, 6).

The Flag, Flagism, and Artistic Representation

> Andrés has a Puerto Rican flag on his car's front bumper. Andrés has a Puerto Rican flag on his outside antenna. Andrés has a Puerto Rican flag on his car's front plate. Andrés has six little, beautiful Puerto Rican flags on his car's wipers and one on each window. Andrés has another Puerto Rican flag on his steering wheel that helps him drive and another Puerto Rican flag on the dashboard. . . . Andrés has a big Puerto Rican flag in the living room. Andrés has a Puerto Rican flag in his bedroom. Andrés has a Puerto Rican flag in his dining room. . . . Andrés bought a beautiful t-shirt bearing the Puerto Rican flag in the Puerto Rican parade at Humboldt Park. Andrés bought pretty t-shirts showing the Puerto Rican flag at the center with a greenish "coquí" playing the "cuatro," as well as a "pava" and El Castillo Del Morro calling to him.[5]

The story I have just cited was written by a wistful observer of the Chicago Puerto Rican scene in a book of vignettes that at least some of which are worth another, better printing, another, closer read by more people. For at least in some of these vignettes, and certainly this one, author Leonardo Rodríguez is able to trace symptoms of a quasi-medical condition marked by extremes of self-deprecation and self-affirmation that has affected the psyches of all too many as part of the legacy of Puerto Rico's troubled hundred years (and surely, of its diasporic history), and that was characterized by Albizu Campos, but also others before and after him, as symptoms of "Puerto Rico, patria infermiza"—an ill country that Albizu and others proposed to cure.[6]

The Puerto Rican flag is at least overtly the center of the work developed by Elizam Escobar, Ramón López, and Juan Sánchez presented in a joint exhibition commemorating but certainly not celebrating one hundred years of Puerto Rico's second colonization. So while the origin of the flag grows out of the struggle against Spain, it also defines Puerto Rico as a U.S. colony. The flag has come to embody the diversity of national feelings of the people of Puerto Rico. It is at once a symbol of immense pride—heroic, nostalgic, and otherwise—as well as an unspoken burden. Through the flag, the artists in question can begin to raise questions beyond the image.

The exhibition was a manifesto in relation to the flag—a Puerto Rican appropriation of Jasper Johns's aggressive play on the U.S. stars and stripes, but it was also a manifesto in relation to flagism—*banderismo*. The three artists are *independendistas* who have all led lives of political as well as artistic struggle. For them, the variations of the Puerto Rican flag have their importance, as does the relation of that flag to another one of fifty stars whose current symmetry and form they would like to see maintained. But these are not "fetishizers" of flags. These are political artists whose visions go far beyond any narrow nationalism or even the frustrated national aspirations of their colonized space of imagination and aspiration. From their barrio and prison worlds, these artists can see what amounts to a fascination of Puerto Ricans with their flag as a form of affirmation and resistance, but they can also see this fascination as an obsession—an expression and not an affirmation of colonialism, an expression too not of resistance but of capitulation to commercialism and commodity consumption—and all this if only because the flag and all the other icons are clearly and necessarily (and of course dangerously) implicated in the seductive circuit of commodities that dominates our lives and the overall world in which we live, and especially the lives of those who have been trained to accept commodity fetishism as one of the religious options available in a colonized object world.

The images of flags, of Albizu, of toy Yankee soldiers, palm trees, *coquís,* carved wooden saints, rosaries, lizards, and whatever all speak to the complications and contradictions, the impositions and fragmentations—indeed, many of the multiple dimensions and problems to be found in plotting Puerto Rican struggles at the end of this century, one hundred years after . . .

Who are the Puerto Ricans, and what is their relation to the symbols of nation and community, to their Latin and Anglo-American, to their Antillean and U.S., their Spanish and African American, as well as Amer-Indian and specifically Taino roots? And what are these relations to questions of life and death, to Christian and camouflaged African practices, to the island's sounds and colors, its well-known music and her less-known visual arts?

The seemingly simple, direct, and overt political works in this exhibit run a gamut extending from political affirmation to questions of flag, leader, and commodity fetishism, to questions of dependency and metaphysical as well as political freedom. In the work of each of the three artists in this exhibit, the political messages read loud and clear; but in each case, the works cry out for some kind of aesthetic understanding, some valorization that is not dependent on strictly political but also artistic attraction. The delicate relation between art and politics, icon and artwork, will be at the center of our discussion of the artists, their life trajectory, and their work on Puerto Rican flags and related icons as part of the Puerto Rican commemoration of its one hundred years of solitude.

Juan Sánchez in his Brooklyn studio. Photo by Jorge Bustos, courtesy of Guariken Arts, Inc.

Juan Sánchez and His Unflagging Work

> Juan Sánchez is one of the most important Puerto Rican artists working today. . . . Although the ingredients of [his] compositions seem familiar to us, [his work] seeks to make us believe in what still doesn't exist. The ordering of images, words and references that Sánchez proposes does not come out of journalistic writing or ethnography. It's not a political strategy, nor a Puerto Rican promise framed in a federal budget. . . . It is a door toward the zone in which things are new and still lack names and birth dates, although one can note the traces of past journeys. Nevertheless, in spite of all the novelty and uncertainty, we can see ourselves facing this mystery. This is what art's all about; it permits us to see what we are still not. Imaginary coherence. Construction of another belief system. In this future that extends itself each day. (Ramón López 1997, 3)

In the view of art critic Shifra Goldman, Juan Sánchez should be seen first as a product not only of José Luis González's four floors of Puerto Rican history

(1980), but a fifth floor she extrapolates that was of "the interactions between the cracked structure of the 19th century style capitalism imposed on the island after 1898 and the opportunistic populism which emerged out of but then transformed that structure," involving as a culminating gesture the implementation of Operation Bootstrap, which turned increasing Puerto Rican out-migration into a virtual system of massive proportions. Goldman points out that the Puerto Ricans who had been arriving, especially after 1917, congealed as a population that had experienced a level of job and housing access comparable to urban U.S.-born African Americans. "Those, like Juan's family, who were black and dark-skinned, suffered racial as well as economic discrimination" (Goldman 1994, 434).[7]

Born in 1954 to Afro–Puerto Rican migrant, working-class parents, Sánchez grew up in Brooklyn, where he continues to live and work today. His artistic and political convictions were largely influenced by the social and economic conditions of the predominantly working-class neighborhoods of his youth. Sánchez's contact with various Puerto Rican political and grassroots organizations greatly shaped his ideology as an artist and cultural worker, starting with his politicization while a teenager in high school by the Young Lords, a Spanish Harlem–based political and social group formed in the late 1960s by Puerto Rican activists, which served as a Puerto Rican counterpart to the Black Panthers and Brown Berets, and worked to improve conditions in the barrios.[8]

By this time Sánchez had an already developed interest in the arts, fostered by his father, who was a maker of wooden altars. The altar format, whether single or multiple panel or utilized simply as painted frames around an image, remains an important element in the artist's compositions. Now, learning his politics through the Young Lords newspaper, *Pa'lante (Right On)*, "he was already moving toward a political conversion of his father's religious-centered path" (Goldman 1994, 435). Sánchez's involvement with the Young Lords, along with his active participation in various proindependence organizations from 1978 to 1985, played a major role in defining his political views. In 1974, Sánchez, with some education in graphic design and photography, enrolled as an art student in Cooper Union, entering painting classes, where he absorbed some lessons of mainstream abstraction—including the use of shaped canvases that reinforced his altar-influenced forms and strengthened his command of composition. Nevertheless, he insisted on figurative and political imagery; he began to produce posters on canvas and began to incorporate texts into his works—all of which led him on a collision course with most of his teachers (Goldman 1994, 435).

Even as he embarked on his formal studies, he met Jorge Soto, Gilberto Hernández, and Marco Dimas, members of the Taller Boricua, a cultural center founded in Spanish Harlem to foster community access and participation in the visual arts, music, poetry, and dance. The Taller Boricua's culturally rooted and socially conscious art had a significant impact on Sánchez and continues to influence his work to this day (Nieves 1997, 6). Living in the ambiance of the Cuban Revolution and the emergent Black and Latino movements, Sánchez, like other Latinos coming to maturity in the 1970s, turned to Che Guevara and Malcolm X as iconic figures of resistance; he, like other Puerto Rican youth, turned to Albizu Campos as the prime icon of Puerto Rican independence, using his image and texts as an essential part of his art (Goldman 1994, 435).

Attending Rutgers University in New Jersey and completing his formal education in 1980, Sánchez emerged as a politicized artist committed to opening communication to and about his community "by employing an artistic language and

Albizu es cultura negra (Albizu is Black Culture), Juan Sánchez. Pedro Albizu Campos, long imprisoned for his nationalism and opposition to colonialism and statehood, is here surrounded by chains and of course the larger flag/palm tree context. As in Sánchez's other images, "the palm tree appears to be dangling down from the flag or it could be said that the palm tree grows out of the stripes. . . . The act of turning upside down is often a sign of disrespect; or if the palm tree is read as a flag, it could be interpreted as a distress signal according to U.S. flag protocol (here recalling Jasper Johns's flags)." (Piazza 1998, 6). In a note to me, Sánchez adds: "The upside down palm trees . . . also symbolize the instability, colonization and ambiguity of a Puerto Rico's national and cultural identity; [the trees] . . . represent a people in a state of limbo."

a variety of symbols and images familiar enough to them so that they would enter his space (the poster, the painting, the print, the photograph) with anticipation, and emerge with heightened understanding" (Goldman 1994, 435). Since then, armed with the technical skills and visual vocabulary of contemporary art, fully attuned to his community's ongoing struggle for self-definition and historical reconstruction, Sánchez began crafting his own personal style, firmly based on a belief in the ability of art and culture to "transform lives and serve as a powerful catalyst for individual and communal change" (Nieves 1997, 6).

In Sánchez's work, Goldman finds the influence of Mexican muralism as filtered primarily through their influence on Puerto Rican printmakers (especially Tufiño and Homar) of the 1940s, intermingled and dialectically emerging through a tug and tussle with New York mainstream artists like Rauschenberg, whose minimalism emerges even in Sánchez's fascination with Nuyorican popular culture forms—the *botánica* with its *santería* paraphernalia, the Spanish-language and religious calendars, the Puerto Rican parades with floats and fancy dress, the *bomba* and *plena*, the *santos,* home altars, inexpensive religious chromoliths of folk Catholicism, and finally the Island love for brilliant color, tropical flowers and plants, and ocean-reflected light. The seamier side of the New York barrio environments—its cracked, crumbling, stained, and graffitied walls larded with the remains of generations of commercial and political posters—offered a prototype for Sánchez's layered methods of painting, tearing, pasting, scratching, and scribbling, and of graffiti-like texts appearing and disappearing into the various layers. Total surfaces are activated in this manner; even prints may have as many as four layers. In this case, the medium itself provides a message situating the human and symbolic imageries within their New York context (Goldman 1994, 435–36).

Thus, for Goldman, Juan Sánchez's fifth floor has "glass windows that let him look out at Puerto Rico's past and present." She says, finally:

> It is the back-and-forthing, the free association of disparate historical and formal elements, the interweaving of personal and political attributes, the switching from Spanish to English texts, the references to widely known powerful personalities and unknown humble persons, which constitute the dialectical interactions occurring in the whole corpus of Juan Sánchez's work. His symbolic and formal usages are positioned to make most effective a complex and didactic view of Puerto Rican history, culture, sensibility and politics. With time, his vision is broadening. He is attempting in his art and in his activism, to synthesize the existing bifurcated view that separates Island form mainland realities. . . . Beyond that, he reaches

out to the entire Third World, the macrovision derived from his New York micro-cosm. (1994, 437–38)

Speaking about his art for his RICAN/STRUCT traveling exhibition, Sánchez notes:

We as people must deconstruct the colonized history that is oppressing us and reconstruct the false reality to give testimony to our real history and truths. We must re-create ourselves and give light to our virtues and strength in order to really appreciate who we are and be proud of it. We must RICAN/STRUCT our path toward self determination and freedom. . . . My commitment is to express significant concerns and contents through the investigation of aesthetic and formal practice. To search for racial, cultural, social, and political definitions rooted in and erupting from a hostile environment is a necessity in my creative process. To dig deep into the history of the colonized and the colonizers. And to take back what is rightfully ours. The multi-layering of this process also expresses the complexity of the Puerto Rican people. To be responsible and responsive to a culture challenged by

De tantas rosas una especial (Of so many roses a special one), Juan Sánchez. As elsewhere in the series, "the joint banners act as a frame for the collaged images which are comprised of bits of ripped photographs, newspaper articles, political pamphlets, buttons and painted marks. It is these images that determine the meaning of the background. . . . [Here], Sánchez . . . paints a heart diagram around the image of independentista [activist and prisoner] Lolita Lebrón" (Piazza 1998, 7).

genocide is to make art that serves progress and not reactionary forces; to be with the oppressed and not with the oppressors; to deal not only with protest but also with recuperation and regenerative healing, to take sides with victory in affirming life and not embracing death. (cited in Nieves 1997, 7 and 10)

Characterizing key aspects of the artist's opus, Nieves makes much of the iconography manifest in virtually every Sánchez piece:

Sánchez' works suggest virtual palimpsests. . . . The use of color, altar-shaped canvases or wooden panels, layered surfaces comprised of painted images, assemblage elements, collage, fabric, photography, laser prints, and text, as well as the physical process of cutting and tearing, while simultaneously reconstructing what has been previously broken or torn—are just some of the many formal and compositional devices employed by the artist. . . . Graffiti-like texts inscribed on these worn surfaces along with a vast array of images, some partially faded or torn, evoke the effect of crowded public walls that have been covered over with posters and advertisements. Sánchez' visual repertoire spans a broad range of artistic and cultural sources including . . . Taino symbols, Afro-Caribbean religious practices, Catholicism, Puerto Rican popular culture and folk art traditions, and American and European painting, all of which reflect the complexities of Puerto Rican culture and its colonial history. Crosses, vejigantes . . . masks, flags . . . petroglyphs, poems, old family photographs, and portraits of Puerto Rican cultural and political icons are just some of the many ruptured fragments that Sánchez carefully weaves together in his mixed media works in an effort to reconstruct individual and collective histories. . . . The formal process of pealing, scratching, and tearing the multi-layered surfaces of his paintings, collages and prints to expose these hidden stories, suggests a political strategy intended to get beneath the surface of what has been previously concealed or repressed, to challenge previously held "truths" and thus construct meaning anew from the vantage point of resistance . . . and cultural affirmation. (Nieves 1997, 6–7)

As Nieves notes, Sánchez's entire artistic career has involved a "commitment to elaborating a complex aesthetic and visual language geared not only towards political protest, but focused on recuperating the many individual and communal narratives previously silenced or erased by the devastating effects of colonialism." The artist's work speaks " . . . from a space of resistance and creativity, challenging the colonizers' authority and reconstructing the Puerto Rican community's history . . . from a position of strength, renewal, liberation, and hope." So it is, Nieves concludes, that irrespective of one's overt politics, "Sánchez' emotionally charged works inspire and challenge us to get beneath the surface of our beliefs— to confront our feelings . . . in order to take responsibility for defining our future

Girl in Vejiganta Mask, Juan Sánchez. "Sánchez gives . . . us . . . an uncertain surface that he can respond to or act upon. [He] is always changing the color scheme which questions the national attachment to prescribed symbolism. His choices are left to interpretation. The shade of blue on the triangular field changes from work to work. The blues vary from traditional, to popular, and official flag tones revealing unspoken regulations regarding Puerto Rican flags. Here we have a black and white photo of a young girl in a vejigante mask made from coconut in [the Afro-Caribbean town of] Loíza, Puerto Rico. Traditional imagery . . . resonates in creating . . . a counter mask to the prevailing climate that ideologically masks important questions that need to be asked. Santería spirals, arrows, crosses overrun the image of the flag turning it into an overall pattern of the soulful rhythm of life [in] an act of love, a determination for liberation, an ongoing search beyond what has been rendered meaningless" (Piazza 1998, 8).

as individuals as well as within a broader communal context. Perhaps therein lies the truly transformative potential of his work. Sánchez's quest to uncover and reclaim individual and collective narratives previously hidden or devalued as a strategy against cultural marginalization is evident in . . . several of [his] recent works [that] address the urban condition, [and] . . . those social problems which plague the Latino community and threaten its very survival" (Nieves 1997, 7–8).

Ramón López. Self photo, 2010.

Ramón López: A Clear Message in Mixed Media

One hundred years after the invasion by the United States of Puerto Rico, Ramón López presented a selection of his mixed media works that serve as an expression of his stubborn cultural affirmation and resistance. Here in his new work, Puerto Rico's one hundred years of receivership shout out with great insistence and urgency; and yet also, in this work, he reaches a new level of vision and expressiveness.

Artisan and artist, anthropologist and essayist in Puerto Rican publications such as *Claridad* and *Diálogo,* López "lived his first years in Luquillo next to sugar cane fields and very close to the Yunque rainforest. Later he lived in a Barranquitas neighborhood."[9] He studied anthropology at the University of Puerto Rico and went to New York to take graduate classes in cultural anthropology. On his return to the island, he lived for various years in Villa Margarita near Trujillo Alto, teaching anthropology at the University of Puerto Rico and Inter-American University. For several years, López worked with the popular Santurce-based musical group, *Los plenaros de la 21 Abajo,* as an artisan and organizer of popular education projects. In several subsequent years, he lived in Chicago's Puerto Rican community doing cultural work, especially as a weaver of works rich in design as well as color, in cultural and religious as well as political implications.

A lover of the expressionist forms and colors of Vincent Van Gogh, of the writings of anthropologists like Eric Wolf, Claude Lévi-Strauss, and Fernando Ortiz but also Alejo Carpentier's *real maravilloso* and the magical realism of García Márquez, López not only studied art but also history, literature, and art theory, especially through his readings of his favorite thinker, John Berger. Early in his career, he investigated pre-Colombian textile techniques, as well as the contemporary work of Mexico's Huichol Indians and other tribes, trying to express his relation to powers alive in and yet beyond the history and everyday life of his country-colony. Perhaps more important in his artistic development was when he read Berger on Van Gogh and the painter's orientation to art as a form of work that approaches and transforms a world of objects.[10] At some point along the road, López decided to dedicate himself to weaving tapestries, a "pedestrian" artisanal art, with clear limits and advantages, with qualities that also retain an artisanal dimension, always tied to everyday materials.

Would it be an exaggeration to suggest that today an educated Puerto Rican who weaves is one who, consciously or not, links himself to the deeply rooted (and often domestic) and that he simultaneously struggles against the one-dimensionality and artificiality that invades the island? To hand-weave materials is almost like mounting a campaign not only against the fabrics of mass production and indeed every manufactured flag: it is to struggle against flagism, as much as against whatever superficial and reductive fetishism of nationalism, and also against the ecological abuse suffered throughout the world, but nowhere more intensely than in sites of colonization and economic deprivation. Of course, it is just another of López's many contradictions that he prefers acrylic, "which is nothing else except petroleum converted into textile fiber" (López 1988, 7). But using a synthetic product, he shows how he can put the achievements of modernity at the service of a struggle not for a community of nostalgia but rather for one that can combine vital traditions with all that the globalizing world can provide.

López is an artist with political ideas in a line that is not hegemonic, at least in the surface politics and even psychology of his country. But what his recent work shows is that his surface politics is only one aspect of a more ample vision that is metaphysical and spiritual, poetic and, of course, in the end, artistic—from which one can deduce anger and love, as well as personal and public morality. And it turns out that the work of Ramón López registers as art and as unconscious and subterranean expression in many people, no matter if they're Puerto Ricans or Chinese, supporters of independence or statehood. López, in his weavings and in all he does as essayist as much as visual artist and religious practitioner, communicates from a multidimensional perspective that corresponds to certain key characteristics of the popular imagination of his people—and other people as well. All this emerges clearly in this exhibition of López's political mixed media works, because he smuggles into them bits and pieces of his tapestries and the totalizing vision that emerges in his work as a master weaver. But while his weaved pictures commemorating 1898 feature the mixed media alone, and these are worth their own autonomous exhibition and explication, it is nevertheless important to underline the relation of these pieces to the full tapestry work if only because they place the more fragmentary media pieces in context.

As Héctor Monclova puts it (1995, 18), López has become an artist-shaman, one who not only presents but also conjures, evokes, and realizes a magical world of plenitude to a public that becomes (at least for a time) a collective chorus and quasi-congregation. The unconscious desire to achieve or experience this plenitude is the attraction of much of López's work, especially in a postmodern time when, for many, national projects, as well as visions of totality and utopia, have been lost. In this sense, López's tapestry pieces have not only presented but also evoked the popular and unconscious aspiration for fullness and coherence through symbolic patterns, including, most recently, one embodying or referring to a symbolic grid based on Cuban Santería and its Puerto Rican appropriations. Increasingly, this tapestry world has veered away from its earlier mimetic function with respect to ritual; it is the world of Van Gogh–made Caribbean–Puerto Rican and also African tapestry. Because it is a key characteristic of López's art that the national, the historical, and the everyday of Puerto Rican life in the island and the diaspora are a frustrated and distorted expression of a more universal vision that includes African identities so often repressed or stereotyped in dominant ideological forms. In the last analysis, López's art escapes colonial categories and seeks relations between the imagination and the forces of nature—beyond the history men and women construct, although of course, for good or ill, as a German-Jewish philosopher now supposedly out of fashion said, under well-determined and determining conditions.

If, in his early tapestries, López emphasized political and daily life, now they seem more focused on metaphysical matters; and it is the mixed media pieces that are charged with the responsibility of mimetic, historical, and political expression. It is in the context of the tapestries and the partial, fragmented tapestry elements that appear in the mixed media pieces that represent the confrontation of Puerto Rican icons with everyday life: the problems and disturbances that we find on all levels and in all directions; the multiple blockages, limitations, knots, and distortions affecting Puerto Rican life—the political struggles over statehood/no statehood, and, above all, in the pieces presented, the question of foreign and imperial power.

Symptomatic of all López's concern with Puerto Rican icons is his use of the flag in these pieces and elsewhere. Like the Three Kings, like the landscapes of his island, the flag, in itself and in relation to other icons, figures considerably in López's work. The messages, the play of flag images in relation to Albizu, Ochún, or whatever point to the complications in making a map of Puerto Rican struggles . . . one hundred years later . . .

However, what are most important are the military figures in their juxtaposition or confrontation with the Puerto Rican icons. López gives us a vision of the nation invaded by plastic soldiers that are not only toys, nor are they all *yanquis*, but rather they seem all too real, and can include among them (as in each military force made-in-USA) many sons and daughters of Borinquen. Here, the soldiers are not products of capitalist machinery in its most terrible form: they are cheap dolls or plastic toy models for children—to feed their taste for violence—as if the violence provided by Puerto Rico's one hundred years plus were not sufficient. These military figures are seen firing on San Francisco de Assisi, the figure of the Virgin, the figure of Albizu, a rosary, a lizard, and a great number of objects that are also disguised African gods reaffirming their power, even under a constant attack. Of course, there are other ways to explain what the artist represents—for example, as a portrayal and rejection of the inert, artificial forms of soldiers unable to affect the cultural forms they have unsuccessfully opposed and tried to kill. But however one might wish to interpret them, it is clear that in the midst of the soldiers and the other symbols of the mixed media pieces, the elements of weaving project us to López's tapestries, and to all the other levels and dimensions of his overall work, representing the African roots of Puerto Rico and representing also, as Monclova suggests throughout his essay on López, "the threads of Puerto Rican survival."

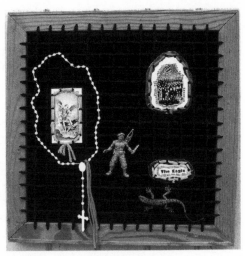

Left: *Orula y el mercenario*, Ramón López. Here, Orula, the African god or *orisha* of divination, related to San Francisco de Asís, usually seen as a figure of peace and love, is confronted by the U.S. military. We have stamps, as "yarn is woven through the wood to create patterns of a personal spiritual iconography or to bind objects to the wood surface" (Piazza 1998, 13). Photo of picture by the artist, 2010.

Right: *Ogún, Aguila Blanca y Rambo*, Ramón López. Ogún, an African god or *orisha* of metal and warfare, connected syncretically to the Arch-Angel San Miguel, is confronted by a U.S. mercenary. "Everyday objects invade or replace the woven images [found in López's tapestries. So, here we have] an assortment of . . . objects such as plastic toy soldiers or lizards, plastic rosaries and religious cards" (Piazza 1998, 12). Photo of picture by the artist, 2010.

Ramón López shows his work in restaurants, on the streets, wherever. Sometimes he does his work before a public, as a pedagogical or shamanistic act à la Claude Lévi-Strauss. He is a street artist in the best sense, using his art as a transforming object in the face of destructive forces, using his art to evoke the cosmic plenitude that he sees through his religious and artistic visions.

As Michael Piazza notes, "In reflecting life, every artistic endeavor is both liberating and constrictive. So whether it is through weaving or unraveling, Ramón López continues to bring his life and his world together. How to use the techniques of weaving to explore the world, and especially the Puerto Rican world; how to express the universal, the national and the person in a productive art which communicates and also shines for its aesthetic quality: these are the challenges in López's overall project, as well as in his paintings commemorating one hundred charming years of U.S. control" (Piazza 1998, 12).

Left: *Retrato de mi país #1* (Portrait of My Country #1), Ramón López. This includes a picture of Pedro Albizu Campos, as maximum figure and icon of Puerto Rican resistance. The sí-yes-no refers to the U.S.-slanted votes taken on Puerto Rico's status, perhaps represented by the tropical lizard. According to Piazza, "U.S. stamps attesting to the [1898] colonization dangle around the neck of a toy soldier. . . . López's vision of the centennial of the U.S. invasion of Puerto Rico, resembles tapestries in production or a weaving gone awry. The armature is left on—exposed as that which confines the work. The string grid is revealed and defines the picture plane as a map (aerially), a cage or net (spatially). It appears that the tapestry process begins to mark out territory on the picture field but is, for some reason, abandoned. It is as though there is a loss of trust in or suspicion of the very act of making art [as] López allows us to see through the grid to the bare wall only interrupted with objects that are entangled or bound to the grid" (1998, 8).

Right: *Retrato de mi país #2* (Portrait of My Country #2), Ramón López. "The image of the Puerto Rican flag is at once emerging and disappearing. It reflects the popular craft of beaded flags that many artisans make for sale to supplement their income in Chicago. . . . Strategies of working within structures are questioned as it is the practice that ultimately gives in to the structures. [Here] one is reminded of certain predominant discourses that herald the endgame of modernism and in turn are illustrated by turning paintings to the wall in order to gaze at the wooden bars and the canvas back . . ." (Piazza 1998). Photo of picture by the artist 2010.

Elizam Escobar. Photo by René
Rodriguez. El Hatillo, Venezuela,
May 21, 2008.

Elizam Escobar and His Free Prison Transfixions

In an essay he wrote several years ago, Elizam Escobar[11] (1988) notes how his particular situation has made him a rather atypical representative of those third world or minority artists within the visual art world who are excluded for having a supposedly "dependent" relation to hegemonic forces—artists who, as Cuban performance artist Coco Fusco puts it, "reject the implicit paternalism of the assumption that their borrowing [from the cultural dominant] is necessarily a symptom of dependency while similar gestures in the first world [supposedly] enrich the vocabulary of High Art" (in Fusco, ed., 1988, 1). With respect to this question, Escobar warns "not to reduce the new and authentic" to a colonial reactive mode vis-à-vis "Western" or to the "modernism of the mainstream," for this reduction only "perpetuates the resentment perspective of the colonialized" (1988, 27). As he writes in a subsequent essay:

> We live in a new historical moment within the frame of capitalist domination where ideological and class struggle is going through a series of convulsions. . . . In . . .

artistic creation, that which contains . . . new and necessary truths forges itself in the heat of contradictions; it . . . pierces through the merely epochal and ideological, actively resisting the seductive attraction of that culture of simulacrum that functions, as never before, as a screen where the imaginary fulfillment of unsatisfied necessities and the explosion of contradictions under controlled conditions are allowed to take place. If "postmodernism" could be conceived . . . as the ambiguous "revolt" and reification-of-confusion of [a] new economic-cultural international order, every artist that refuses the reduction of art to an instrumentality, as well as to a mere surface design or ornamental trivialization, must, by necessity, simultaneously distinguish and connect art praxis and social-political role. (Escobar, in Piazza and Zimmerman, ed., 1998, 190–91)

Elaborating on his situation, he adds: "My own experience of adversity leads me to propose an anti-theoreticist theory which purports to be a combat weapon derived from the praxis of art. My proposal opposes theory-*about*-art with theory-*from*-art. My intention is far away from repeating the doctrines or theoretical works of many artists within modernism, which ended up dogmatizing art praxis under one style, a movement or aesthetic school. Neither style, movement, school, nor 'regional language,' but the praxis of art is at the center of my work" (1998, 197).

What has been Escobar's experience of adversity that has made him a crucial Puerto Rican artist and art theorist? Above all, it is his experience as a Puerto Rican painter and writer imprisoned in the United States from 1980 into the new century for his participation in the struggle for Puerto Rican independence.[12] Born in Ponce in 1948, he abandoned his university studies at the University of Puerto Rico and worked briefly as an elementary school art teacher. Immigrating to New York, he worked as a garbage sweeper and sign painter in a Brooklyn-based community program, while he took the classes at City College that he needed to earn a UPR fine arts B.A. From the late sixties on, Escobar's New York jobs included working as an art, history, and Spanish language teacher at the School of Art of El Museo del Barrio and the Art Students League, as well as in the public schools. He also worked as an artist in the CETA-funded Hispanic Arts Association; and he was illustrator and cartoonist for several radical journals, including *El Socialista, El Correo de la Quincena, Desafío, PL Magazine,* and *Libertad.* He participated in numerous painting exhibits in the New York area as well as in Puerto Rico, at the Instituto de Cultura Puertorriqueña and his alma mater. Meanwhile, he involved himself in political work centered on Puerto Rican independence politics.

In 1980, Escobar was arrested and tried for seditious conspiracy in connection with his work for Puerto Rican liberation, allegedly as a member of the Armed Forces for National liberation. Convicted, he was sentenced to sixty-eight years in state and federal prisons. He had served more than twenty years when he was

granted a parole through the efforts of countless Puerto Ricans and their peti-
tions to President Bill Clinton. During this same period, he produced a considerable body of artwork that appeared in any number of galleries and museums;
and he also published poetry in several journals and anthologies, as well as in a
collection of his own, *Sonia Semenovna* (1985). Furthermore, he wrote and published a wide range of critical and theoretical essays on art and society—involving himself in contemporary debates on postmodern culture and its implications
for Latin America and Puerto Rico.[13]

In his years as an imprisoned visual artist and national resistance representative, Escobar produced a remarkable range of large paintings and varied mixed
media pieces using the resources available to him (for example, prison photos
sent to loved ones) within the restrictions of the penal institution. His artist's
life was one of subverting the rules to create striking self images in relation to

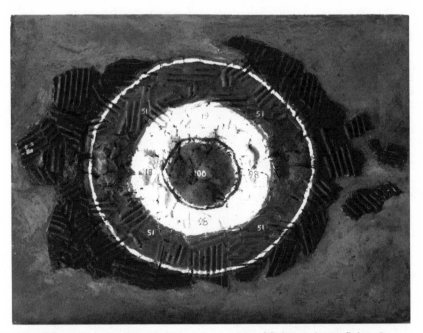

Target/Map, Elizam Escobar. The target is a means of fixing and transfixing. It
is "a point system diagram for practicing or measuring levels of focused skill.
[Here,] Escobar alters the point system on a target to reflect relevant numbers
and dates. In the outer region the player can score 51. It is mostly used as a
game of predator competition. The target is placed over the map of the island
which is made of disposable corrugated cardboard to simulate a topography"
(Piazza 1998, 10).

a variety of groupings and settings that explored domination through a poetic erasure of authority.

Writing of his art work in those years, Lucy R. Lippard notes how, in his most impressive paintings, Escobar "parallels the coexistence of individual and society by revealing the substance of an image . . . in the process of forming or deforming." As his works trace processes of disintegration, they increasingly resemble the deconstructions of images in the early mythological paintings of the Abstract Expressionists" (Lippard, in Escobar, ed., n.d., 8–16). And yet his images never go down the Jackson Pollock path but remain poised in a state of becoming or dis-becoming, perhaps a state reflective of how Escobar saw his life and the world (and of course Puerto Rico) in his "mind-jail."

Inevitably, there are varied and often problematic modes of interpreting Escobar's artwork in relation to Puerto Rico's insertion in postmodern consumption patterns and discourse—and this question simultaneously fascinated and troubled him. Thus, according to Carlos Gil, cofounder of Puerto Rico's first postmodern journal, *Postdata:* "What sums up [Escobar's work] is . . . transfixion, a dual act that can signify both the ability and inability to overcome fixation. The central problem of the work . . . is the problem of time" (Gil 1995, 238).

For Gil and other Puerto Rican postmoderns, contemporary culture means the end of the island's macro-narratives of independence and nation building seen as a utopia in the name of which one resisted U.S. powers of hegemonic cooptation. So, his view of Escobar's problem: "Escobar has been deprived of his liberty. . . . But there is a suffering even greater than this—a dimensionless suffering because it lacks the profundity which consolation provides; a unidimensional suffering, a flat suffering: that of the loss of utopia. . . . But why has this incredible thing happened to Elizam Escobar, to him, an alleged member of the FALN, standard bearer of a prefiguration of a better world, a future of transparency. . . . Because the utopia of Elizam Escobar, the utopia of our generation, lost its time and the clock kept ticking. . . . And it was not a question of time as an empty sequence . . . but the time of the martyr, the time of prefiguration" (1995, 238).

To be sure, Gil's view falsifies how Escobar constituted his own situation and attitude. Escobar refused to be limited or imprisoned within a discourse that credited a particular enunciation of his only to the degree that it could be construed as being in conformity with postmodern practices. For him, sitting, pacing, reading, and creating in his prison ambiance, the emergence of postmodernist perspectives and their particular Puerto Rican turn represented a fascinating adventure and challenge, raising questions he felt he had to answer in his visual artwork and writing. Dealing with postmodernity in art and in theory became this prisoner's mode of being in the world, his mode of freedom as artist and intellectual, militant and human being. Thus he was able to enter the discussion and sustain positions. So, if the logic of standard Puerto Rican postmodernity like Gil's led to a renunciation of nationalist and *independentista* positions and the assumption of a posture designated as "radical statehood," Escobar positioned himself in a way that enabled him to critique this stance and answer with his own (see his three-part essay on these matters in *Claridad,* summer 1997). Beyond theoretical answers, however, he remained an activist resisting in 1998 as he had resisted before, even as prison authorities threatened to cut off his communication—his flow of words and images.

It is the particular life and struggles of Escobar confronting the current, relativistic/pluralistic, politically tepid ambiance of postmodern hegemony that distinguishes his concerns from other, more academically oriented students of Latin American cultural studies—and makes his effort to constitute a left-activist appropriation of postmodern themes all the more striking and compelling.

Even as he kept up with postmodernist thought in first world, Latin American, and specifically Puerto Rican contexts, Escobar was especially wary of postmodernism as the latest guise and continuation of cultural domination with all its ramifications for artistic practice. He opposed contemporary trends that trivialized the force of art as "continuation" and reduced it to mere "imitation" of life. In the postmodern context, class conflict and praxis get lost among the multiple logics and ideologies of hegemonic transnational formations. As theorists attempt to develop adequate structures in which to describe certain situations, artists feel the shackles extending from those situations and must then struggle for some means of liberating action in a world that has seemingly lost traditional or previously constructed parameters. In constructing his oppositional stance, Escobar sought to maintain and promote the "subversive permanent force of the political imagination"—fending against directly ideological and political art on the one hand and empty formalistic and market art on the other hand. Against all this, he proposed his "anti-theoreticist theory" which, most influenced by another imprisoned radical, Marxist philosopher, Antonio Negri, was able to link with an "art praxis" aimed at breaking through late capitalist structurations (Escobar, in Piazza and Zimmerman 1998, 209–10).

And what then became the nature of Escobar's praxis? In this respect, he notes that the "postmodern condition" left only three steps for radical art practice and aesthetics:

1. *resist* critically by continuing the "political art" tradition within the existent or experimental practices.

2. *intervene* critically by using the same "postmodern" devices (tactical/strategic homeopathicism) in order to "undo postmodernism" itself.

3. *pierce through* these two, understanding that . . . it is not only possible to over-come the-theoretical-*about*-art, but [that] to . . . transfix—heuristically—the debate itself . . . means to allow the "modernism"/"post-modernism" debate to annul and annihilate itself and for us to continue our . . . search. (ibid., 212)

In an essay on Escobar's work, Iván Silén particularizes Escobar's "piercing" or "transfixing" operations in ways that are particularly germane to the artist's "medi-tation" on or play with the Puerto Rican flag for his "98" exhibit, when he argues that the artistic confrontation and "triumph over the colony and neo-colony" con-stitute . . . our artistic ('human') liberation" (Silén 1992, 51). Because this victory is achieved by using hegemonic, postmodern art techniques against the very system those techniques would seem to represent, it is no wonder that in his work for PR98, Escobar evokes the work of artist Jasper Johns to make satirical commentary about the obsession and fetishism with a negated flag. It is also no wonder that the flag images Escobar provides seem to play with every ambiguity and every confusion that would problematize the apparent simplicity of his flag-painting project.

Flag/Trojan Horse, Elizam Escobar. "Escobar asks how would the U.S. flag be designed . . . if Puerto Rico were to become a state. [So here], the U.S. flag is the surface of work. . . . The color of the red stripes is dark like dried blood. The white stripes appear as crypts for corpses. There are now 51 stars arranged in an awkward pattern to accommodate the latest acquisition. Certain stars are made out of cheap aluminum foil and on second look reveal the number 51. The Trojan horse becomes an ambivalent symbol for the craftiness of U.S. policy or the resourcefulness of the Puerto Rican diaspora" (Piazza 1998, 9).

Commenting on Escobar's technique, Bertha Husband notes: "The constant creation of variations of [Escobar's] images may be seen as an act of freeing himself from a double incarceration—not only was he imprisoned by the U.S. government, but he was in exile from his own imprisoned country. . . . For Escobar, the process is as important as the finished product; the journey and its discoveries are equal to the arrival at the destination. Everything in his painting process is confined to manipulating acrylic paint with brush or knife on canvas. In this, we are in the presence of "real" painting, painting in which the decisions are made as the work is carried on within the violence of the process" (Husband in Escobar, ed., n.p., n.d., 22).

Final Thoughts

In her essay, cited above, Husband argues that "To be a Puerto Rican artist is to inherit the exclusion from the official history of art of all colonized people. Their work becomes stigmatized as 'folkloric,' 'primitive,' or special in some way, rather than the embodiment of another aspect of the human spectrum. But to be excluded from the mainstream can also be viewed as freedom from the constraints of a ruling ideology in decline. And to be excluded from 'official history' is, after all, not the same as being excluded from living history, the arena chosen for our struggle to reach a higher level of social development and human discourse" (n.d., 23).

What, beyond this general perspective, and after all is said and done, after all the play of flags and icons, do the three artists exhibited here have in common? Writing about his relation to Juan Sánchez some years ago, Ramón López takes up the theme of the Puerto Rican diaspora Shifra Goldman articulates above, and extends the diaspora perspective in ways that clearly link his own work to Sánchez, but also, rather directly, to Elizam Escobar as well:

> We are the voices of a migrant people. In every household we rent, we live the uprooting and pain of migration: distance, absence, sacrifice and perseverance. . . . We have lost much in order to win our survival and when we open our hands we see a map of wounds. But look how we love to dance and eat. Look how we write Puerto Rico instead of America. . . . Look how we struggle with the pronunciation of Albizu Campos' name until we pronounce it well. Look at the light in our eyes when we discover that we really had a history before we were colonized. Look what happens to us when we learn to see. . . . To hold history in your hands, you have to believe in a world that is still for the making. And if you're an artist, you have to unite the pieces of life that you find along life's road and place them in such a way that you become a mirror [able to] see yourself in the other

so that this beautiful lie we call imagination and this painful human pleasure we call creation permit us to see the truth when it still doesn't exist because we still have so much to understand. The artists who articulate the new belief world of a people are chroniclers of the future. Through their lying will to truth, a mother is a flag and a rag doll, and both are words in an almanac of victories. A photo placed before a mirror is the vision of a new face. (López 1997, 3–4)

López notes how Sánchez uses the necklaces of Ochún, Taino petroglyphs, a Christian heart of Jesus, and a machete embossed with laser ray sparks. Sánchez, Ramón López himself, and of course Elizam Escobar show us how to create a world of past and future—how to use Puerto Rican icons and, yes, Puerto Rican flags, to pierce through Puerto Rico's commodity-dominated, plastic world, to get beyond the flag and flag fetishism, to explore the deeper roots and deeper issues of Puerto Rican being and becoming, during one hundred–plus years of Puerto Rican colonial solitude and the years of Puerto Rican struggle that will not be stopped by any vote in anyone's congress and that continues into the next decade of the new millennium.

Chapter 3

U.S. Puerto Rican
Literature

···

To the memory of Pedro Pietri (RIP)

Some years ago, in his introduction to an anthology of U.S. Puerto Rican poetry, Efraín Barradas (in Barradas and Rodríguez 1981, 11) went to great lengths to point out the lack of continuity and community between Nuyorican and Island writers. One of the most difficult tasks in explaining U.S. Puerto Rican writing, he argued, is to distinguish between island-oriented literature (even when it is written in New York and/or is about the U.S. diaspora), which is a branch of Caribbean or Latin American literature, and continental U.S. Puerto Rican writing, which, no matter where written, at least tends to be a U.S. ethnic literature. In attempting to make a bridge between island and continental expression, we cannot overlook the differences, which have been felt so keenly by those on both sides of the divide.

Because of his concern with unity, Barradas refuses to evade the differences and their bases in fact. Above all, he notes the tendency of "Nuyorican" writers toward heretical demystifications and/or mythmaking constructs with respect to Puerto Rican culture and national identity. The reasons for these constructs lie in the root causes for the migration of Puerto Ricans to New York: the island's colonial status and the economic upheaval caused by efforts of modernization, and of course the very negative and demoralizing circumstances most Puerto Ricans have encountered in the United States. So we have a mythifying of the island and a search for alternative role models and identifications; and we have, above all, the assertion of an injured, denied, and hence defiant sense of national and cultural pride.

At times, continental Puerto Ricans have resisted identifying themselves as a U.S. minority, because to do so would seem to imply a negation of a focus on their island's colonial status. Even as unemployment, poor housing, drug and welfare dependency, gang and school dropout rates, and so forth, became increasingly endemic in the Puerto Rican community, such problems could only be seen as legitimate to the degree that they were subsumed in function of the situation of Puerto Ricans as a colonized people. And the entire migration process, seen from the island intelligentsia's struggle to preserve a fragile, jeopardized national identity, could only be construed as loss. This sense of loss, felt in the very bones of those having their base in a U.S. enclave, and unable to recapture fully their island roots, has led to sometimes extreme alternatives—from a full-blown romanticism with respect to the island, to a rejection of the island and a search for other worlds.[1]

Indeed, perhaps for their smaller numerical size as a population (or as a tiny writer/artist subculture), and perhaps also for the fragility and difficult-to-specify character of their sense of nationhood, U.S.-based Puerto Rican writers, more than their Chicano counterparts, tended to decenter or go beyond national identification to Latino and third world/minority identifications, even to the degree that they affirmed their nationhood. So, the first Puerto Rican writers in the United States learned to project their visions of island independence in terms of union with Cuba and the broader Caribbean world. And, in this century, it is no accident that in the Chicago area, where the Puerto Rican population exists in the context of a much larger Mexican presence, a major contribution to the developing national scene was *Revista Chicano-Riqueña,* cofathered by U.S. Puerto Rican Nicolás Kanellos.

Though recent Chicano writers have attacked, abandoned, or transformed the *Aztlán* construct as the armature for their poetic explorations, the problem for Puerto Rican writers has been the elaboration of a series of partial, fragmented mythologies in the face of a lack of an abiding and binding Ur-myth that could give depth and unity to the epiphenomenal thematics of their work. So the occasional and topical feel and at least appearance of much U.S. Puerto Rican writing, and also the tentative and melancholy nature of the writers' heresies and mythologies; so the apparently more limited volume and elaboration of U.S. Puerto Rican literature compared with the Chicano counterpart. This is the viewpoint articulated rather arrogantly in Bruce-Novoa's *RetroSpace.* But if there is some truth in this contrast, stemming as it does from the lost past, or broken memory, of Caribbean cultures (as opposed to the at least partial continuities involved in Mexican history), and from a lack of long-term residence or rootedness (through workforce or proprietary relatedness--through a standing as permanent workers, businesspeople, or homeowners) in a land that they have felt theirs by some deep and at times sacred pact (the case of at least some people living in the Southwest, and part of the mythic structuration of much Chicano literature), nevertheless, this very situation helps to define the profundity behind the sometimes facile appearances.

We have in fact just designated "the space of U.S. Puerto Rican literature" as one primarily for the exploration and forging of a new sense of identity and nation in the face of loss and disorientation, multiethnicity, and multi-Latino identifications, in the face of the loss of myths that is increasingly the postmodern condition for Chicanos just as for others in contemporary life. The space of this literature separates even as it relates it to Puerto Rican island writing; the space is where the Puerto Rican colony or barrio is related to the city and its majority and minority populations, to the island, the Caribbean, Africa, and the world. Gender will also emerge as a crucial concern. In this context, the main contribution of much recent Puerto Rican writing is the insistence we have pointed to on a broad Latin and even internationalist focus even in the midst of developments emphasizing U.S. Puerto Rican nationalist, broadly minority, and feminist trends. And in this context too, the question emerges (in a way it hardly ever does for Puerto Rican island writers) about what may have been *gained* by Puerto Ricans in spite of the obvious negative dimensions of the diaspora.

To be sure, Puerto Rican literature in the continental United States does not begin with the massive Puerto Rican diaspora of economic refugees to New York known as Operation Bootstrap or "*Manos a la obra*." In a well-known article, Juan Flores divides Puerto Rican literature to the United States into three phases, preceded by a kind of "pre-phase."[2]

The "pre-phase," extending from the last century, consists of exiles from the independence struggle against Spain. These include major intellectuals like Eugenio María de Hostos, Ramón Emeterio Betances, and so forth, but also "a solid base of artisans and laborers," who spent varied lengths of time in New York, forming Puerto Rican and Antillean independence support groups and writing mainly about their Caribbean struggles (such might be considered the case of Hostos and Betances, as well as Lola Rodríguez de Tió, Arturo Alfonso Schomburg, and Sotero Figueroa), but also (in the writings of Francisco Gonzalo "Pachín" Marín) reflecting critically on the New York experience of arriving Puerto Rican nationals.

The first phase, extending from 1917 to 1945, is mainly of autobiographical and journalistic works expressing the efforts of first-generation migrants, many of them with the feelings and attitudes of foreign nationals and subject people (and here their difference from immigrants), to adjust to U.S. life. This period is most fully and richly represented by Jesús Colón's *A Puerto Rican in New York and Other Sketches* and *The Memoirs of Bernardo Vega*. But, as Flores notes, it is also represented by fragments from a vast, still-accessible stream of oral history, and a still more accessible volume of popular music (*boleros, plenas,* and so forth) in which Rafael Hernández, Pedro Flores, Ramito, Mon Rivera, Cortijo, and Tito Rodríguez as well as other talented popular songwriters, identified or anonymous, expressed a wide range of feelings about the experience of Puerto Ricans coming to the city. However, as I mention in the preface, this perspective leaves to one side a broad if understudied range of other writers who were part of the early wave but whose work did not feed into what was seen by some as an effort to construct a "left wing resistance" approach to Puerto Rican literary studies.[3]

Recently the resistance approach has led to considerable attention being given to the writings of *tabaquera* union activists Franca de Armiño and Luisa Capetillo (Acosta-Belén and Santiago 2006, 183)[4] in the context of other women such as Clotilde Betances Jaegger (niece of the famous nineteenth-century leader), Margot Arce, Concha Meléndez, Carmen Gómez Tejera, Antonia Sáez, María Cadilla Martínez, María Teresa Babín, Nilita Vientós Gastón, María Mas Pozo, Pura Belfré, Carmela Antonia Marrero, Aimee García Cortese, and Leoncia Rosado among Puerto Rican women writers emerging during the first half of the twentieth century.[5]

After the initial development of agribusiness during nearly fifty years of U.S. occupation, industrialization efforts under Operation Bootstrap (or "manos a la obra") were responsible for the massive movement of poor, country Puerto Ricans off their land and into a migratory process that brought them to U.S. cities. The period of this migration, from 1945 to 1965, constitutes the second phase of developing U.S. Puerto Rican literature. The Puerto Ricans of this period arrived too late to the feast of U.S. industrial expansion. Whereas many Mexicans, lacking legal status and having to take whatever job became available, gradually integrated themselves into the U.S. workforce (albeit in marginal roles), all too many Puerto Ricans, lacking minimal skills and suffering from cultural and racial discrimination as well, failed to find permanent niches in a declining industrial base; and, as U.S. citizens, they found their modes of survival in low-paying, temporary jobs, and (the subject of Oscar Lewis's notorious study of the "culture of poverty," *La Vida*), the famous U.S. systems of welfare and the "informal economy."

The circumstances of emergent lumpenization and what many saw as a loss of Puerto Rican/Latin American values, along with the attendant defense of the very system that was undoing them, led to the emergence of two predominant literary modes. First, there was a very powerful, negative "view from the island"—a perspective focusing on the problems of working-class Puerto Rican immigrants shared by writers, whether living in San Juan or New York, and represented most famously by Pedro Juan Soto, René Marqués, Enrique Laguerre, José Luis González, and Emilio Díaz Varcárcel.

Second, there was a "view from within the community" by a group of radical exile writers with long residence in New York (Clemente Soto Vélez, Juan Avilés, Emilio Delgado, Jorge Brandón, José Dávila Semprít, and Julia de Burgos among them—but also including Juan Antonio Corretjer, his wife, Consuelo Lee Tapia, and Vicente Geigel Polanco [Acosta-Belén and Santiago 2006, 177–79]), writing mainly a literature of exile with hardly any bilingualisms and only limited reference (for example, in Pedro Carrasquillo's *jíbaro décimas*) to the migration experience—with only Guillermo Cotto-Thorner's novel, *Trópico en Manhattan,* and various works by Jaime Carrero turning toward the depth exploration of the migration experience and the linguistic and cultural *"neorkismos,"* which were to become common in the next stage of Puerto Rican literature.

This third, or Nuyorican, stage of U.S. Puerto Rican literature "arose with no direct reference to or evident knowledge of the writings of the early period. . . . But nevertheless in prose at least [it] effectively draws together the firsthand testimonial stance of the 'pioneer' stage and the fictional, imaginative approach of the writers of the 1950s or 1960s" (Flores 1988, 43). Clearly, this definition applies to such narratives of male becoming by Piri Thomas, Lefty Barreto, Nicky Cruz, Humberto Cintrón, Edwin Torres, and Edward Rivera, as well as much of the work of the best-known Nuyorican woman writer, Nicholasa Mohr, whose most famous narratives are, as Arnaldo Cruz-Malavé points out, "narratives of formation," or *bildungsroman* exploring the fate of outsiders caught often between one or more sets of conflictive polarities: Puerto Rico/New York, city/suburb, Latin culture/ Anglo culture, semifeudal patriarchism/capitalist feminism, and so forth.[6]

According to Cruz-Malavé, New York Puerto Rican writers have been most prolific in poetry, where, more than in other genres, they have mapped out the polarities specified by Barradas between mythification and heretical demythification, which "constitute a dialectic that may be said to have its origins in the New York Puerto Rican awakening of the late 1960s" in the work of the Puerto Rican members of the Last Poets and in a group known as the Young Lords (Cruz-Malavé 1988, 48).[7]

Early Nuyorican poetry draws on militant African American poetry (especially the rebel poets who tended to group around Amir Baraka), on the Beat poets, as well as one of the Beat gurus with a special Puerto Rican connection: William Carlos Williams, seen as a rebel within the modernist tradition. The young Rican poets speak for a community, more than an individual, and seek to strip away false consciousness about the "American Dream" and Puerto Rican colonial status in a third world ghetto; they seek to promote action in the direction of nation building.

Gradually Nuyorican writing becomes freer of prior models and develops its own voice. Tending to portray the New York ghetto world against a mythified view of an interracial utopia identified with a liberated Puerto Rico, these poets begin to break down the mythified strand (what Piri Tomas cynically called "kitchen yak") and move in a richer, more complex frame of polarities and contradictions, which they portray not only in poetry but in plays as well. Indeed, for Miguel Algarín, by the mid-70s, Nuyorican poetry had already developed three modes that he saw also as an overlapping continuum of phases in Nuyorican writing (Algarín 1975). First, there was "outlaw poetry," involving expressions of hostility, rage, and violence; second, there was "evolutionary poetry," entailing a growing consciousness of the external determinations of outlaw moods and acts, as well as a movement toward transcendence; finally, there was "dusmic poetry," tracing the transformation of aggression into spiritual strength, wholeness, and freedom.

Even in Algarín's last phase, U.S. Puerto Rican literature does not leave specific national and ethnic considerations behind.[8] But this begins to happen in what may now be considered as almost a fourth phase of Puerto Rican literature, which seems to mark a kind of middle sector, postmodern literature of exploration on the part of college-educated U.S. Puerto Ricans who, mainly in English but also in Spanish, now explore themes of transculturation, feminist, queer, and overall gender studies, in texts that tend to stretch the normative limits of prior literary work Among these writers, several like Esmeralda Santiago, Luisita López Torregrosa, Abraham Rodríguez, and Ernesto Quiñónez have maintained elements of the tradition of autobiographical *Bildungsroman* so prevalent in U.S. Puerto Rican writing; and others like Victor Hernández Cruz (in his latest work), Gianani Braschi, Ed Vega, and Magadalena Cruz represent a continuity with the college-educated, Spanish-dominant island writers of a previous generation. But they all seem to share a concern with forging a literature that is cosmopolitan and transnational even as it continues to focus on social concerns of colonialism, racism, stereotyping, and so forth as found in the literature of the Nuyoricans.

Island-Based Puerto Rican Literature
on the U.S. Migration Experience

Early writing by Puerto Ricans in New York is best exemplified by Pachín, who more than any other Caribbean writer transplanted to New York, with the exception perhaps of Marti, has a feel for everyday U.S. urban life and its possible impact on future Latino life and literature. As noted, between Pachín and the writers of the 1940s on, there seemed to have been an enormous historical gap that is now being filled in by the publication of a few texts and the examination of forgotten writers by Ph.D. candidates, many of them drawing on the archives of Nicolás Kanellos's Recovering Hispanic Literary Heritage Project.

In poetry, Pedro López-Adorno's anthology *Papiros de Babel* (1991) helps to fill the historical gap with selections of several writers from the first half of the twentieth century; Roberto Márquez's comprehensive anthology (2007) presents these poets in the context of a historical arc that extends from the Conquest to the twenty-first century. *Songs of the Simple Truth,* Jack Agüeros's anthology of Julia de Burgos's poetry (1997) reveals the transformations one very gifted Puerto Rican writer undergoes in form and orientation as a result of her life in New York City from the 1940s until her death in 1953. Jaime Carrero's *Jet Neorriqueño: Neo-Rican Jet Liner* (1964) is a book that anticipates the development of Nuyorican literature, by a writer who spent much time in New York and whose perspective, while still island-based, shows continuing interest in the New York *colonia* and empathy with the Nuyorican perspective (Flores 1988, 43, and Márquez in Márquez, ed., 334). Víctor Fernández Fragoso's *Ser Islas/Being Islands* (1976) represents the kind of poetry written by Iván Silén, Manuel Ramos Otero, and many others, which provide a Spanish-language treatment of the migration experience that is still primarily a "view for the island" even as it flirts with Nuyorican perspectives. Nevertheless, the connection with the city, especially as a space of homosexual exploration, in many works, prose as well as poetry, by Manuel Ramos Otero, led to his featured inclusion with Martí and García Lorca in Dionisio Cañas's book, *El poeta y la ciudad. Nueva York y los escritores hispanos* (1994).[9]

As far as fiction is concerned, New York and other U.S. places enter in and affect the work of many prose writers who partake of the immigrant experience even if they ultimately maintain or return to their island roots. This is especially evident in the *Generación de 1940,* which lived through and experienced the vast Puerto Rican diaspora developing in the late 1940s and in the decades that followed. Indeed, the literary production of this group was very valuable and in many respects anticipates the subsequent wave that would occur of writers who are almost completely diaspora figures, most of them born or raised in the United States and known, however inaccurately, as "Nuyorican."

José Luis González's *Paísa* (1950), and then his fine collection of stories, *En Nueva York y otras desgracias* (1973), offer biting, negative portraits of the effects of the "U.S. experiment" and what he considers to be the growing Anglo-Americanization of Puerto Rican values and norms. However, one of González's greatest stories, "La noche que volvimos a ser gente," in *Mambrú se fue a la guerra* (1972), portrays a New York community victory over racialization and subalternization. Pedro Juan Soto's *Spiks* (1956) presents classic short stories from New York that views the diaspora experience as degradation and negation. Soto's later book, *Ardiente Suelo, Fría Estación* (1961), is one of the best treatments to date of Nuyorican return migration to the island.

Manuel Méndez Ballester's *Encrucijada* (1958) provides still another negative image of the U.S. migration experience. Enrique Laguerre's *El Laberinto* (1959), mainly set in New York and Santo Domingo, portrays Puerto Ricans who make pan-Caribbean identification with Dominicans plotting to overthrow the Trujillo regime. Compared with the portrayal of the immigrant experience by other island writers, Guillermo Cotto Thorner's *Trópico en Manhattan* (1959) provides some depth in depicting "the shock of arrival and first transitions . . . [as] individual traumas and tribulations are woven into a more elaborate interpersonal and social context." The novel's Spanish "is . . . interspersed with bilingual neologisms— what Cotto-Thorner calls 'neorkismos'" (Flores 1988, 45).

Author of a novel about return migration to Puerto Rico, *Raquel tiene un mensaje* (1970), and also *Los nombres* (1972), Carrero is an island-based writer with strong U.S. ties who uses cross-cultural code switching as the mark of his style. Carrero was one of the first to use and develop the term "Neorican." In *El hombre que no sudaba* (1982), he uses stream of consciousness and other techniques to tell about a man who resists societal restrictions. Emilio Díaz Valcárcel's *Schemes in the Month of March* (1979a) and *Harlem todos los días* (1979b) are both fine examples of Latin American–style Puerto Rican writing, although set in New York and focusing on the urban U.S. scene.

Of course U.S.-related themes appear in all of the more contemporary Puerto Rican prose writers, including the work of Ana Lydia Vega, Edgardo Rodríguez Juliá, Mayra Santos, Mayra Montero, and many others. The most striking and complicated contemporary example is probably Rosario Ferré, who has lived in the United States for years and portrays characters fully interpenetrated with U.S. concerns. She wrote one of her most fully island-oriented books, *The House on the Lagoon* (1995), in English, marking her full move from her early *independentista* politics to her full embrace of her father's statehood orientation.[10] The distortion, rearticulation, or persistent assertion of Puerto Rican traditions and values by U.S. norms is the ubiquitous theme of much of Luis Rafael Sanchez's work in theater and narrative, most emphatically in his brilliant novel, *El guaracha del Macho Camacho* and in his short story about Puerto Ricans en route to New York, "La guagua aerea," which became subject to a mediocre, stereotyped film version by Luis Molina.

To this day, playwrights Francisco Ariví, René Marqués, and again Luis Rafael Sánchez have offered some of the most provocative portrayals of the U.S. impact on Puerto Rican life and identity. Ariví's *Vejigantes* portrays questions of island racial prejudice deepened by contact with the U.S. South. Marqués's play *Los soles truncos,* a fine recycling of Garcia Lorca's *La casa de Bernarda Alba,* is the classic treatment of the effect of the U.S. occupation on traditional creole society; his most famous play, *La carreta* (1955), is the classic portrayal of a family that moves from the countryside to New York, in a work that became famous for its view of the Puerto Rican migration as total disaster and defeat, as exile from sacred land, as loss of family identity and integrity. While best known as a playwright, Marqués also wrote many prose works treating U.S. influence and the New York experience, including his controversial essay on the supposed docility of Puerto Rican identity—a perspective recently and definitively trumped, finally, by Arcadio Díaz's collection of essays, *El arte de bregar* (2000).

Filmmakers Zurinaga and Morales at times seem intent on avoiding or evading U.S.-related thematics for the sake of exploring Latin American, Caribbean, and even European connections often obscured by U.S. hegemony. Such would be the case of Zurinaga's *La gran fiesta, Tango Bar,* and *Lorca,* as well as Morales's *Dios los cria* and *Linda Sara.* U.S. references indeed have weight in Zurinaga's work (for example, the impact of U.S. involvement in World War II in *La gran fiesta* and the satire of Hollywood appropriations of Latin American musical forms in *Tango Bar*) and are present if not central in Morales's *Lo que pasó a Santiago.* However, Morales's *Nicolás y los demás* is the most important film to date about an effort of Puerto Rican return. Finally, of course, Luis Molina's film version of Luis Rafael Sánchez's *La guagua aerea* loses itself in silly *costumbrismo* and clichés, but that nevertheless confirms Emilio Pantojas's view that the only place Puerto Ricans of the diaspora feel at home is not in their place of origin, nor in their place of destination, but in the airplane itself.

All this said, even as the above Puerto Rican writers and filmmakers inevitably portrayed U.S. influences and experiences in the course of their developing opus, what is essential for our concern here is the full emergence of U.S. Puerto Rican writing.

U.S. Puerto Rican Poetry

Without question, the most famous poet of Puerto Rican descent in the United States was the doctor-poet William Carlos Williams, who, Puerto Rican on his mother's side, apparently disassociated himself from the cultural traditions of the island, even after his visits there and his translations of poetry by Luis Palés Matos. Only today are critics taking seriously his Puerto Rican and broader Caribbean and Latin roots as a means of understanding his relations with U.S. elite poets like Eliot and Pound on the one hand and "New World" writers on the other.[11] The lack of recognition of Williams's own "Puerto Rican" identity may be taken as a sign for the broader series of questions having to do with the recognition of continental Puerto Rican poetry as part of U.S. and U.S. Latino literature. The second question is as important as the first, but the first will be our main focus here, in a survey that must turn away from the remarkable case of the Ivy League–educated Williams and the Great Modernist Tradition, to the urban poets of New York and elsewhere emerging in the 1960s and beyond.

Some of the first Nuyorican poets, like Felipe Luciano Jr., were members of the Young Lords or "The Original Last Poets," "an ensemble of African American and Afro-Puerto Rican poet-performers . . . known for the powerful and vigorous vernacular immediacy and rhythmic, spoken word presentation . . . of its street-wise, nimble verse which . . . early anticipates the rap compositions of a later era" (Márquez in Márquez, ed., 2007, 408). Others, like Lucky Cienfuegos, Jesús Papoleto Meléndez, Américo Casiano, and Sandra María Esteves, were members of El Grupo, a collective of touring, New York-based musicians, performers, and poets (Márquez in Márquez, ed. 2007, 423) with links to the New York wing of the Puerto Rican Socialist Party (Hickman 2008, 148); some of the other poets were rebels like Bimbo Rivas, "who along with Chino García . . . rechristened the Lower East Side as 'Loisaida'" and worked with local organizations to rebuild their gutted community (ibid., 149). Other writers identified as Nuyorican poets—Ángel Figueroa, Miguel Algarín, Victor Hernández Cruz, Tato Laviera, Pedro Pietri, and Miguel Piñero—had early connections with rebellious groups or trends in the 1960s and '70s.

Jesús Papoleto Meléndez's *Street Poetry and Other Poems* (1972) features people of the barrio. His more recent book (1993) and his CD (2002) confirm his continuing presence as a Nuyorican performance poet. José Angel Figueroa's *Noo Jork* (1981) is probably the most accomplished volume by one of the most anthologized Nuyorican street poets of the 1970s. The author's surrealist bent becomes more marked here than in his earlier (and publisher-bowdlerized) volume, *East 110th Street* (Detroit: Broadside, 1973), as he projects craziness, chaos, romanticism, and sometimes humor as an expression of the Nuyorican experience.

Clearly the great masterpiece of the early phase of the Nuyorican literary experience is Pedro Pietri's *Puerto Rican Obituary* (1973). The famous title poem and others constitute one of the early classic statements of Nuyorican poetry. As Cruz-Malavé says:

> Pietri uses irony, a scathing humor and the grotesque to awaken Puerto Ricans to the social realities around them (segregation, unemployment; exploitation by em-

ployers, merchants, and slumlords; drug addiction; and criminality) and to expose the illusion involved in the "American Dream." But mostly his poems address "false consciousness," the "colonized" mentality of Puerto Ricans who have "bought into" the "system." . . . [Pietri's book] is an attempt to help Puerto Ricans "kick" the consumerist "habit" . . . ; to help them withdraw from the false images of America and of themselves produced by the media to a space of resistance outside consumerism. . . . This space of resistance is identified . . . with a "true self," a true ethnic identity, an idyllic Puerto Rico or a "tropicalized" urban space transformed into a mythical Puerto Rico. (Cruz-Malavé 1988, 48)

Pietri's *Traffic Violations* (1983) is a compendium of eighty poems, including "I Hate Trees," his acclaimed elegy. The poet's verve and originality emerge, even as he shows more of himself and his dreams in his constant moves against the oncoming traffic. Harsh, deep laughter, tragicomedy, and irony permeate a key Nuyorican work that shows "a disappearance of the utopian element that served as a counterpoint to [Pietri's] demythification of 'false consciousness' and . . . of the didactic persona" of Pietri's earlier work (ibid., 49).[12]

Along with Pietri, Miguel Algarín, Miguel Piñero, Tato Laviera, Victor Hernandez Cruz, and Sandra Maria Esteves are core figures of the Nuyorican renaissance of the 1970s. Cofounder of the Nuyorican Poets' Café, where established and neophyte poets read and slam, Algarín has produced a body of poetry related to the theoretical stance outlined earlier in this article. First, *Mongo Affair* (1978) presents a virtual trip in search of freedom through the Nuyorican Poets' Cafe to various places in the United States and Europe. In his first volume of poetry, Algarín asserts that Puerto Ricans are poetic by nature, but muffled by U.S. domination. He seeks to replicate and reveal Nuyorican speech. Accessible and performative in style, the poems are marked by code-switching and underscored by repeated rhythm patterns that Algarín considers central to Nuyorican talking style. Two years later, in Algarín's *On Call* (1980), street people, musicians, dancers, and poets from New York and San Francisco join in an aesthetic celebration and exploration of roots. Then comes *Body Bee Calling from the 21st Century* (1982), where the poet takes risks in sexuality as he embarks on a bionic journey through his own body in a search for transcendent experience and love. Then Algarín's *Time's Now/Ya es tiempo* (1985)—and winner of that year's Before Columbus Foundation American Book Award—combines interior and street experiences that transport the writer to Central America and other fields of action on his way to spiritual breakthrough. His own production seems to have cooled down, though he coedited two key anthologies of Nuyorican poetry in the 1990s.

Best known as a playwright (see below), and the subject of a recent film about his drug- and prison-troubled life, Miguel Piñero had his greatest poetic success with his "Lower East Side poem" and his overall collection, *La Bodega Sold Dreams* (1980). The poet urges those who survive him not to bury him in Puerto Rico (the usual dream of the diaspora) but to bury him near the shooting and killing that have become so much part of his life in New York's urban underworld. The late writer's best work in *La Bodega* presents an angry and ironic view of city life and its marginal types, mixing ghetto slang, macho posturing, and a rough-exterior sentimental quality that disarms criticism.

Another representative of the New York scene, Victor Hernández Cruz, began his work by developing free-form poetry and prose poems that used bilingual and bicultural motives that brought together New York and other U.S. value worlds while emulating popular Caribbean musical rhythms and forms in their search for a rich poetic language based on barrio speech but reaching toward a more introspective orientation than most other Nuyorican writers. Hernández Cruz's *Rhythm, Content and Flavor: New and Selected Poems* (1989) presents nineteen new poems forming a chapter entitled "Islandis," plus a selection from *Snaps* (1968), *Mainland* (1973), *Tropicalization* (1976), and *By Lingual Wholes* (1982); his *Red Beans* (1991) is a collection of chants, prayers, celebrations, testimonies, and prose poems, covering the poet's years in New York, San Francisco, and Puerto Rico. Remarkably, in his recent work, reflected in *Panoramas, Red Beans,* and *Maracas,* he has gone through a more complete transformation as an island-based and centered poet (for some years he divided his year between the town of Aibonito and his teaching position in Colorado; now he spends considerable time in Morocco) more representative of Puerto Rican transnational than strictly U.S. settlement processes.

Reversing the negative vision of Rene Marqués's *Carreta,* Tato Laviera's first book for Arte Público Press, *La Carreta Made a U-Turn* (1979), uses New York Boricua rhythms to transcend Nuyorican cynicism and celebrate what has been and can be preserved, transformed, and gained after cultural pain and loss. In *Enclave* (1981), Laviera uses rhythmic songs and skillful and graceful bilingualisms to celebrate Rican life struggles and present sharp portraits of New York's enclave dwellers. Introduced by Wolfgang Binder, Laviera's third collection, *AmeRícan (*1985), portrays New York ethnic diversity and examines the traditions of several cultural groups, while exploring the effort to forge a new Puerto Rican identity. If, "in the past Laviera redirected Hispanics to invest culture and emotion in the reality of the Metropolis," his *Mainstream Ethics* (1988) "affirms that Hispanic language and lore, art and history are transforming the national culture and identity of the United States. It is not the role of Hispanics to follow the dictates of a shadowy *mainstream,* but to remain faithful to their collective and individual identities

. . . to either lay claim to mainstream territory or disprove its very existence" (back cover blurb). Then, after years without a new book, Laviera finally published *Mixturao and Other Poems* (2008), where he celebrates Latino and Puerto Rican men and women in function of borders and the overall diversity and complexity of their lives.[13]

Among the first-wave Nuyorican writers, only one major woman emerges, Sandra María Esteves. In her first collection, *Yerba Buena* (1982), the questions of definition and affirmation as an urban, U.S. Puerto Rican (colonized but struggling) woman are the major themes of poems that are strongly influenced by African American musical forms as well as the work of militant black poets of the previous decades. In a second collection, *Bluestown Mockingbird Mambo* (1990), Afro-Cuban fusions with spirituals, blues, and jazz are transposed into Puerto Rican feminist critique and poetic aestheticism.[14] A second woman poet to emerge in the 1980s is Luz María Umpierre, a university literature professor and feminist lesbian whose bilingual collection *Y otras desgracias* (1985) evokes and transforms José Luis González's famous title to frame unconventional, often aggressive and biting poems about the U.S. Puerto Rican experience. Also in the 1980s, the prolific and talented Iris Zavala wrote an important body of poetry (1982);[15] and a Puerto Rican mother, Rosario Morales, combined with her Puerto Rican/Jewish daughter, Aurora Levins Morales, to write *Getting Home Alive* (1986), a collection of poetry and prose exploring their complex cultural weave that involves geographical, political, ethnic, and specifically feminist dimensions of identity. Umpierre and Levins both went on to write additional works that gave them some standing in U.S. Puerto Rican letters,[16] while Zavala continued to turn out some fiction and poetry in the midst of her vast critical production.

Related to but also very different in poetic style from women writers who preceded her, Judith Ortiz Cofer followed William Carlos Williams as a poet identified with Paterson, New Jersey (though Williams's Paterson was Rutherford), and the New York area. Her *Terms of Survival* (1987) presents cultural icons, customs, and rites of passage in the course of portraying the dialectical conflict between adherence to island memories and traditions and a feminist impulse toward liberation. She followed this first volume with the *The Latin Deli* (1993) and *Reaching for the Mainland and Selected New Poems* (1995a) that are imagistic, ironic, and thoughtful but often narrative in style as well, pointing toward the prose works that preoccupy Ortiz Cofer throughout the 1990s and beyond (see below).

More political in his preoccupations is Elizam Escobar, the brilliant POW *independentista* painter and polemicist imprisoned for twenty years for his political activity, who produced a vast body of important painting but also numerous essays (see chapter 2) and a collection of poetry, *Discurso a la noche y Sonia Semenovna* (1985) during his prison years. As discussed in chapter 2, he has, since his release in 1999, renovated his career as an artist, now based in Puerto Rico.[17]

Another political writer, but one more fully committed to poetry as his prime expressive mode, is Martín Espada, the Brooklyn-born son of a Puerto Rican diaspora photographer (Frank Espada), who left his University of Wisconsin law degree and his people's lawyer practice behind to pursue a career as a Boston-based professor and poet. He has produced a series of books that evoke key aspects of U.S. Puerto Rican diaspora and overall U.S. problems.[18] *The Immigrant Iceboy's Bolero* (1987), originally published by Editorial Cordillera in 1982 and accompanied by some of his father's expressive photos, reveals Espada's capacity for creative transformations of his own life experience. *Trumpets from the Islands of Their Eviction* (1988) depicts the personal eviction—the unfulfilled dreams, the insanity, the drinking, pesticide poisonings, Vietnam wounds, firing squads, and other ways of dying, as well as overall questions of language and identity—common to thousands of Puerto Ricans who, starting with Operation Bootstrap in the 1950s, were encouraged and pressured to leave for the United States. With a forward by poet Robert Creeley, and a lengthy introduction by Diana Vélez including backgrounds about the Puerto Rican and personal contexts affecting his work, Espada's third collection, *Rebellion Is the Circle of a Lover's Hands/Rebelión es el giro de manos del amante (*1990) mainly portrays the tradition of resistance and rebellion rooted in the *independentista* movement of the 1930s and extending to contemporary East Coast struggles. Hands appear in poem after poem, marking continuities and connections among countless strands of U.S. Puerto Rican life and the many concerns of the advocate lawyer-poet, as he generalizes beyond his own people's problems to those of Nicaraguans, Chicano farmworkers, and others put upon by the powers that be, in a book of victories in the face of countless reasons for defeat. Espada's universe continues expanding in his next collection, *City of Coughing and Dead Radiators* (1993), which prolongs his ride as a reflective left poet of the down and out and oppressed, here including a poem related to continuing problems in El Salvador. The expansion and return to earlier themes continue in his volume *Imagine the Angels of Bread* (1996). His poetic production has recently been capped off by *A Mayan Astronomer in Hell's Kitchen* (2000), which continues his exploration of radical perspectives in a post–cold war context, and *Alabanza* (2003), a selection of his overall work. And he has also written his own critical meta-commentary, *Zapata's Disciple: Essays* (1998).

In some ways parallel to the emergence of these East Coast poets is that of those based in Chicago—a first wave led by David Hernández and including Salima Rivera as well as Alfredo Matías, Eduardo Figueroa Condes, Cesar Quiñones, Carmelo Rodríguez, Julio Noboa Jr., Emma Iris Rodríguez, and other poets in the 1970s; then a second wave including Adolfo Colón, Rane Arroyo (who also wrote plays), Frank Varela, Lourdes Lugo, Eduardo Arocho, Tony Del Valle, Juana Georgen, and Sonia Báez Hernández, who emerged in the 1990s (see chapter 4). There is also the isolated and very special case of Carmen Pursifull from Champaign, Illinois, and with very little contact with the Chicago writers (see chapter 5).

In the meantime, some of the East Coast Rican poets mentioned above have continued to write. Piñero died some years ago, and Pietri died in 2004; the Nuyorican Café went through several changes, expanding beyond its Rican and Latino roots to reach out to a broader, multicultural group, with Miguel Algarín, Jesús Papoleto Meléndez, Willie Perdomo, Ed Morales, and others holding down the fort.[19] At the same time, several poets, veteran and neophyte, have found their way into print. Jack Agüeros put together his poetry in *Correspondence between the Stonehaulers* (1991), *Sonnets from the Puerto Rican* (1996), and *Lord, Is This a Psalm?* (2002), works mainly centered on New York experience. Gloria Vando's *Promesas: Geography of the Impossible* (1993) heralded the arrival of a new and sophisticated voice to the U.S. Puerto Rican poetry world; Giannina Braschi's previous poetry collections, brought together and translated as *The Empire of Dreams* (1994), established her as a cutting-edge New Wave Puerto Rican postmodernist (see below). Louis Reyes Rivera published an award-winning collection, *Scattered Scripture* (1996); Naomi Ayala published her striking first collection, *Wild Animals on the Moon* (1997); and Julio Marzán followed up his earlier books (for example, *Translations without Originals,* 1986) with *Puerta de Tierra* (1998), his first book of poetry in Spanish (Márquez in Márquez, ed., 2007, 372, 467, 390). In 2002, Lydia Cortés published her first volume of poems, *Lust for Lust*; and Alba Ambert capped off her previous volumes of poetry with *Alphabets of Seeds* (Márquez in Márquez, ed., 2007, 354 and 396). A few years later, Frances Negrón-Muntaner, one of the most brilliant lights of the Puerto Rican diaspora, published her first volume of poems, *Anatomy of a Smile and Other Poems* (2006).

To conclude this very partial list, we turn to a dynamic hip-hop poet and performance artist known simply as Mariposa (María Teresa Fernández de Rosario), who presents her work at the Nuyorican Café and became involved in Vieques-related cultural politics in the early days of the twenty-first century. Known for her high-powered, dramatic performances featuring her shouting-pouting-rapping style, she published her first volume, a record of her early efforts, *Born Broxeña: Poems of Identity, Survival, Love and Freedom* (2001). Mariposa's work continues the underclass Nuyorican poetry tradition and projects it into the new century. All of this to say that U.S. Puerto Rican poetry continues to develop, evolve, and in some cases thrive in patterns of recuperation and change in relation to changes in U.S. Puerto Rican life.

In this respect, I may here do violence to Roberto Márquez's rich vision of U.S. Puerto Rican poetry—a vision that, even in its truncated form, to a certain degree may be said to represent U.S. Puerto Rican writing in its entirety. According to Márquez:

> The general refusal . . . of the poets of the diaspora to conform to established insular linguistic, literary or patrician . . . protocols . . . would . . . [generate a] new poetry [that] called into question the . . . parameters . . . [of] "Puerto Rican literature" and "U.S. poetry." . . . The poets challenged . . . notions of nation and citizenship in the context of (im)migration and the realities of a . . . commuting population. . . . These "new Creoles" demanded "new definitions" . . . of Puerto Rican . . . identity [and] nationality. . . . [in an] AmeRícan sancocho or diaspora-seasoned Puerto Rican stew [of] poetry . . . [whose] worldview, voice and place [was and is] . . . both *here and now* and neither *here nor there* but in some hovering and still fluid . . . *in-between*. . . . The . . . diaspora and . . . "commuter nation" [of which the] poets write stand as . . . [a] rebuke of the unfulfilled promises of meaningful citizenship by not one but two now complexly entangled societies, as well as testimony to its inhabitants' refusal . . . to reconcile themselves . . . to . . . marginality. . . . The poets of the diaspora . . . bring entirely new dimensions, perceptions and challenges . . . to "the Puerto Rican experience," [as their poetry] . . . intimates, dwells in, and yearns for a future realm of . . . communal possibilities. (Márquez in Márquez, ed., 2007, xxxv–xxxvii)

U.S. Puerto Rican Fiction and First-Person Narrative

An early Puerto Rican novel of U.S. migration has been recently discovered by Nicolás Kanellos, who assures that the book contains every major topos of the migration novel. However, for now, a consideration of New York–based Puerto Rican book-length fiction and first-person narrative should probably begin in 1931 with Pedro Caballero's *Paca Antillana,* a novel of migration, and Pedro Juan Labarthe's *The Son of Two Nations,* a third-person autobiographical story of a young man who leaves Puerto Rico to study in New York, and who stays on to win success and good fortune. Labarthe's text represents an early pre-Depression conformist and naively optimistic phase of New York–based Puerto Rican writing comparable in some respects to an education-centered text by Juan B. Huyke (1925). In stark contrast, we have a book dealing with roughly the same period but from a left, working-class perspective that was stronger in the community than its early commentators acknowledge: *Las memorias de Bernardo Vega* (1977), edited by Andreu César Iglesias. This important volume, a literary find, tells the story of Vega's life as an early-twentieth-century immigrant from Puerto Rico who comes to New York and makes his way as a worker and then labor leader in the years before the great Puerto Rican diaspora and the slum-dwelling process that was to dominate the Nuyorican experience.

Iglesias, Bernardo Vega's alter ego–editor knew Jesús Colón, a first-generation immigrant who saw duty as a tobacco worker, community and union activist, and journalist and whose *A Puerto Rican in New York and Other Sketches* (1961) is a series of short prose pieces written for the Communist Party's *Daily Worker*. The book is a treasure house of reminiscences and reflections about the New York Puerto Rican community before the Great Diaspora, in many ways paralleling Vega's *Memorias* and anticipating many of the problems that will come to the fore in the writing of Piri Thomas or the Nuyorican poets. Although suffering from a sometimes abstract preachiness that was part of the *Daily Worker* ethos, the work transcends its limitations through the elaboration of vignettes that constitute virtual "atoms" of ethnic tension, with far-reaching implications for Puerto Rican/U.S. conflicts and possible resolutions that prove, as in the title of one of the more remarkable pieces, that "Little Things Are Big." A second volume of Colón's work, *"The Way it Was" and Other Writings* (1993) is an autobiographical collection portraying the author's life in relation to the evolution of the Puerto Rican community in New York, including a portrayal of major figures and organizations. Still another collection, *Lo que el pueblo me dice* (2001), shows this gifted, self-taught Puerto Rican managing a body of work in Spanish that surely adds to his standing as the precursor of Nuyorican literature.

Early in our new century, Nick Kanellos's Recovery Project published *Pioneros puertorriqueños en Nueva York, 1917–1947* (2001), a book by labor activist and political organizer Joaquín Colón López (1896–1964), a contemporary of Andreu Iglesias and Bernardo Vega, as well as being the brother of Jesús Colón. The founder of important mutual aid societies, Hispanic political organizations, and civic groups, this Colón was an indefatigable fighter for Hispanic civic participation and suffrage and an early Hispanic activist in the Democratic Party of Brooklyn. He was a pioneer in organizing and motivating political action by New York Puerto Ricans, and in brokering their power for improvements in their lot as a national minority. Always at the center of community culture, Colón was an acclaimed speaker and a widely read columnist in Spanish-language newspapers, where he served as a public conscience writing under his own name, as well as under the pseudonyms of Tello Casiano, Momo, and Farallón. It was only in his later years that Colón felt compelled to recount the history of the first large wave of Puerto Rican immigrants making a life for themselves in New York City. *Pioneros Puertorriqueños* is an original, richly detailed, and provocative Spanish-language text that, while sometimes quirky in its criteria, portrays the previously unknown personalities who led community struggles of labor and political organizing in the early twentieth century.

In the 1960s and '70s, Nuyorican prose writers followed minority trends in producing a body of works dealing with alienation, criminality, incarceration, and return. Manuel Manrique's *Island in Harlem* (1966) portrays a black and a light Puerto Rican fighting over the same woman, in a stilted novel about class and race in *el barrio*. Nicky Cruz and Jamie Buckingham's *Run, Baby, Run* (1968) deals with the protagonist's trajectory from gang member to evangelist preacher. Cruz's life story is designed to woo the reader to the author's religious obsessions. In Cruz's *The Lonely Now* (1971), our evangelist author responds to letters from people in pain in a book that manages to tell us much about the U.S. Puerto Rican experience. Just a year later, Humberto Cintrón's *Frankie Cristo* (1972), tells how, as Spanish Harlem rival gangs go to war, the protagonist comes to see the destructiveness of *barrio* life and decides to "better himself" through education.

Without doubt, the major Nuyorican prose work of the period, Piri Thomas's *Down These Mean Streets* (1968), is the classic of all Puerto Rican stories about growing up in New York. This book is Thomas's memoir about life in Spanish Harlem in the Depression and after—his identity crises, his cultural and ethnic problems, his initiation to gangs, drugs, sex, and violence. From his perspective as an ex-con turned juvenile counselor, Thomas tells of initial disorientation and deviance followed by prison and reintegration into the community. Dark-skinned, he has to deal with his father's rejection and come to understand his own self-rejection. As a privileged observer of self-defeating and contradictory racist and machistic attitudes within his own community, Thomas perhaps disappoints by his position in favor of rehabilitation and "adjustment." His sequel volume, *Savior, Savior, Hold My Hand* (1972), tells of Thomas's efforts at social and personal reintegration after being released on parole. Resolved not to return to criminal activity, he must now find other ways to deal with the tensions that continue to plague his life, seeking solutions in his marriage, charismatic religion, and youth counseling. Thomas attacks the parole system and underlines the need to fund innovative community work. Thomas's *Seven Long Times* (1975) continues his self-documentation by detailing his seven years in Comstock Prison. Published in the wake of Attica and often compared with examples of prison literature like *Soul on Ice,* the book nevertheless accepts the conventional norms of penal rehabilitation. Thomas's *Stories from El Barrio* (1978), his first collection of short fiction, returns to his childhood years in Puerto Rican Harlem, but this time with a lighter, less violent tone, with more tenderness, humor, and compassion.[20]

Underworld Nuyorican narrative reaches another level with Edwin Torres's *Carlito's Way* (1975), which portrays a Puerto Rican criminal and his underworld life. This is the first of three novels by Torres, which have been criticized as exploiting Puerto Rican stereotypes but praised for their rich portrayal of Nuyorican culture and life, for their thriller-style plotting, their inventive detailing, and their skillful use of popular traditions and newly emerging slang. A judge in the New York County Criminal Court, Torres portrays Puerto Ricans profiting on the informal economy in marginal, illegal, and directly criminal activity. The same hustling criminal hero appears in *After Hours* (1976), now confused by his years in prison; in a third novel, *Q and A* (1977), the hero becomes part-owner of a salsa club and takes us through the New York Caribbean jazz world in a manner that exposes the Cuba-centrism of Oscar Hijuelos's *Mambo Songs of Love.*

Comparable to both Thomas's and Torres's work is Lefty (Manuel) Barreto's *Nobody's Hero* (1977), an autobiographical novel about coming of age in the New York barrio. The book presents the cultural problems of U.S. Puerto Ricans, as they attempt to hold on to their language and values. But in the main the work centers on housing, employment, and family problems that lead to crime, run-ins with the law, and imprisonment. Barreto's book has been used in classes of social work education because of its emphasis on neighborhood relations with police and social service workers.

However, the persistence of barrio realism is jolted first in the late 1970s and then throughout the 1980s. Richard Ruíz's *The Hungry American* (1978) is the autobiographical story of a young Puerto Rican barrio boy who breaks with his community to seek economic success and assimilation. Pedro Pietri's *Lost in the Museum of Natural History/Perdido en el Museo de Historia Natural* (1981), the poet's first published story in a bilingual edition, shows his narrative force in exposing the false illusions inherent in Puerto Rican acceptance of U.S. consumer values.[21]

Edward Rivera's *Family Installments: Memories of Growing Up Hispanic* (1983) presents a young Nuyorican reconstructing his family's island roots, their move to the United States, and then his own life experiences growing up and oscillating between Puerto Rican and emergent Anglo identifications. Written in fine style and moving beyond the raw realism of Piri Thomas and disciples, Rivera tells a moving story especially notable for a carefully drawn father/son relation, the situation of generational sacrifice, and the *maromas* or tricks required to survive in the tragic "New York experiment." Growing up between mafia kids and Irish nuns and priests, our young hero pees at his graduation ceremony, and is forced to wallow in excrement for trespassing black turf in his search for a statue of his great white father, George Washington. Our narrator also has a go at understanding *Julius Caesar* in an Italian mafia school environment, producing language and cultural confusions that rival those found in the classic chapter about a Jewish immigrant group's English class encounter with *Macbeth* in Leonard Q. Roth's *The Education of H*y*m*a*n K*a*p*l*a*n.* (1938). The father works himself to blindness, plays his alternative Puerto Rican national anthems, studies Spanish-language oratory, and experiments with fraudulent relief checks—or "real-ifs"—only to find himself humiliated and brutalized on the New York streets. The son, seeing what happens to those around him, returns finally to Puerto Rico to bury his father, explore his roots, and begin to sort out the forces that have made him who he is and will be.

In another effort, Ed Vega's novel *The Comeback* (1985), a Puerto Rican–Eskimo college ice hockey star is treated by a team of mad Freudian therapists for his extreme identity crisis. Vega's parody of the ethnic novel, a satire about revolutionary politics and racism, with undercover police, professors, shrinks, and upwardly mobile athletes, is considered a gem by his publisher-enthusiast, Nick Kanellos. *Mendoza's Dreams* (1987) is Vega's collection of short stories brought together by a *Decameron*-style "frame story." Replete with zany New York characters, Vega's book draws on García Márquez, Cortázar, and other Latin American writers to give us a comic portrayal of the major issues facing U.S. Puerto Ricans--independence, poverty, assimilation--as he portrays struggles against bureaucratic systems that subjugate and oppress.[22] Vega's *Casualty Report* (1991) is another innovative collection by an inventive Nuyorican writer who presents traditional Latino themes with distance and satire—the defense of honor, the pathos of migration—as characters waver between death and rebirth. Still more recent works by Vega, now using his full name (Edgardo Vega Yunqué), are his novels of 2003, 2004, and 2005.

Throughout the 1990s and into the new century, U.S. Puerto Rican volumes of narrative were few and far between. Oswaldo Rivera's *Fire and Rain* (1990) treated the Vietnam War in a first novel by a New York–based writer. Then Víctor Rodriguez's *Eldorado in East Harlem* (1992) follows a teenager, René Gómez, and his coming of age through his affair with a friend of his mother and his friendship with a Jewish recluse living in his barrio world. The next year, Jack Agüeros published *Dominoes* (1993), a collection of telling stories about barrio life. But the most important new Puerto Rican short story writer was Abraham Rodríguez Jr., first with *The Boy without a Flag* (1992), and then with his celebrated *Spidertown* (1993). Including eight short stories equally divided between Puerto Rican and New York settings, *The Boy without a Flag* is notable for its portrayal of the conflict between traditional values and technological progress on the island and the conflict between processes of creativity and those of cultural disintegration in New York. A departure from the ethnic biographies Nick Kanellos sees as dominating much U.S. Latino and specifically Puerto Rican literature, the collection is a kind of prelude to *Spidertown,* which Juan Flores (2001, 200–201) and others have heralded as the most realistic and powerful, indeed "Balzacian," portrayal of key dimensions of New York Puerto Rican life—certainly the most important Puerto Rican fiction collection to appear in the 1990s, where the deepest and most terrible problems of Puerto Rican life in New York are portrayed in the most cutting and penetrating ways. With *The Buddha Book* (2001) and most recently, *South by South Bronx* (2008), Rodriguez has gone in new directions, with the latter book receiving considerable acclaim as the author's entry into the detective story genre, but with an acute New York Puerto Rican accent, which leads to his effort to escape broadly Hispanic stereotypes and the market-driven reduction of Latino fiction to a few simplistic models.

Turning to writing centered on women, the first portrayal to emerge was Nicholasa Mohr's *Nilda* (1986), a story of a young Puerto Rican girl growing up in the city and barrio in the early 1940s. Including some well-etched vignettes, this volume shows the signs of labored style and technique—but it also shows the storytelling drive that would lead to several books and open the gates for the beginnings of Nuyorican women's literature. A second reading of this novel reveals a rather knowing sense of the political and social landscape (for example, the Puerto Rican support for charismatic radical Italian politician Vito Marcantonio) a young Latina has to traverse.

Mohr's *El Bronx Remembered* (1986) is a series of stories portraying the Puerto Rican community emerging during the 1940s and 1950s, mainly from the perspective of children, in a book replete with good characterizations and humor. Her *In Nueva York* (1988) presents a sequence of interrelated stories about the fragility of Puerto Rican life in a world where survival is an achievement, while Mohr's *Rituals of Survival: A Woman's Portfolio* (1985) is a moving group of stories dealing with the struggles of Nuyorican women, proving that no one model can provide an adequate picture of the different ways different women face difficult situations. A breakthrough work for Mohr, the book portrays iconoclastic women who defy traditions, dare to express their sexual desires, and seek their own realm of freedom away from domestic definitions imposed by men and those women who affirm a male-centered universe. A still more recent work, however, *A Matter of Pride and Other Stories* (1997), is a collection of seven works that portray key aspects of diaspora life but fail to present any new take on the field.

In 1989, Judith Ortiz Cofer's *The Line of the Sun* and Carmen de Monteflores's *Singing Softly/Cantando bajito* appeared; then in 1991 came Carole Fernández's *Sleep of the Innocents*. In reverse order, Fernández's book is a first novel depicting the disruption of rural family traditions caused by Puerto Rican internal divisions and U.S. influence; Monteflores's book portrays the protagonist Pilar's scandalous love affair in Puerto Rico as reconstructed by her granddaughter Meli, who must return to Puerto Rico to reestablish her familial identity, in this first novel by a San Francisco–based practicing psychotherapist, poet, and lesbian. Praised by Roberto Márquez (who should know) for opening new locales and class relations with respect to U.S. Puerto Rican experience, *The Line of the Sun* is a "national allegory-cum-autobiography" involving the story of three generations of the Vivente family as told by a young woman, Marisol, but based also on countless stories told around the kitchen table. Perhaps more than any other Puerto Rican narrative to date, this one portrays the back and forth flows of people, family relations, and identifications between Puerto Rico and the United States, and the power of island matriarchy. It opens with a fine portrayal of the mythic town of Salud in a series of chapters that mix ethnography and magical realism and mainly tell the story of Marisol's uncle Guzmán, who falls for an *espiritista* and eventually flees to New York. In the second part, Marisol tells of her childhood in Paterson, New Jersey, as she is torn between her assimilationist father and island-oriented mother, and only finds her own hybrid identity as woman and writer at least partially through the mediation of Guzmán. This story, told in function of Marisol's identification with the island's spiritist culture pervading "El Building" where she lives, culminates in the portrayal of a perhaps overly symbolic if richly described conflagration that destroys the project. Though marred by contrived and clumsy plotting and story transitions, the novel contains passages of lyricism and power, telling descriptions of Puerto Rican folk culture, and rich characterizations.[23]

Ortiz Cofer's *Silent Dancing: A Partial Remembrance of a Puerto Rican Childhood* (1990) presents essays interspersed with poems of personal recollections and character portraits in a book communicating the power of storytelling and a writer's struggle to maintain her bilingual/bicultural heritage, and depicting, as well, a young girl's communion with a grandmother, problems of migration and cultural dislocation, Puerto Rican female role-formation, and other themes of interest in recent years. A subsequent collection of short stories, *An Island like You* (1995), contains some telling stories of life in the barrio and on the island; and *The Year of our Revolution* (1998) shows Ortiz with some fine kaleidoscopic work, but fails to live up to *Silent Dancing*.

At the opposite pole is Sandra Benítez. Born Sandy Ables in 1941 to a Puerto

Rican mother and an Anglo-midwestern father, a U.S. State Department official, Benítez spent most of her early life in Mexico and then El Salvador—wherever her father was posted. During her teens she lived on her paternal grandparents' farm in northeastern Missouri, where she attended high school and college. At thirty-nine, after years working in the corporate world, Benítez launched her late-blooming career with *A Place Where the Sea Remembers* (1993), a story about a Mexican family in a small fishing village. She subsequently wrote two novels rooted in Salvadoran history, *Bitter Grounds* (1997) and *The Weight of All Things* (2000), the first taking place during the uprising of 1932 and the second during the civil war of the 1980s; she then published *The Night of the Radishes* (2003), which "involves a Minnesota woman who, haunted by family tragedies, travels to Mexico in search of her estranged brother. The novel is the first in which Benítez deals with her bicultural heritage" (Barillas 2004). Benítez has recently finished a nonfiction book *Bag Lady: A Memoir of Illness and Recovery,* which tells of her thirty-year struggle with ulcerative colitis and her turn to leucotomy surgery as a remedy. She has won countless awards and honors; however, she has yet to present a narrative centered on her mother's Puerto Rican roots.

Other works by women have appeared in the past several years, including a novel about New York and San Juan Puerto Rican life, perhaps most notably Alba Ambert's *Porque hay silencio* (1995—see also her collection of stories published in 1997); and Giannina Braschi published her postmodern pastiche, *Yo-Yo Boing!* (1998), a work heralded by such gurus as Jean Franco, Doris Sommer, and Diamela Eltit and seen as the most complex and experimental of U.S. Puerto Rican fiction yet to be written. In the same year, Aurora Levins Morales published a collection of stories and a related group of essays that added her name to the list of poets turning to prose (1998). In the new century, Judith Ortiz Cofer had a burst of productivity, publishing her *Woman in Front of the Sun: On Becoming a Writer* (2000), *The Meaning of Consuelo* (2003), *Call me Maria: A Novel* (2004), and *A Love Story Beginning in Spanish* (2005).

In this same period, still another woman, Luisita López Torregrosa, published *The Noise of Infinite Longing* (2004), an intimate, lyrical memoir portraying "ruptures produced by migration and family dispersal" while revealing a "rejection of . . . a dominant patriarchal social and family structure," and a questioning of "nationality and cultural hybridity" as well as gender (Torres-Padilla and Rivera, "introduction," in Torres-Padilla and Rivera, eds., 2008, 11).

Nevertheless, in the years between Ambert's first book of fiction and Ortiz Cofer's second wave, there is no question that the only bona fide publishing success was that of Esmeralda Santiago, first with *When I was Puerto Rican* (1993), and then with

América's Dream (1996) and *Almost a Woman* (1998). The first book was a smash hit because it was not bogged down by political or reformist social thinking, but seemed to present as rich a portrayal as possible of the effects of a family's life on the island and in New York. A presentation of family disruption, spousal abuse, and youthful discovery, the book registered with many readers, Puerto Rican or otherwise, with its nostalgic portrayal of rural poverty as well as its direct presentation of urban adjustment. *Almost a Woman* continues the author's story with a portrayal of her departure from the barrios of New York to the wider world of Manhattan theater and upper-class schooling at Harvard and Sarah Lawrence University. For its part, *América's Dream* is an idyllic fictional narrative that shares many qualities with the memoirs that sandwich it. While very popular with readers, these works received a less favorable response from critics, who found them to be without bite or depth, presenting, they felt, a commoditized Horatio Alger–style version of Puerto Rican adjustment in the United States while evading the complexities of colonialism and ethnic stigmatization. And Santiago was indeed a publishing phenomenon, producing not only three ample narratives but collections of work that sustained her writing career and kept her on the pages of reviewing presses. Without doubt, many Puerto Rican and Latino readers related to her narratives as they had not to those by Nicholasa Mohr or Judith Ortiz Cofer, not to mention Piri Thomas. And this sense of going beyond seems confirmed by what is probably her boldest effort, *The Turkish Lover* (2004), which portrays a complex love affair in function of gender and overall cultural clash and accommodation. But what did these successes tell us about what the future held for U.S. Puerto Rican narrative and especially the writing of Puerto Rican women, so much in the shadows for so many years?

As if to answer (though with no direct reference to Braschi's Bakhtinian dialogism and appearing too early to cover the most recent work by Ortiz Cofer, López Torrregrosa, and Santiago), Lisa Sánchez González's *Boricua Literature* (2001) critiques the extended narratives of several of the female writers, noting the "mainstreamed" and "nonconfrontational nature" of their texts as they "narrate personal experiences of the feminine condition to the near total exclusion of a collective predicament that entails growing problems within racism, poverty, reproductive rights, education, and Colonial *maldevelopment*" (2001, 140). Thus, Sánchez ultimately dubs these works as "failed feminist allegories" for "[the] inability of the protagonists to save anyone's lives but their own" (158–59).[24]

Whether there is some truth to these rather severe claims, it is the case that just when the U.S Rican tradition of the urban narrative seemed to be fading away, and as the new Puerto Rican middle class was announcing its full entry into the Latino literary world, Ernesto Quiñónez published his *Bodega Dreams* (2000), followed by *Chango's Fire: A Novel* (2005) and thus joined with Abraham Rodríguez in showing the continuing power of a literary mode that still paralleled the experience of many urban Puerto Ricans.[25] Similar developments would mark Chicago's Puerto Rican scene in the new century, alerting us to the fact that, while liberated women writers might project in new directions, the Puerto Rican urban male narrative was far from being a thing of the past.

We may also look for new trends, however, by pointing to how overtly homosexual U.S. Puerto Rican fiction in English emerges in the writings of Robert Vásquez-Pacheco (1999), Emanuel Xavier (1999 and 2002), and Larry La Fountain-Stokes (2009).[26] Marking a new direction are the short story collection *The Speed of Darkness* and the novel *When the Shark Bites*, written by Hawaiian Rican Rodney Morales—works of great diasporic hybridity pointing to the continuity and diversity that mark the ever-expanding horizons of Puerto Rican writing.[27]

U.S. Puerto Rican Drama and Cinema

Puerto Rican theater has a long history in New York (see Kanellos, ed., 1984 and Kanellos, 1990). We may recall previous references to plays by Luisa Capetillo and Fernando Sierra Berdecía's *Esta noche juega el jóker* (see note 5). Reviewing the 1920s and 1930s, Acosta-Belén and Santiago (2006) note that Gonzalo O'Neill's *La Indiana borinqueña* (1922), *Moncho Reyes* (1923), and *Pabellón de Borinquen o bajo una sola bandera* (1929) "upheld the proindependence and anti-imperialist ideals of the Puerto Rican nationalist movement during its burgeoning years." They also note that Erasmo Vando wrote and produced a work of *teatro bufo*, *De Puerto Rico al Metropolitano o el Caruso Criollo* (1928); Franca de Armiño wrote *Los hipócritas*, a play that focused on the Great Depression; and Frank Martínez anticipated *La carreta* with his *De Puerto Rico a Nueva York* (1939).

Between *West Side Story* and *Capeman*, two well-known Jewish American efforts to glamorize the underside of U.S. Puerto Rican life on stage,[28] U.S. Puerto Ricans have themselves produced a small but significant body of work—first by some of the early Nuyorican poets and then others representing other U.S. Puerto Rican sectors and dimensions.

Pedro Pietri's *The Masses are Asses* (1984) is an absurdist tour de force portraying a pretentious and superficial upwardly mobile couple subjected to wide-ranging, rueful, and politically insightful satire. Far more prolific as a playwright and indeed the major Nuyorican dramaturge, Miguel Piñero managed to produce several plays in the 1980s. His volume, *The Sun Always Shines for the Cool* (1984), portrays ex-con street people doing their numbers on every one in the urban jungle of the title play. His *Outrageous: One-Act Plays* (1986) brings together six works all vying to be worthy of the volume's title, as they seek comedy, pathos, and paradox in the projects, subways, and subway bathrooms, sleazy bars and drug dens, that make New York what it is for Nuyoricans, including the hungry writer at work. Piñero's award-winning *Short Eyes*, a full-length effort that later became a powerful PBS film, is the most famous play by a U.S. Puerto Rican. A work somewhat in the mode of Jean Genet, it portrays what happens when a white child molester is thrown in among prisoners whose machistic code makes them hate and ultimately kill him. The play is famous for its raw portrayals and for its grasp of racial/sexual dynamics that speak to the transformation of core cultural patterns in terms of lumpen ritual identification and violence. It may be seen as a kind of ritual killing of the pariah other whom the ethnic others must sacrifice.

At the end of the 1980s, Edward Gallardo published *Simpson Street and Other Plays* (1990), a collection of three plays showing how urban socioeconomic and political conditions affect Nuyorican working-class psychology and behavior. The title play was produced and toured nationally and abroad by the New York Shakespeare Festival; "Women without Men" portrays female/male relations on the worksite and in the barrio. Theater groups such as the Pregones have enlivened Nuyorican theatrical life for years.

Meanwhile in Chicago, Puerto Rican Billy Zayas teamed up with Chicago Cubans Achy Obejas and Jorge Casuso to produce a bright, Spanish-language political satire, *Carnicería Rodríguez* (see chapter4); and still another Chicago production in the 1980s was *El viejo y el mar*, a bizarre Spanish-language adaptation of Hemingway's *The Old Man and the Sea* taking place in Chicago's Puerto Rican Humboldt Park area in which the old Cuban lassoes a Rican gang kid and engages in a long, titanic struggle to haul in his catch.

In the 1990s, John Antush published a Nuyorican drama collection, *Recent Puerto Rican Theater: Five Plays from New York* (1991), which included *Bodega* by Federico Fraguada, *Family Scenes* by Ivette M. Ramírez, *Midnight Blues* by Juan Shamsul Alam, *Ariano* by Richard V. Izrizarry, and *First Class* by Cándido Tirado. Antush's second collection, *Nuestro New York: An Anthology of Puerto Rican Plays* (1994), reveals the wide array of burgeoning talent for this difficult genre in plays produced from 1958 to the 1990s portraying aspects of diaspora life, attempts at return, rejection of assimilation, and the search for new identifications. The collection starts with *The Betrothal* by Roberto Rodríguez Suárez, the director of the New York premiere of *La carreta*, in a work about Puerto Ricans reaching the cultural crossroads. Other works, by Oscar Colón, Carmen Rivera, Reuben Gonzalez, Eduardo Ivan López, and others, round out a fine collection. However, the two most exciting Nuyorican theatrical writers of this historical period, Carmen Rivera and Magdalena Cruz, are not represented. Rivera wrote *Julia*, "a feminist play that challenges traditional women's roles and evokes the poetic rebelliousness of Julia de Burgos"; she "also won an Obie in 1996 for *La Gringa*" (Acosta Belén and Santiago 2001). Cruz wrote a brilliant sexy play, *Fur*, a study of gender relations and power without any Puerto Rican or Latino references. She brought the play to Chicago, but then stayed on in the city to work as resident dramaturga with Teatro Latino Chicago, in developing scripts and productions dealing with Lolita Lebrón and Che Guevara. Perhaps Cruz was not fully successful in taking on political and ethnic-infected materials removed from the talents manifested in *Fur*. She and Teatro Latino Chicago had great difficulty in making political and historical sense of the two great protagonists they had chosen; repeated variations of the Lolita materials failed to achieve a fully satisfactory form. Nevertheless, Cruz's talents were evident in every scene. She eventually returned to New York, presumably to continue her work as one of the most important U.S. Puerto Rican playwrights today.

In the new century, perhaps the standout playwright is José Rivera, best recognized for his award-winning screenplay *The Motorcycle Diaries,* but with a long list of successful plays, starting with *The House of Ramón Iglesias* (1983), continuing with Obie-winning *References to Salvador Dalí Make Me Hot* (2000), and culminating with *Boleros for the Disenchanted* and *Human Emotional Process* (both produced in 2008).

The Puerto Rican Traveling Theatre of New York kept on with its work of featuring new U.S. Puerto Rican playwrights, perhaps most notably *Piragua Papa* by Ed Cardona (2006). The biggest Puerto Rican success of the decade was *In the Heights,* Lin-Manuel Miranda's musical about Puerto Ricans and Dominicans in the Washington Heights area of New York, which started off-Broadway then moved to Broadway, and has received prize after prize while playing to large audiences and going on a national tour as the new decade began.

In film, U.S. Puerto Ricans have had few opportunities to develop their wares, and have often been left to one side as non–Puerto Ricans have directed and produced the few works about U.S. Puerto Rican life. One of the most telling documentaries, *Sures,* was directed by a New York–based Chilean, Diego Echevarría. Similar in structure to the Bolivian film *Chuquiago,* about the city of La Paz, Bolivia, this film shows the variety of experiences and attitudes found in one of the poorest and most drug-ridden Nuyorican communities, and also shows how a monolithic interpretation such as Oscar Lewis's (in *Five Families* but also the notorious *La Vida*) cannot adequately account for all the variations. Another film on U.S. Puerto Rican life, directed by an Anglo documentary filmmaker but with great participation by the Puerto Rican cast, is *Nuyorican Dreams/Sueños nuyoriqueños,* which follows the narrator/protagonist schoolteacher on his return to his family and his effort to deal with the problems of drugs, criminalization, and psychological dependency he finds at home and in the alternative school where he is attempting to make a difference. As in Echevarría's film, the Puerto Rican characters learn to act so naturally in front of the camera even as they reveal some of their most intimate and difficult experiences. We see confessions of drug abuse; we watch the mother break down from the pain of the negative lives her children have lived. Ironically, it seems that the protagonist has been spared the most horrendous aspects of the Nuyorican experience (gang recruitment and involvement, informal economy participation, and so forth) by virtue of being gay. Surely, important aspects of U.S. Puerto Rican diaspora life have reached the screen in feature films such as *Popi, Carlito's Way, I Like it Like That, Piñero,* and *The Blue Diner,* one of the most positive presentations of Cuban–Puerto Rican interactions (there is also a great Cuban–Puerto Rican confrontation in Iván Acosta's U.S. Cuban gem, *El Super;* and the Cuban–Puerto Rican question is central to *Popi*).[29]

In spite of all the criticism directed by Puerto Ricans and others at the Hector Lavoe bio-pic, *El cantante* (see my snide comment in chapter 1), I believe the film provides some important visual perspective on the imaginaries of many Nuyoricans of the period in question and continues some of the fine work Cuban American writer-director León Ichaso developed in *El Super* and *Piñero.* Yes, Ichaso's decision to frame Lavoe's story with an interview with the singer's wife, Puchi, creates a problem, as Jennifer Lopez's brittle performance almost steals the film from Marc Anthony; but Anthony is indeed remarkable in his portrayal of Lavoe; and the frame gives greater gender-based depth to a presentation that many decried probably because it all too graphically portrays the drug world that came to dominate and destroy Lavoe as a diasporic icon and hero and to represent all too many others who lost their way in the cauldron of New York.[30]

A still more recent film on U.S. Puerto Rican life is *Nothing Like the Holidays,* which portrays a Chicago Puerto Rican family getting together for Christmas dinner in the city's Humboldt Park. Written by Chicano Rick Nájera and Anglo-American Alison Swan, the film was directed by Alfredo De Villa *(In the Heights),* shooting on location and attempting to portray the urban snowscapes, customs, and problems of the area. But the script is full of clichés; actors like Alfredo Molina, John Leguizamo, Elizabeth Peña, and others have never seemed so lame; and Puerto Rican questions are leveled to Latino generalities that fail to grasp the more specific dimensions of an embattled community, with perhaps the best part of the film involving the story of a son returning from military service in Iraq.

Representing greater Puerto Rican production control than the above instances are the filmed comedy routines of John Leguizamo and Luis Caballero. Leguizamo's *Mambo Mouth* and other projects manage to capture typical aspects of New York Colombian, Puerto Rican, and overall Latino life. However, Caballero's *Puerto Rican Mambo: Not a Love Song,* more a film than a filmed comedy special, is perhaps more deeply important. As noted in the introduction to this volume, his film is a very negative Woody Allenesque portrait showing the disrespect and negative internalization processes common in the Nuyorican community. Caballero asks the Linda Chavez question: why it is that of all Latin Americans coming to the United States, Puerto Ricans have done least well?

Although Nancy Dos Santos and other trained U.S. Puerto Rican film specialists have worked on several Latino (mainly Chicano) productions and other Puerto Ricans have taken on key roles, we have long awaited a film on the Puerto Rican experience more directly controlled or directed by Puerto Ricans. Of course there have been exceptions, like Frances Negrón-Muntaner's *Bricando el charco* (1994) and Rosie Perez's documentary, *Yo soy boricua* (2006). Even with Puerto Ricans in the driver's seat, we shall have to wait to see how well they portray the U.S. Puerto Rican experience in the years to come.[31]

Concluding Thoughts:
Whither U.S. Puerto Rican Literature

In recent years, with Hernández Cruz's stylistic and thematic experiments and with the gender explorations of Sandra María Esteves, Luz María Umpierre, Judith Ortiz Cofer, and others, we see new modes and new cultural horizons only hinted at in earlier days, but in no way signaling an end to Spanish and collective orientations, in no way signifying accommodation or assimilation. Piñero is gone, but others have arrived. Ed Vega and others may parody the earlier immigrant narratives and may search for new narrative paradigms; but this, far from signaling an end, just points to the fact that, in Tato Laviera's wonderful phrase, the *carreta* has been making a U-turn. So, in concluding his overview essay on Puerto Rican literature, Juan Flores notes that, like Chicano and other "'minority' or non-canonical literatures of the United States," continental Puerto Rican literature since its Nuyorican phase has been, while intensely national in orientation, also "a literature of recovery and collective affirmation, . . . of 'mingling and sharing,' of interaction and exchange with neighboring, complementary cultures." However, while paying homage to African American literature as influence and Chicano literature as cross-fertilizing parallel and presence, Flores adds that, most distinctively among these minority literatures, "Puerto Rican writing today is a literature of straddling, a literature operative within and between two national literatures and marginal in both. In this respect" he concludes, "Nuyorican writing may well come to serve as a model or paradigm for emerging literatures by other Caribbean groups in the United States, such as Dominicans, Haitians and Jamaicans" (Flores, 44).

Noting the broader perspective, Cruz-Malavé (50) argues that "Because of the diversity of the Puerto Rican experience, encompassing both the Third and First Worlds, underdevelopment and advanced capitalism, oral and written traditions," Puerto Rican writing has not just been a matter of survival stories and poems "in the fringes" of U.S. society, but "the space where . . . the strategies for change—the many attempts to find a space of resistance and freedom outside (and inside) [first and third world] modernization and [first world, late capitalist] consumerism—are taken to their ultimate consequences."

As we project to future phases of U.S. Puerto Rican literature, we should simply note what I believe this essay has made obvious: that from the perspective of Chicago and the Midwest, the designation by Flores and Cruz-Malavé (but not Barradas) of the third phase of Puerto Rican literature in the United States as "Nuyorican" was misleading in the first place and more so now, because it leaves out a significant area and all the other centers where the new literature has developed. Future studies must include these other communities in and around New York, but the Midwest and even Hawaii—wherever Puerto Ricans have gone and will be going. In further efforts, and above all in developing a more sophisticated critique of the remarkably slow and limited emergence of a Puerto Rican woman's and specifically feminist literature, however, the perspectives specified above will continue to serve as significant guideposts.

It is perhaps disturbing but revealing in this context to note the reemergence of essayistic narratives dealing with the most negative dimensions of the Puerto Rican experience. Philippe Bourgois's treatment of a Puerto Rican crack community (1995) seems a postmodern throwback to Oscar Lewis's work—and the same may be said about the two books by Chicago's Rey Sánchez, on his life as a Latin King gang member (see chapter 4), as well as the new book by Timothy Black, *When a Heart Turns Rock Solid* (2009). Other such narratives on their way will confirm the persistence of criminality and anomie, in spite of the rise and success of many U.S. Puerto Rican intellectuals of the current generation and in spite of the ever greater diversity marking the diasporican experience. Above all, the written word, whether on page, in song, in film, or electronic media, will provide spaces for framing and plotting Puerto Rican trajectories as time goes by.

Chapter 4

Puerto Rican
Poets in Chicago

···

To the memory of Salima Rivera and Rane Arroyo (RIP)

Where are the Latin poets?
Maybe at the neighborhood tavern,
like the rest of the Latins
drowning their thoughts
on American beer or wine.
Thinking about back home
where the land is warm.
Yes, thinking about mi viejita.

Wine is fine when the mind unwinds
thoughts such as, why?
Sleeping in the snow when
our country
is so warm,
where are the Latin poets?
I don't know, maybe sleeping in the snow
or vacationing down at Cook County Jail.

In an article published several years ago (Zimmerman 1989, 77), I cite the above poem published in the late 1970s by a then-young Chicago Puerto Rican, Alfredo Matías, that bears the provocative title, "Where are the Latin Poets?"[1] Today, after so many years of Latino literary development, we may feel we no longer have to ask Matías's question. Latino literature has fully emerged as a significant minority presence that has forced some critics to redefine the U.S. literary canon, and has even impacted social scientists as they have attempted to understand Latinos and their importance for the United States as well as the Americas as a whole.

Indeed, even focusing on the specifically Chicago dimensions implicated in Matías's question, the record, though far from spectacular, is at least beginning to change. There are not many Chicago Latino writers with a large national standing and exposure; but, yes, at least four are considerable voices in the overall U.S. constellation: there's Carlos Morton, the playwright; Laurence Gonzales, a prose-writing mainstreamer; and, of course, the best known figures: Ana Castillo and Sandra Cisneros. Nevertheless, a central aspect of Matías's question still holds. All four of the writers mentioned are of primarily Mexican origin, and there are many other important Mexicano and Chicano writers in Chicago. The question then remains, "Where are the *Puerto Rican* poets?" And what is their contribution to the Chicago Latino and overall U.S. Puerto Rican and Latino scene?

To approach this matter from a different angle: some years ago, in his introduction to an anthology of U.S. Puerto Rican poetry cited in chapter 3, Efraín Barradas (1980, 11) went to great lengths to point out the lack of continuity and community between Nuyorican and Island writers. The Chicago Puerto Rican writers have been cut off from both sectors, and only one of them appears in the anthology cited. So, where have these writers been and what has their work meant?

What follows in this chapter is a look at the emergence of Chicago Puerto Rican poetry in function of a developing Latino world. My assumption is that it is impossible to understand Chicago Puerto Rican writing without a sense of the larger context. And indeed, this need for a broader Latino perspective is true for the overall Midwest and Chicago Puerto Rican social context, as well, as Félix Padilla (1985) argued cogently. Inversely, of course, a Chicago Puerto Rican perspective is also necessary for an understanding of the overall national Puerto Rican and Latino reality.

With reference to the Chicago scene, it may well be that the ability of Carlos Morton to go beyond his specific ethnic and geographic origins is related to his effort to pass as a "puertorican" (Morton, 1971, 4).[2] The constructions of Latina liberation in Ana Castillo (1988) and Sandra Cisneros (1988) also benefit from alternative Latina models, often Puerto Rican ones. The Chicago Puerto Rican writers almost always refer to their specific roots, but they also relate them and their experience of oppression to African American and Mexican or Chicano orientations.

From the beginning, Chicago Puerto Rican poets were to speak of Latin or Latino identity, Latin or, increasingly, Latino poetry. Indeed, perhaps for their smaller numerical size as a population (or as a tiny writer/artist subculture, and perhaps also for the fragility and difficult-to-specify character of their sense of nationhood), they, more than their Mexicano counterparts, tended to decenter or go beyond national identifications to Latino and third world/minority ones even to the degree that they affirmed their particular parameters of identity. It is no accident that the major Chicago-area contribution to the developing national Latino scene was *Revista Chicano-Riqueña,* headed by U.S. Puerto Rican Nicolás Kanellos. Thus, the question of Latino as opposed to strictly Puerto Rican identity is one of the major contributions of Chicago Puerto Rican writers to an overall national Latino literary scene.

This chapter will provide an overview of Chicago Puerto Rican writing as a means of establishing a frame for our central object: a look at the first consolidated wave of Chicago Puerto Rican poetry as represented by David Hernández, Salima Rivera, and the other Chicago poets appearing in the *Nosotros* issue of *Revista Chicano-Riqueña* (1977).

Chicago Puerto Rican Writers: An Overview

Puerto Rican texts written in Chicago may well exist prior to the major settlement wave of the 1940s and 1950s, with the first Puerto Ricans to come to the area. It seems safe to say that there were *décimas* and *plenas,* poems of nostalgia and exile and so forth, written in Chicago, and some appearing in early Puerto Rican and more generally Latino publications long before the 1970s. These materials should be found, collected, and examined if the whole story of Chicago Puerto Rican poetry is to be told.[3] Chicago Puerto Rican writing and overall literary development have been relatively limited; but there are a few players in recent years who deserve mention here.

Long a Chicago fixture first as the codeejay (with Chicano band leader Víctor Parra) of a widely popular local PBS radio program entitled *Mambo Express,* then as a member of Chicago's Latino Institute staff, emcee, ad writer, political campaign manager (for mayoral candidate Larry Bloom and others), and overall cultural entrepreneur, Billy Zayas was also the cowriter of a play entitled *Carnicería Rodríguez,* a work about Chicago Latino politics on the eve of the Harold Washington years and in a deep sense expressing some of the Latino-related issues that would be involved in his campaign. *Carnicería* is an at times brilliant effort cowritten with two talented local Cuban writers, Achy Obejas and Jorge Casuso, which is perhaps one of the few works of Latino science fiction, if only because it deals with a Puerto Rican (performed superbly by Zayas) who owns his own market and employs a *cubano* and even an *argentino.* In the course of the play, Latinos are taught to unite and to join with others to fight against those who seek to use and exploit them. in this respect and others, the play anticipates not only the years of Harold Washington as Chicago's first black mayor, but Jesse Jackson's call for a" rainbow coalition."[4] Zayas also wrote a body of mainly unpublished poetry; he developed and performed innumerable comic routines; and, over the years, he published a series of sketches in a local Latino newspaper. But his main work appeared in the 1980s.

In that same time period, another writer emerged—Ralph Cintrón, a native of Mayaguez, who grew up in the Chicano world of Mercedes, Texas (the hometown of novelist Tomás Rivera, after all), before coming north to develop as a promising poet with strong metaphysical inclinations who nevertheless sought to maintain and deepen what was left of his Puerto Rican roots, both as the editor of the short-lived Latino journal *Ecos,* but also as the sometime writer of poems with clear ethnic markings, in which he reflects on what has happened to his island since the years of Luis Muñoz Marín. Cintrón was later to write a telling ethnography-based book, *Angeltown*, a study about Latinos (mainly Mexicans, it should be noted) struggling for "respect in a world that denies them respect," in the Chicago suburb of Aurora that is more brilliantly and dramatically conceived and written than many a novel or play.

A few additional works round out a period when U.S. Puerto Rican women writers finally came to the fore. First there was the poet Marta Collazo, who sometimes did athletic dance performances of her largely unpublished body of evocative poetry. Aurora Levins Morales and Rosario Morales include some Chicago memories in their *Getting Home Alive* (1986). And then, during the same year, Chicago's Clementina Souchet self-published *Clementina: Una historia sin fin* (1986), an autobiography detailing her odyssey from Peñuelas, Puerto Rico, to her years in Chicago as wife and then divorcée who then built a career for herself as a Puerto Rican journalist and community worker and was eventually appointed representative of the "Hispanic Community" by Republican Governor Jim Thompson several years ago. According to the author's account, her husband was a naive dupe of Chicago's sinister independence movement of the 50s; and in perhaps the book's most fascinating pages, we watch as he gets involved with local *independentistas* in conspiratorial meetings and planned activities that are part of the background of the Puerto Rican *independentista* 1954 assault on Congress.[5] Appalled by her husband's friends and the danger in which they were placing him and above all their young son, Souchet proudly describes how she saved her husband and perhaps Harry Truman as well by reporting the group to the FBI, spying for that organization, and indeed helping, she claims, to thwart the overall conspiracy and to place behind bars many of those misguided and deranged souls, including her husband, who were giving their place of birth and people a bad name in the land of opportunity.

This floridly written and self-serving book is, even in these senses, an extremely valuable document for giving us at least one perspective on Chicago's Puerto Rican world of the 1950s and 60s. It is a world of *independentistas* and social conformists, of revolutionaries and opportunists. Above all it depicts Puerto Rican Chicago, mainly in the era of the Daley machine. Clementina is a woman formed by her class and time, living out all the pretensions inscribed in her name, hobnobbing with Anglo dignitaries, machine politicians, Latino businesspeople, and the Mexican and Latin American celebrities who came to the city and in turn invited her to their homes. Filled with copies of letters, documents, photos, and so forth, this narrative makes of its protagonist a Puerto Rican female Lazarillo de Tormes, a self-righteous Moll Flanders, or Fanny Hill Boricua-style.[6]

Two years after the emergence of Souchet's book, another prose writer, Leonardo Rodríguez, found support from the Puerto Rican Parade Committee and other sources to publish a slim volume of vignettes entitled *They Have to be Puerto Ricans* (1988), which tells of Chicago Puerto Ricans living on welfare, manifesting a crude, superficial flag-waving nationalism, wasted on U.S. dependency, with the lowest sense of self worth, and yet struggling (at least some of them) to maintain some kind of cultural identity and integrity (for examples, see chapter 2, part 2, and chapter 6).

In the 1990s and into the current century, several other Chicago Puerto Ricans produced a body of writing worthy of mention. Adolfo Colón published a book of rather traditional, island-centered poems, *Cantos de Seboruco,* including *décimas* and other traditional forms, in a work that reveals a poet with commitment and skill whose romantic portrayal of *jíbaro* life would seem nourished by his many years of urban residence. He also wrote some short fiction, including two stories, "Una obra maestro" and "La gran ciudad," published in John Barry's posthumous collection, *Voces en el viento* (1999, 20–24, 101–4). Lourdes Lugo López published a volume, *Poemas que me desnudan y me definan* (1992), presenting her *independentista* and feminist sympathies, and also including provocative photos reflecting aspects of her politics and personal trajectory. In addition, four advanced-degree Puerto Ricans, Eduardo Arocho, Sonia Báez Hernández, Juana Goergen, and Frank Varela, have been giving new life to the Chicago Puerto Rican poetry scene but clearly moving away from the street poetry model developed by the Nuyorican poets and Hernández's early Chicago group. A Spanish professor at DePaul University, Goergen has written *La sal de las brujas* (1997—finalist for the *Letras de Oro* prize), *La piel a medias* (2001), and *Las ilusas* (2010); she has also appeared in anthologies of Chicago Latino and Midwest Latina writing—the first, edited by Chicago Mexican poet Olivia Maciel (1998), the second, edited by Chicana Brenda Cárdenas and Boricua Johanny Vázquez (2001). In the same volume, Báez Hernández published "Container" and "There Is Something"; she published "Born Equal" in the *Centro de Estudios Puertorriqueños* Chicago issue. But she was just beginning to publish in Chicago when her fight against cancer and family circumstances caused her to embark on a new phase of her life in Miami. A committed community worker with a graduate degree in social work, Arocho published two poems in the *Centro de Estudios puertorriqueños* Chicago issue (2001), and he then published his first chapbook, *Poems Behind the Mascara* (2002) followed by *Paseo Boricua Renaissance* (2003); and *The Fourth Tassle* (2006) works centered on celebrating aspects of Puerto Rican life in Chicago and on the island.

Frank Varela, a poet trained at the Universidad Católica in Ponce, but with a long

U.S. residence, first in the New York area then many years in Chicago and now in Cleveland, worked as a fundraiser and librarian in his Chicago years and served on the board of the Movimiento Artístico Chicano, the publisher of his early books of poetry. Varela's first volume, *Serpent Underfoot*, introduced and with some translations by Luis Felipe Díaz, portrays some key moments in the author's life, as well as Puerto Rican life in the Humboldt Park area of Chicago. His second volume, *Bitter Coffee* (2001), continues some of the directions developed in Varela's first book but also presents the author's reflections on key figures of Puerto Rican and U.S. history, culture, and literature. Included are William Carlos Williams, Arturo Alfonso Schomburg, Pablo Casals, José Campeche, Julia de Burgos, Pedro Albizu Campos, Ramón Emeterio Betances—even Ezra Pound appears in a collection that projects in different directions but is primarily focused on reconstructing Puerto Rican memory. A more recent book, *Caleb's Exile* (2009), may well be his best.

More directly political than the work of most of these writers is the poetry written by and sometimes about Chicago's Fuerzas Armadas de Liberación Nacional (FALN) POWs—poems by Carmen Valentín, Alejandra Torres, and Luis Rosa. Usually published in FALN and Movimiento de Liberación Nacional (MLN) newspapers and newsletters, most of this poetry constitutes another mode of militant expression, communicating the plight of the group and perhaps providing therapy for the prisoners and their most intimate supporters. But at times the writers rise above conventional language to give vivid testimony of their revolutionary ideals or their situations as fervent believers and prisoners. Genuine products of a Chicago urban experience that lumpenized and marginalized many, while it led others to varying forms of political and cultural resistance, the writers of Chicago FALN poetry, whether the POWs themselves or their supporters, represent a dimension of Chicago Puerto Rican poetry and reality that requires further study to grasp the totality of Boricua poetic expression in the diaspora.

Finally, a few years ago, Johanny Vázquez produced a new bilingual collection of poetry, *Poemas callejeros/Streetwise Poems* (2007), that reaffirms but also moves beyond some of the main trends noted in Chicago Puerto Rican literature and poetry. Section I, "Tránsito pesado/Heavy Traffic," presents this "hija de la ciudad" walking through streets and alleyways, or riding on the El, always moving with "paso firme," even as she meditates about Latino family and self, as she makes her way through Chicago. Section II, "Adoquines/Paving Stones," contains meditations on birth, life, African dimensions of identity, the problems of using words, of missing her island home and family; but it also contains poems about the Puerto Rican island of Vieques and the sea that remind us of one of her favorite poets, Julia de Burgos. Section III, "Calle sin salida/Dead-End Street," returns us again to the city and its rough streets, but with heightened subjectivity in relation to themes of longing and loneliness, the tedious routines of everyday life, moments of passion and indifference. Section IV, "Luz verde / Green Light," returns to African associations to speak sensuously of the body, dance, and sexual adventures. It affirms sexual revolution in a postrevolutionary era. There's a poem about "the night after," another relating the island to body geography, another expressing conflicts of feminism and passion. This, then, is a collection that brings together the work of a poet who, after years of living, experimenting, and sometimes failing, has finally found her voice and who speaks out from her urban space, projecting us toward her Caribbean and African roots as well as the broader world beyond.

Still another phenomenon in Chicago has been the emergence of first-person narratives that may be classified as *testimonio* and have an ethnographic value somewhat parallel to that of Philippe Bourgois's New York crack narrative of 1995. First, Félix Padilla presented a book full of first-person narratives but analyzing Chicago Puerto Rican gang life as an entrepreneurial exercise (1992); then he gave us some entry into a Chicago Puerto Rican woman's life on the fringe of the gang world, as told to him by Lourdes Santiago, in *Outside the Wall: A Puerto Rican Woman's Struggle* (1993). More recently, Reymundo Sánchez has published two successive volumes on Chicago Puerto Rican gang life constituting an autobiography of his participation in Chicago's Latin Kings. The first volume, *My Bloody Life: The Making of a Latin King* (2000), is a vivid portrait of growing up in a poor Puerto Rican barrio, the effects of families and neighbors, just a few blocks from where this author and his Puerto Rican family live, and yet what a different world it is. Sexual obsession, loyalties, and betrayals are all portrayed in one of the stronger accounts yet written by a former gang member. The sequel volume, *Once a King, Always a King: The Unmaking of a Latin King* (2004), portrays the narrator's subsequent life and his ever-difficult efforts to leave the gang world behind. Bill Barillas notes that "Sánchez, whose mother brought him as a child to Chicago from Puerto Rico, sought refuge from an abusive household by joining the Latin Kings, a notorious gang often as brutal toward its own members as toward rivals. Sánchez's books act less as cautionary tales than as indictments of society's failure to assist disadvantaged children. A perpetrator as well as a victim of crime, the author does not spare himself in truth telling about gang violence" (Barillas 2004).

The two volumes constitute one of the most vital accounts of gang life written to date, with the feel of everyday life and the entrapment to which life in the poorest Puerto Rican neighborhoods can lead. One further narrative not to be omitted from this account is the autobiography of Josefina Rodríguez, as told to Carlos Quiles, *Memorias de Josefina* (2005), the story of a Puerto Rican mother in Chicago who fought for more than twenty years to get her two daughters out of prison for their activities in favor of Puerto Rican independence.

All this said, one of the most prolific and important Chicago-origin Rican writers was poet and playwright Rane Arroyo, who had little contact with his home community in recent years because of his work as a professor in Youngstown and Toledo, Ohio. Writing of Arroyo, Bill Barillas notes:

> The parents of poet and playwright Rane Arroyo (b.1954) met in Chicago, each having come from Puerto Rico seeking work. They lived in Lincoln Park and other North Side neighborhoods, moving to Chicago's western suburbs when the future writer was a teenager. In his doctoral dissertation at the University of Pittsburgh (1997), Arroyo examines how the Harlem Renaissance writers were admitted into the canon only after critics had displaced their politics in favor of aesthetic issues. He also compares their critical reception to that of contemporary Latino/as. In addition to several chapbooks, Arroyo has published three larger works: *The Singing Shark* (1997), *Pale Ramón* (1998), and *Home Movies of Narcissus* (2002). Frequently alluding to popular as well as literary culture, these books reflect Arroyo's complex identity as a gay man, a Puerto Rican, a teacher, and a writer. These personal dimensions converge in the Midwest, particularly in Chicago, which Arroyo [always referred] to as home though he live[d] in Ohio. His work challenges outdated notions of Midwestern character. As he writes in the poem "Being: An Essay on Being a Midwestern Writer" (in *Midwestern Miscellany* 30 (Fall 2002), "A gay Latino helping / a straight student write a love poem / for 'his woman' isn't used in brochures—/ why not? It's rude that Hart Crane / hasn't visited me—he who now wears / the Caribbean Sea and I his Ohio" (xx). In addition to his poetry, Arroyo also wrote several plays, some of which have been produced in New York, Los Angeles, and other cities. He [was] director of creative writing at the University of Toledo (Barillas in his manuscript 2003).[7]

Arroyo died in May 2010, and his life's work was slated for presentation in a volume edited by his best critic, Betsy A. Sandlin. He and many of the other writers mentioned above are worthy of further study. However, this chapter now turns to a closer look at the core of Chicago Puerto Rican poetry—the work of David Hernández and the group that emerged with the 1977 *Nosotros* issue of *Revista Chicano-Riqueña*, which brought Chicago Puerto Rican poetry to the fore and made it an essential part of Chicago, Midwest, and U.S. Latino writing.

The Emergence of Chicago Puerto Rican Ethnic Writing

For our purposes, the context for the emergence of a specific U.S. Puerto Rican ethnic literature in Chicago stems from the conditions of economic and social marginalization and alienation that produced the so-called "Puerto Rican riot" on Division Street in 1966 and led to the formation of new organizations and groups attempting to generate social, political, and cultural empowerment in the Puerto Rican community (see Padilla, 1985, chapter 2; also Padilla, 1987, 117-143; Gina Pérez 2004, especially 183–89). Organizations such as ABC, Aspira, and other community action groups developed; so did gangs such as the Latin Kings and Young Lords, and the Chicago branch of the FALN, whose legacy is reflected in today's urban activism against gentrification, as well as in the emergence of Luis Gutiérrez, Chicago's Independentista *independentista* congressman.[8] From the late '60s on, Chicago Puerto Ricans created several high school, university, and community centers, groups and projects that involved cultural expression as at least one dimension of their work. The emergence of collective publications is clearly part of this story.

From 1971 until its demise in 1975, Samuel Betances's Chicago-based publication, *The Rican: A Journal of Puerto Rican Cultural Expression,* was to produce many seminal articles on questions of Puerto Rican island and immigration history and experience, and usually included at least some poems, primarily those written by young Chicago Puerto Ricans. A number of these poets were also involved in the new social organizations, while some would become members of community arts organizations such as El Taller (The Workshop) and ALBA (The Association of Latino Brotherhood of Artists) and would be among the *Nosotros* writers. In this latter category were David Hernández, Julio Noboa, Carmelo Romero, and Emma Iris Rodríguez; but Chico Rivera and Shabazz Pérez were other young Puerto Ricans who wrote poetry for the journal. Some of these writers, and above all Hernández, would be among the first Chicago Latino writers to appear in the pages of *Revista Chicano-Riqueña*. But clearly, the key early continuity between the two publications was between the poets of *The Rican* who found their way, through the *Nosotros* collective, into *Revista Chicano-Riqueña's Nosotros* issue.

If up to the time of these publications, few people had heard much about "Chicago Hispanic poets" or even "Chicago Hispanics," now Chicago *Latinidad* was to come of age with a newly heightened Latino definition and thrust. *Nosotros* is crucial to our story because it brought together poets in a nationally distributed Latino journal and because it highlighted Puerto Rican talent in a city that, in terms of things Latino, was mainly seen as Mexican. While *Revista* had carried some Chicago poets and artists from its earliest days; now, with its *Nosotros* issue featuring ten Latino poets and several visual artists, Chicago Latino and specifically Puerto Rican poetry and art were finally on the national map.

Above all, *Nosotros* specifically and consciously articulated Chicago's pan-nationalist Latino perspective, using the militant language of the times but nevertheless summing up issues that remain crucial to this day:

> We are the Latino poets and artists. As Boricuas and Chicanos we have struggled to define ourselves and erase the stereotypes imposed on our minds by the forces of oppression. The Latino communities of America have said, "Basta/Enough!" No longer will Latinos in the U.S.A. be identified and stereotyped with images of what Puerto Ricans, Cubans, Mexicans should act like as seen through the eyes of the world. We will identify ourselves. We will decide who we are and what we will be about. We exercise the right to express our identity so that no exploiter could confuse and use us. . . . Our poetry and art is born of love, of suffering and of every experience that delights and torments our people. We are the magicians who weave glorious spells of thought images, depicting the lives, moods, struggles and hopes of the people who populate the Latino barrios of Chicago. We print rainbows of thoughts and feelings that range from the darkest hues of anger and bitterness to the brightest fantasies and dreams. . . . We speak with the voices of a rainbow underground that is beginning to surface from the pitfalls of racism; for we will not eliminate but harmonize our Afro-Indio-Hispano roots and our children of every color will set an example of brotherhood to all mankind (*Nosotros,* 1).

Where did the *Nosotros* poets come from and where were they going? In what way were they typical of their moment, or at least the Chicago Puerto Rican experience at this time? To what degree do they culminate past developments and anticipate the future? As a means of exploring Chicago Latino and Rican poetry, we should examine the *Nosotros* anthology and poets in relation to the forces that went into its making—that is, we should use this publication as a basis for exploring how the social and literary past of Chicago Latino poets leads not just to nationalism, but to perspectives that move beyond it to a vision of *Latinidad,* and then still further toward internationalism as well as the possibility of a future multiracial coalition. This approach will give us an encapsulated view of some of the key dimensions of the story of Puerto Rican literature in Chicago.

Gamaliel Ramírez, *Self Portrait,* 1976. Acrylic on canvas, 54 in. × 56 in., which served as the cover image for *Revista Chicano-Riquena*'s *Nosotros* issue on Chicago Latino (and mainly Chicago Puerto Rican) poetry and art.

Nosotros and Other Puerto Rican Dimensions

The *Nosotros* collection is a diverse representation of Chicago Latino life seen (with the exception of Chicana writer Yolanda Galván and Mexicano Rubén Sánchez)[9] from the perspective of young Puerto Ricans, the majority of whom have grown increasingly hostile to the situation of their compatriots in the city and on the island and who explore through their poetry possible sources of opposition to further negative change. Written in Spanish and English, the poems speak of pride in cultural heritage and loyalty and love for the island they see as homeland. All of them rebel against the situation in which their parents and they have been placed: the injustice that rules their misery and pain, the experience of leaving one's homeland, the cruel reality of their life in the inner city, the drugs and violence that have become part of their everyday life and against which they rebel.

This volume is the product of articulate young people who had experienced the worst situations of the Chicago Puerto Rican diaspora, who were involved in cultural and social programs attempting to better that situation. Subject to endemic unemployment and some of the worst housing in the city, Puerto Rican youths turned to gangs, to drugs, to crime, to independence groups, to grassroots advocacy programs. The poets turn to none, some or all of the above, but also to poetry, to cultural work, as crucial to any project for transforming the Puerto Rican situation. To be sure, their poetry is a matter of patter, dance rhythm, street sound. Ragged lines tear down the printed page. Parentheses and dashes speak to the jagged process of their making. Often bilingual, but not always "correct" in either language, the poems struggle for expression, struggle to make their points, sometimes succeeding, sometimes not. While the poetry is clearly influenced by contemporary African American and Nuyorican writing, not all the poets are the same in content or style. First, there are Matías's simple ironies, in tightly formed poems pointing to the situation of Latino injustices and questioning both the divine and social order. Stylistically more ambitious in his bilingualisms, rhythms, and points of attack, Eduardo Figueroa Condes recalls peasant women who helped him in Puerto Rico, recalls working in New Jersey fields, and pays homage, in effect, to key examples in his Puerto Rican past that can help him to struggle on in the future.

Cesar Quiñones, writing in Spanish only, bemoans how some Puerto Rican men and women have betrayed or distorted their behavior to survive. For Quiñones, Carola sings to the sound of the radio and the street; trapped in a world of consumerism and escapism (locked into a world of Latin music as evasion and not confrontation), she sings but doesn't know, "Carola canta y no sabe . . . no lo sabe, no lo sabe." In another poem, a nun goes "bla, bla, bla." In still another poem, "you are not you, . . you don't exist." In many other poems, people are not what they seem, or disappear, or can't disappear because they have ceased to exist or perhaps never existed. But then too, in the poem "2 x 2," there is the new woman, who has a warrior inside her. The new Puerto Rican woman waits to be born in the desert and hell of today's barrio life.

Emma Iris Rodríguez speaks perhaps too directly to the worst poverty in the Puerto Rican community:

> And, the cockroach that crawls
> slowly
> down the tubes of my stomach
> finds the remains of yesterday's
> rice and beans.

The junkie needs his fix
broken dreams
rattling bones
cold, cold
cold like the
ice before death.

I am the broken glass in the
windows of
poisoned schools.

Sitting here
under the eyes of whites,
I think in who I am-
Latin woman
(life with a double chain)
(Rodríguez, in *Nosotros*
1977, 86–87)

A few years before, in a contribution to *The Rican,* vol. 2 (October 1, 1974): 62, "Tuley Products," Rodríguez reflected bitterly on the educational system for Puerto Ricans in the Daley years:

Year in, year out
Spanish children grow
INTO
Gang bangers, drug pushers,
Street hangers, night walkers.
Devoured by monstrous
8 til 4 factory jobs
Haunted by eviction notices
Chased by cockroach tribes
Enclosed within Latin sounds,
Bacardi, happy wine-filled dreams
of
'I never go back to Georgia'
Which means, never leave, always die
And the only crib they will ever
own
In Puerto Rico is a death crypt.

In *Nosotros,* seeking still stronger images, Rodríguez seems all but locked ever more completely into a habitual ghetto dirge. Perhaps that is why she seeks other thematics, other modes of dealing with the problems that consume her. So she takes an imaginary voyage, anticipating one by the most touted Latina writer from Illinois (Sandra Cisneros 1987), trying to leave her chains behind, free herself of the ghetto blues, and break into the future. We leave the mundane world of insufficient money, of cold and hungry nights, of barrio sites and frights, and we enter a realm of poetic time and space. We return to the island, we even go to Africa. But, and here is the problem: the island is the conventional paradise of childhood memory; Africa is the cliché site of sensuous drums, of ancient rituals, of primitive dance, of pure and black blood running through veins and heating men's passions. Is there nothing in our Chicago realities that points to any genuine transcendence of its miseries?

Carmelo Romero provides another kind of affirmation of blackness. Pointing to the Latin Kings and asking, "where is our nation?" he explores the African dimension of salsa, the Latin dimension of jazz, the sources linking Puerto Ricans to the rest of the Caribbean. In proud defiance of the effort to identify Puerto Ricans with a white racist image of blacks, he writes:

> the man
> sees no
> differences
> between
> us
> in spanish
> in english
> we are niggers
> we must be ruled
> or
> destroyed
> his nation demands it
> his nation demands it
>
> let us stop
> killing
> each
> other
> let
> the
> spirits
> of Afrika
> our
> Afrika
> be
> the

spirit
of
our
nation
let us build nests!
(Romero, "Nests to be Built,"
in *Nosotros* 1977, 102)

Surely Romero's black solution is a romantic one, another exotic falsification of U.S., Caribbean, and African black cultures, a one-sided view of musical and human history. But if Romero misconstrues black history and reduces salsa to its African components, his distortions are simply the reactions to imposed ones. If all else fails, if the syncretic union of the oppressed does not lead to a transformation of life itself, he poses a dream of guerrilla attacks and confirms, in the voice of Portuguese Africa: A LUTTA CONTINUA (Romero in *Nosotros* 1977, 110).

Not all the poets speak the same language, have the same message, or have had precisely the same experiences. Within the same general orbit as his fellow poets, Julio Noboa Jr., literary editor of *The Rican,* confronts us with difference. Here is a poet who is also intent on giving expression to the problems of identity facing second-generation Puerto Ricans in the years after 1967-68, but whose writing is less directly tied to everyday speech and everyday life. Born in the Bronx, but far from projecting a Nuyorican voice in his poetry, he perhaps never developed such close ties to Puerto Rico as a place to remember and mourn as did other *Nosotros* poets. His poetry seems to reflect a broader perspective of the U.S. Puerto Rican experience, as he seeks and provides explanations for the events that shape Latino lives. His is a more overtly historical perspective involving economic, political, and religious interests. Unlike the other poets, whose work echoes everyday barrio life, Noboa's poems are more developed on the overt conceptual level, and reflect a degree of formal education that differentiates him from his fellow poets. If anything, his poetry suffers from a kind of defensive abstraction, as if he is everywhere attempting to fight stereotypes and project the image of a Puerto Rican who is well-educated and well-versed (he even has poems that rhyme). In one poem, he writes of the continuing historical exploitation of some groups (of which Latinos are just one example) by powerful ones. But he affirms the eventual triumph of the oppressed soul over the oppressor. Truth is found through knowledge of one's history, and freedom must exist first in one's mind and soul. And Noboa sees a solution to the problems of Puerto Rico's colonial dependency and the internal colony status of U.S. Puerto Rican barrios in a righteous struggle for education, for spiritual and humanistic growth. His poem "The Entire Scope of

Humanity" points to the contradictions of attempting to find truth through the institutions created by those who would use knowledge to control others; but he suggests that for Puerto Ricans, there is no other alternative.

Noboa affirms his Puerto Rican identity in a poem like "Comiendo Cerebro"; then in another poem, he affirms his African roots, but he warns against Puerto Ricans trapping themselves in narrow frames that simply counter one stereotype with another or express defiant pride for what others have sought to impute as negative group attributes (for example, African roots). "Oración" indicates his continuing efforts to find and understand his Puerto Rican past as the key to any renewed identity; and in "Reincarnation" we find that that identity is found in grasping Puerto Rican diversity as well as its unity:

> What forms of life did my spirit inhabit
> Before its rebirth as a human being?
> . . .
> From . . . a multitude of lifetimes/
> my spirit can recall
> Only one thing is certain, I was each and all!
> (*Nosotros,* 48)

Paradoxically, Noboa's poem "Identity" might not seem to have any specifically Puerto Rican content at all; and yet it is this poem that may have ultimately the most to say on the Puerto Rican drive for spiritual and cultural affirmation, even if other forms of dependence continue:

> I'd rather smell of musty, green stench
> than of sweet, fragrant lilac.
> If I could stand alone, strong and free,
> I'd rather be a tall, ugly weed.
> (*Nosotros* 1997, 49)

Finally, in this light, we might look at a poem called "Survival of the Species," which Noboa published in *The Rican,* vol. 1 (May 4, 1974): 51. This poem exhibits Noboa's problems in poetic expression, as well as his ideological importance in the development of Chicago Puerto Rican poetry. It is probably because of its distance in diction and poetic concreteness from the "down to earth" standards of *Nosotros* and of most urban Latino writing in general (as well as from dominant and countercultural poetic norms) that this poem was not included in *Nosotros.*[10] But it may well be that these very qualities or problems highlight the poem's significance as a statement of ideology that was clearly typical of

Noboa, and that as Félix Padilla (1987, 190) has suggested, typified the fullest sense of Chicago Puerto Rican aspirations in the 1970s. Indeed the poem may be said to express the value frame from which frustrations about the social and educational realities of Chicago Puerto Ricans were sensed most keenly: the effort to move through and beyond (yet without negating) a sense of nationhood, to a defiant affirmation of the Puerto Rican's right to the fullest range of human historical experience:

From the seed of Intelligence
Could emerge and develop
The plant of wisdom
Only when the roots are
Firmly embedded in the
Rich soil of Knowledge,
The leaves are lit by the
Radiant sunlight of Truth
And both are bathed in the
Cleansing rainwaters of Experience.
Many good seeds not nurtured in rich soil
Nor blessed with sunlight and rain
Never develop into mature, healthy plants,
But when knowledge nourishes,
Truth illuminates and Experience
Invigorates, the growing plant of
Wisdom blossoms into full maturity,
Capable of procreation and expression.
Only by this ultimate achievement,
The ability to create, spills its
Own seed, with the spirit within
The plant of Wisdom forms a link
In the cosmic chain of life
And stakes a claim for immortality.

David Hernández in the 1970s. Photo
by Gamaliel Ramírez.

David Hernández and his Chicago Street Poetry

The central poet in the *Nosotros* group, the writer who encouraged many of the
others and served as their mentor and model, was David Hernández, who figured as a major personality and poet in the Chicago Latino scene until his demise. For most non-Latino Chicagoans who know anything about Latino poetry,
Hernández *is* Chicago Latino poetry. He's the perennial ubiquitous representative, the one let in the front door, the talented "token" in citywide, statewide,
nationwide anthologies, our Nuyorican poet Chi-town style.[11] Of course, for some
Latinos and Puerto Ricans, he remains too disreputable, too connected with bo-
hemianism, drugs, booze, jazz, black culture, white culture. He's too much a
paradox—at once the Chicago institution and alternative model for young Rican
gangbangers; yet too anarchistic, too antiestablishment, too Beat, hippie, and
the rest. Some complain about his unwillingness to join a specific Puerto Rican
political group, even as he works for and is identified with the most progressive
political trends in Chicago. Some complain he takes Puerto Rican problems too
lightly. But Hernández has taken on the traditional stance of the poet *manqué*.
Whether in truth or in fantasy, he has taken on the persona of a Puerto Rican
Whitman, singing fiercely democratic and populist hymns to the bums, drunks,

losers, and bag ladies, all those whose fates are somehow among the worst possible in the Puerto Rican diaspora.

Also, by means of his chimerical poetic identity, he has been able to stand for many of the identity possibilities and directions that exist in the Puerto Rican community. He has had, then, the "negative capability" Keats ascribed to a fairly well-known poet, and which has enabled Hernández to represent many—the men if not all the women. Hernández has sought to be Chicago's complete Puerto Rican male voice, has sought to express the entire range of (prefeminist) U.S. Puerto Rican literary themes, from nostalgia over roots, to growing up Latino in the rough part of town, to the struggle for equality and recognition, to an expansion beyond the Puerto Rican and more broadly Latino world to the still larger world beyond. This gamut is present even in Hernández's earliest collection, self-published with friends and significantly called *Despertando* (*Waking Up*) (1971).

As far as I can gather, *Despertando* is the first poetry collection by a Chicago Latino. Not fortuitously, it appeared in the same year that *The Rican* was born, and on the eve of the birth of *Revista Chicano-Riqueña*. The title is derived from the nationalist chant, *Despierta Boricua, defiende lo tuyo* (*Wake up Puerto Ricans, defend what's yours*). The refrain was constantly heard in Chicago's Puerto Rican neighborhoods, especially in the 1970s after the disturbances of the late 1960s. It is present as well in the poems that appear in the *Nosotros* issue and in Hernández's later work.

Despertando itself is very uneven (almost all the best, most realized poems are in the first pages of the book); and in this way, it anticipates not only most of Hernández's themes but also his main characteristics as a writer. Here, with the question of unevenness, we should be a bit careful, however. For, as his first book shows, Hernández's art situates itself as a virtual manifesto of creative improvisation with all the risks improvisation entails.

Capable of rewriting a given poem year after year, Hernández nevertheless insists, through form and overt statement, on the crucial, inviolable status of inspiration and spontaneity. Because part of his art is an irreverence toward academic poetics, his trick is frequently to create a poem that seems unpremeditated and unchecked, even when the effect may prove ultimately calculated. The poems are written as variants of an unstated melody or set of chords, in function of a given rhythm design, with internal rhymes and other poetic devices creating a sense of form, which is then continually violated, usually in a gentle and mocking way, as if the dissonance or rhythmic interruption is a function of life's or society's confusions, disequilibria, and discord. From 1972 on for many years, Hernández usually read his poems with his musical group, *Los Sonidos de la Calle* or *Street Sounds* (often bass, guitar, and congas and other percussion) in a Latin-jazz syncretism that paralleled and complemented the mixing process found in the poems themselves. And because the *Sounds* supplied the unheard undercurrent music and rhythm, the full effect of Hernández's stylistic tricks came to the fore—the half-shaped, purposely offbeat line played out against the more truly formed notes and chord patterns; the dissonance, interruptedness, and tentativeness of one between two cultural systems, belief patterns, and imperatives emerges most fully. Perhaps this is Hernández's challenge as a writer: many of his poems don't work as well on paper as they do against a musical background. Part of this question is one of personality, but in the 1980s, theatrical productions based on his poems proved them effective even when he was not directly delivering them.

The references to music and theater are just indications of the broad artistic orientations sometimes hidden by Hernández's populist thematics and attitudes. So, when asked about his inspiration, his reference is not to music or theater but to sculpture. "Poetry is the tool to change the English language," he says: "I am out to destroy the language of silly fascists and rebuild it for all of us. This sculptor Julian Harr took me into his studio in 1963 and I became his apprentice. Not as a sculptor but as a poet. By watching him carve and chip away, create form out of formlessness is how I learned the craft of poetry. My life was half into my people and half into the artist counter-cultural bohemian life-style that Julian represented. From there on my circle of artists from all races and backgrounds grew larger until all hell broke loose and I found my heaven."[12]

But after this trip into sculpture, the reference seems to go into music after all: "I am a product of the African Griot, and the antenna of the race. Poetry is important to me because it fills the space between my heart-beats."

Born in Cidra, Puerto Rico, in 1946, Hernández arrived in Chicago with his parents, two brothers, and a sister in 1955. As one of his poems tell us, his parents were very poor; they lived mainly on the Puerto Rican north side. He went to three different grade schools, was demoted, displaced, and spewed through and out of the educational system "because no spik English." In the late 60s, he was already a member of the counterculture, into drugs, jazz, and (if we can believe his poetry) lots of hetero-sex. Dedicating his work to all those who he could call his people and community, he tumbled out his poems, half-hacked, half-formed, bits and pieces taken here and there—some impressions on Chicago's train system, vignettes out of Chicago night lights, some personal remembrances that, considered together, might make a little novel, a miniature version of a Latino life, like Eduardo Rivera's *Family Installments*. So, *Despertando* starts in Puerto Rico with a boy climbing up a mountain, tin pail full, dogs barking, and singing behind him.

Next he is on a plane, arriving at Midway Airport. A proud boy but brown, antici-pating the smiles of Americans, he arrives and is hit by the Chicago wind. And as the book unfolds, we see him get to know his new world. There are poems about Puerto Ricans young and old, about lumpens brown, black, and white. There's a Puerto Rican man who loses his fingers and job, swallows his pride, and gets on welfare, a Puerto Rican teen who has no choice but to join the army, a suffering Chicana, a prostitute, a lonely old woman eating alone. The remembrances and vignettes rank among his best work—they are hard, deeply felt portraits of an unjust and cruel reality.

Similar qualities are found in the *Nosotros* materials of 1977. In two poems that he will later weave together as part of a chant that will become virtually his sig-nature, the poet intones:

El fire hydrant	The fire hydrant
es mi playa	is my beach
bajo un calor	in a heat
que hasta desmaya	that makes even
las cucarachas	cockroaches
y los ratones	and rats faint
aqui en Chicago.	here in Chicago.

i
am rican
nigger/
blanco/
indio/
in between
all which
is alive
good/bad.
when
i
was in
darkness
you
turned
me
down.
can i forgive
you for that?
  i can.

i
am
not
like
you.
(Hernández, "Me la Buscaré" and
"White Statue," in *Nosotros* 1977, 3–4).

Some of the longer poems that follow are far from his best, but one, "Tecata"
(Nosotros 1977, 4), gives us a harsh portrait of how country Puerto Rican values
are bludgeoned by the urban nightmares that lead from drugs to death. And finally, in "Fame," we have one of several run-on catalog poems that are usually
his biggest successes:

now that i have been discovered
i will no longer write nasty poems about america.
i will no longer hang her flag in the bathroom.
i will no longer scream that the only good system
is the chicago sewer system even though it clogs up at times . . .
. . .
I will be discussed in english classes,
the types of rhymes I used
the deep-hidden meanings in my lines and
how inspiration hit me in a chicago rain.
(*Nosotros,* 11–12).

In a much more recent poem, Hernández says, "I want to be a real poet/so I
can participate in poetry-discussions." Now that Hernández is more or less famous
(at least in Chicago), here we are dissecting and assessing him. In a telling statement, he notes, "Being from Illinois and Chicago, the environment, the place of
the city definitely influences the images and rhythm of poetry. . . . Being in a
racist town," he adds, "Latino poets must be slicker, tougher and no holds barred
kill with kindness artists." In *Despertando* sometimes the situation leads to anger:

I do not care who you
are or why
here is me from not the united states
of amerikkka in
chicago.
dirt stench
shit whores

wiskey wine
sweat piss time
grass trees sky
("El," in *Despertando* 1977, 52)

But the other side of this harsh attack is the sentimental, populist Hernández, who loves love, gets gushy about the people, and virtually sinks his city rhythms in syrup. If love and truth are to win over a world of hatred and lies, let the victory be hard fought so that it has some genuine equivalency to the problems facing us in life. If David Hernández finds his way out of the dilemma of being "Chi-town brown" in the U.S. belly of the shark, if he never forgets that many of his brethren have not found their way, if those brethren are the real source and stuff of his work, could it be that in finding his way through writing, he has sometimes come to identify the writers or his white-Latin artist-art-consuming audience as his true brethren? "I come from a proud tribal-heritage of artists: The Word-Dealers," he intones to his (sometimes mainly white) audience today. And he thanks his audience for making his performance and life work possible.

Has the bitterness in *Despertando* and Hernández's *Nosotros* poems grown into complacence? Has Hernández mellowed too much? That would seem to be the conclusion one could reach in reading his little collection *Satin-City Lullaby* (1987) or his Elvis collection (1995). But the total effect of a performance of his work belies any negative or nagging impression (even some of the *Satin-City Lullaby* poems come off as better than they seem on paper).[13]

Most of Hernández's major poems became available in *Roof Top Piper* (1991), an attractive publication that presents the poet as a Whitmanesque Rican whose traumatic slap by the Chicago wind opens his eyes to the forces sending Ricans and so many others to poverty, drugs, and loss of security and identity itself. The poems are filled with humor, sentiment, and hope, in what may turn out to be his definitive text portraying the ups and downs of Chicago Puerto Rican life. Much of the same material had come out on tape in their definitive performance form as *Liquid Thoughts* (1988). The tapes reveal that what really keeps his work alive is his capacity in performance in which his irony and his humor, not his indulgent sentimentalism, nor his anger, but that side of him that makes him and his listeners laugh at pain and ugliness. In one of his most disarming off-the-wall narrative poems, "Chicago Sun Times" (a poem he performs without accompaniment—in *Liquid Thoughts*, track 3), he tells of how he is tempted to rip-off a newspaper from a neighbor's doorstep, but chooses not to do so, because he projects step-by-step, how the act could lead to a bitterness that culminates in world nuclear holocaust. Without any overt Latino or Puerto Rican referent yet deeply rooted in the kind

David Hernández recording with the Street Sounds, 2003. Photo by
Gamaliel Ramírez.

of negative anticipation so central to discussions of Puerto Rican colonial identity, this poem speaks comically about an absurd, dread surreality in which one can take nothing for granted, in which uncalculating spontaneity has become impossible, and in which the worst things are ever-ready to happen. In such a world, the refuge of intimate love, the profession of such love in a poem, sentimentalism itself, become dangerous, unmodern, romantic, unhip, and eminently non-Euro-American options. But they are the options chosen by this eminently Rican/Latino poet as he makes his way, twisting and turning through the years.

Salima Rivera and the Construction of Puertorriqueña/Latina Selfhood

Eliana Ortega (1989) traces a pattern by which Puerto Rican women writers identify with an indigenous, pre-Conquest, communal *madre borinqueña* (figured as

Anacaona or Preciosa) to reaffirm an all-but-lost sense of woman-centeredness in relation to an extended tribal family, and to then project beyond the alienated and oppressed position of woman in the context of Spanish and then U.S. domination. Strikingly, in making her argument, Ortega turns to the *Nosotros* issue and draws heavily on one writer I have not yet discussed: Salima Rivera. Specifically citing one of Rivera's *Nosotros* poems ("Ode to an Island"), Ortega notes that

> The lyric "I" in . . . Rivera's poem . . . refers to a "we" [as] . . . poetic discourse emerges from an identification with the indigenous mother, . . . transcending the purely domestic sphere and projecting . . . into a historical-political-national one that [the poet] traces to her origins. [Rivera's] mother-speakers are neither silent martyrs nor tearful *lloronas* . . . but rather rebels with a very specific cause: liberation, not simply individual liberation, but also liberation of their motherland. . . . In this manner, Puerto Rican women poets in the U.S. continue the Anacaonian tradition of song as a rebellious voice and act of liberation. At the same time as these poets demythify the patriarchal discourse of dominant culture, they also produce a dynamic poetic discourse in a dialectic process, creating new myths that are, in turn, a product of the circumstances of a very specific everyday life as Latina women residing in the U.S. (Ortega 1989, 128–29)

Once again drawing on Rivera's *Nosotros* poetry, Ortega notes how Puerto Rican women's writing often shows anger "against the situation of violence and destruction that characterizes the life of Puerto Ricans under U.S. colonialism." And in this context, she shows how in her *Nosotros* poem "False Idols," Rivera scoffs at the view that "It's a man's destiny to rule," as she asserts her disbelief in "weak deities" (ibid., 131–32).

This study draws on the same *Nosotros* poetry to show briefly how Rivera's early work projects an affirmation and then partial, feminist rebellion against standard patriarchal and nationalist myth patterns; the study then turns to Rivera's later work to suggest how (partially through the influence of other non–Puerto Rican Latina role modelings) Rivera matures in function of more generally Latino, internationalist, and feminist perspectives in a poetry that simultaneously grows fresher, more syncretic, and more individual and that paradoxically, in the last analysis, is able to express more successfully core questions of Puerto Rican national and feminine identity and their transformations in contemporary U.S. life. Our subject here, then, is the gradual construction of a Puertorriqueño/a identity in the context of Chicago's multi-Latin American reality.

Clearly, except for Hernández, Rivera was the best-known poet of the *Nosotros* group, the one who could be said to sum up and take to their conclusion characteristics we have already discussed. The oldest daughter of Luis and Florentina

Rivera, she was born in the small coastal town of Isabela, Puerto Rico, on August 19, 1946, and arrived in the United States by way of Salt Lake City in that same year. Her father was employed by the Anaconda Copper Mining Company until the strike of 1948, which forced him to migrate to Chicago, where he found new employment in a textile factory. He then sent for his young family and settled in the near Westside of the city.[14]

Like most Puerto Rican women of her generation, Rivera had only limited formal education. She attended Crane Technical and Richard Vocational High Schools; she also took classes for a year at Columbia College. But she was a largely self-educated poet who began as a graphic designer and brought a strong visual sense to her writing. In addition, perhaps because she was raised for some years by a Mexican family, her work was marked by her experiences not only as a Puerto Rican woman, but also a Latina committed to her community and the larger world. Over the years, she worked with various community organizations, including Casa Aztlán, Movimiento Artístico Chicano (MARCH), the Westtown Concerned Citizens Coalition and, from 1985 on, the mayor's Office of Special Events. Living on the near Westside with her husband, Mexicano artist Oscar Moya and their son, she was probably the first Chicago Puerto Rican writer to deal with many Mexican as well as Puerto Rican, feminist, and nationalist themes, and is for these reasons, as well as others, an essential figure in this history of emerging "Latino" poetry.

Rivera's section in *Nosotros* (53-63) begins in rather standard fashion with a series of poems marked by cliché images of tropical drums, the "fertile womb of the homeland," "proud race," and so forth. Something rings true, when she speaks out against Puerto Ricans killed in U.S. foreign wars: "A poisonous bile of hatred/ fills my veins as I see you sprawled/bleeding into the scorched foreign soil"[15] or when she complains, "you silently condemn me as I seek the freedom you scorn." But then "cadent blood . . . roars thru . . . veins" singing of "verdant rain forests and tawny breasts." Borinquen's presence "lingers like a trembling kiss/A young virgin bestows/on her young lover's brow." The call for Puerto Ricans not to forget their land is compelling; the equation of that land with love is striking. But the message is not writ. Her words are not the "jeweled offerings" she claims they are. Rivera's "Elegy" is hurt by stale rhythms, conventional gestures; her "False Idols," an improvement, is weakened only by its opening line. Then, with "Contradictions," the overall quality rises, as we find a tone that is simple, clear, rueful, perhaps even playful, in expressing basic antinomies that seem essential to many women's lives and situations. "Fruits of War" is also direct and compelling, if not original in imagery. But the tiny poem "A Woman Alone" reads like a fragment from Sappho, very fine in its sufficient way:

The day has faded
an illusion like me
Night creeps in my bed
and whispers: "Alone again?"
Then
covers me
in its cold embrace.
(*Nosotros,* 62)

The problem for the Puerto Rican or Latina woman writer is how to resolve her problems of exploitation by men without ending alone or completely breaking with her cultural base. In "Home Again" the poet says she is able to transcend the lonely night and look to the beauty of dawn. But the point is all too putative; the poem is inferior to the previous one on which it feeds, as it is to "The Silent Minstrel," which follows and in fact fulfills the promise of dawn not through its overt claims as much as through its delicate rhythmic word-weaving that announces a poet who should keep working:

Then softly
play my song
on a quiet starlit night
let your voice take flight
and though the dream is gone
Perhaps the pastel dawn
Will whisper my amends
in sighing harmony.
(*Nosotros,* 63)

This is a poet whose work sometimes falters but who nevertheless rises to moments of intensity, grace, and force. In her early work, Rivera expresses her *desengaño* not only with personal, romantic love, but with the romance of and hope in homeland. Locked into a world that has self-defined itself as Puerto Rico's "mainland," the Puerto Rican woman must face the contradictions of U.S. minority women with the added problems stemming from her nostalgia and outraged sense of loss in the face of the Puerto Rican "national question." Can this turn into some kind of gain? Only when the dawn materializes as higher insight and action in art. This is no easy achievement. But Rivera's work in *Nosotros* suggests future possibilities, future struggles to speak true and strong.

During the 1980s, even as most Latina writers developed an increasingly acute personal and feminist discourse, Rivera went on to publish poems mainly focused on general questions of political and social awareness with respect to U.S. minority and also international Latin American concerns. A poem like "Indio" (*Revista Chicano-Riqueña* 1981, 22) praises the redemptive pride of an oppressed people; "The Crazy Women from Plaza Mayo" (*Third Woman* 1982, 25) seeks to express her empathy for the Argentine women who risked their lives to demand the whereabouts of their missing children; "A Letter to a Friend in El Salvador" (*Ecos* 1982, 56) speaks for those who died in that nation's struggle. All three poems show a poet whose thematic and formal horizons are in a process of expansion. Perhaps more successful than such works, however, are her more city-centered poems of 1982, which are closer to her own direct experience, "Louie the Mongoose, Killer of Snakes" and "Pilsen" (*Ecos* 1982, 16 and 13–14 respectively).

Evoking the *Nosotros* slogan, "WE ARE THE RAINBOW RACE," "Louie the Mongoose" lives by the power of its conviction and pain as it recounts the story of a Puerto Rican nationalist:

> Cutting words honed in resentment
> bouquets of poems
> fashioned lovingly in city blues
> -latin red—battle grays.
> His verses tried to wake us/
> from soured dreams
> warning us of venomous snakes
> crawling in our beds, our heads.
> Exchanging his pen for a gun, . . .
> the poet took aim/
> and Louie the Mongoose, killer of snakes
> was found guilty
> of loving
> the best
> in us,
> our nation
> Borinquen.

As for "Pilsen," though hurt perhaps by references to a city modernization project (Plan 21) that is now a fading memory, it nevertheless speaks to current efforts at gentrification, while providing us a Puerto Rican woman's evocation of the Chicago Mexican world. Here the imagistic power is intense, creating a virtual aesthetic of urban poetry:

> Broken glass glitters
> like old discarded jewels
> under harsh street lights

turning vacant lots
into treasure chests of debris.

Then, in the final stanza, "night surrenders to the gold streaks on the horizon," and the jewel-like shards give way to a dawn revealing graffitied walls and murals and, then, a virtual epiphany of the Mexican Chicago experience:

men in dark clothes
and patient women huddle/
like quiet flocks of blackbirds
waiting for the buses/
to take them to the slaughterhouse.

The patient women waiting, it seems, for their daily dose of murderous exploitation, are not very far removed from those *lloronas* Eliana Ortega invokes in the passage cited above. And, it could be well argued, that Rivera's firsthand knowledge of Chicago's Mexican world and Mexicana-Chicana class and gender victimization helps to project her emergent feminism. This may have directly impacted her poetry through the mediation of that impatient Chicana, Sandra Cisneros, in whose 1983 City Songs poetry workshop (cochaired by African American poet Reggie Young in Chicago's Ruiz Belvis Puerto Rican Community Center) Rivera participated.

Whatever the reasons for her evolutionary trajectory, it seems no accident that in her contribution to the *City Songs* collection (*Ecos* 1983, 5–23), Rivera is able to return to the theme of her homeland and the process of cultural estrangement in "There are no Ceibas in Chicago," a poem that is her most mature and successful evocation of past roots, as well as of the complex struggle of transplantation and Latina identity in a world where *la isla del encanto* is overlaid (and possibly enriched) by images from Alice's Anglo wonderland:

There are no ceibas in Chicago,
those great trees in whose tangled roots
my mother played as a child
She called it the devil tree.
At night, I understood her meaning
as I gazed at the enormous twists of wood/
jagged rents in the raw enchanted earth,
a tropical connection into Alice's Dream.
Crawling in on hands and feet,
raising her ragdoll family.
I searched for the wonderous land
but the White Rabbit had moved/

to the mainland
and the Cheshire Cat didn't speak Spanglish
(*Ecos* 1983, 6).

In the 1980s, while Rivera occupied her very public job in the mayor's Office of Special Events, she did not publish much poetry. However, her friend Lillian Anguiano was busy collecting and word-processing a mainly unpublished opus. In this project, some fine, often piquant poems (personal poems, city poems: "Acculturation," "The Sub-Urban Pioneer," "Victor," "Summer Madness," "If the Shoe Fits . . .," "Erotica Sweet," "The Bag Lady," "Hard Times II," "Herstory") emerged and were read at public meetings, though never published. These poems reassert and deepen some of the poet's most intensely felt preoccupations: patterns of Latino adjustment, selling out, or maintaining and even celebrating some of the worst traditions: drinking, sexism, and violence. It was always hoped that when these poems appeared, it would be time to herald the most important female poet who emerged out of the Chicago Puerto Rican agony of the late 1960s. That moment was never to come because, after a long and painful fight, Rivera succumbed to cancer in 2004. However, on the basis of the few poems she had already published by that time, it seemed more safe to say that Rivera had offered readers some memorable moments from a large poem that, when rooted in personal experience and cross-fertilized by her multidimensional Chicago Latina experience, was able to express a larger social aggregate and stand as testimony to some of the issues and feelings crucial to the Puerto Rican Diaspora.

Concluding Thoughts

In 1974, just as Chicago Puerto Ricans began to articulate their concerns, the late Frank Bonilla made the following observation with respect to the Puerto Rican situation:

> The dialectic of impotence and stubborn resistance, however covert and diffuse, is perceived as a grinding friction shredding individuals and social ties, but is denied any prospect of political resolution. We are, perhaps, developing a dangerous virtuosity in documenting the prostration, insecurity, ambivalence, and ideological bafflement within our ranks and assigning too little value to the contrary signs that point to a remarkable capacity for survival in a context of prolonged and radical ambiguity (Bonilla, speaking at a conference and cited in Padilla 1987, 64).

With the Chicago Puerto Rican *Nosotros* poets, we can perceive this dialectic of impotence and stubborn resistance, as well as hopes and frustrations with respect to apocalyptic political solutions. In their works, they show a growing virtuosity in documenting Puerto Rican prostration, insecurity, and so forth. However, above all, in their greatest achievements, they also point to the Puerto Rican capacity of survival, to make something of their difficult situation and to find new means of growth. This aspiration is present in many of the writers; it is articulated perhaps most directly by Noboa, and perhaps most entertainingly, variously, and fully by David Hernández who, more poet than Noboa or most of the other *Nosotros* writers, not only describes the aspiration but at times realizes it. The aspiration and achievement also permeate the work of Salima Rivera.

The assertion and underlying assumption of this chapter has been that the space of Puerto Rican literature is primarily one for the exploration and forging of a new sense of identity and nation in the face of loss and disorientation, multiethnicity, and multi-Latino identifications. The space of this literature is where the Puerto Rican colony or barrio is related to the city, the island, the Caribbean, Africa, and the world. In this internationalist context (which very centrally includes the question of gender patterns and attitudes in transformation), the main contribution of specifically Chicago Puerto Rican writing may be articulated as the insistence on a broad Latin focus even in the context of U.S. Puerto Rican nationalist, broadly minority, and, recently, feminist phases. With the work of the *Nosotros* poets, and above all, the work of Hernández and Rivera, we have the basis for the core thematics that were to be part of Chicago's Puerto Rican writing in the years to come. These thematics were to become key political ones in the campaigns that brought increased Puerto Rican representation at city and state levels, and in the polemics that led many Puerto Ricans to support Harold Washington and then turn toward Richard Daley, and the local struggle that brought Luis Gutiérrez to Congress as one of the key Puerto Rican and Latino representatives in the country, and also generated a Boricua renaissance and a resistance to gentrification led by community activist José López (see note 8 on these matters). Questions of lumpenization among Rican/black, as well as Rican/Mexican and overall Latino relations, and finally questions of feminism as it cuts across all other issues, continued to be crucial in Chicago and were only brought more to the fore with the emergence of the gang-centered narratives of Rey Sánchez.

As if to sound a final note for this chapter, in the wake of Sánchez's books, Marisol Torres, a Rican student and part-time professor of film studies at Chicago's Columbia College, completed a full-length film, *Chicago Boricua* (released in December 2005), that takes place in the Division Street community and centers on three separate stories: the efforts of a young upwardly mobile Rican willing to sell out his community by rigging real estate rip-offs for the company that employs him; the effort of a young girl to pass as Puerto Rican to compete for queen in the Puerto Rican Day Parade; and the stormy love affair of two young Ricans in the area. A fine first effort, perhaps overly focused on sex, violence, and "making it" versus community loyalty, this film, which features recognizable Chicago Puerto Ricans in key parts, indicates that the community and its cultural growth is still on the agenda just as much as when the Taller group produced the *Nosotros* issue.

A very different image emerges in the disappointing Hollywood treatment of Chicago Puerto Rican life in *Nothing Like the Holidays* (see chapter 3); however, several short documentaries and an eighty-minute effort, *Chicago's Puerto Rican Story* (2008), directed by Antonio and Gloricelly Franceschi, provide commentaries of Chicago Puerto Rican community leaders and members collaged with footage drawn from a wide variety of film and video sources to present the 1966 Chicago Puerto "riots" and successive developments in the city.[16]

Of course as things changed and developed in the barrio, things would not stay the same with those of the original group. Naboa moved to San Antonio in the early 1980s; Matías disappeared for a time, but came back several years ago and has often threatened to publish his work. Condes and others remained in Chicago, but ceased to publish any new work. As noted, Salima Rivera died. Meanwhile, also as noted, David Hernández became a Chicago fixture with his Street Sounds, often performing in schools and night clubs over the years. He continues performing, and in 2004 brought together some of his best old and newer poetry in a volume, *The Urban Poems*. Indeed, Chicago Puerto Rican artist Gamaliel Ramírez, one of the founders of Taller and the artist featured on the cover of *Nosotros* and elsewhere in this chapter, went through a new rush of creative energy involving not only new painting but an outpouring of poetry that seemed to be leading to a book in the near future. In 2010, he announced the reemergence of Taller, only to be stricken a few months later by cancer. In spite of all, Ramírez has struggled to keep on with his painting and related projects, most recently on a trip to Puerto Rico in the winter of 2011. So even as Chicago Puerto Ricans move farther west from the Humboldt area, as a major sector of the community advances in its efforts to renovate and save the core area of what had come to be Puerto Rican Chicago by the time of the uprising of 1966, so at least a few of the artists and writers who emerged from the uprising's aftermath continue to work, while younger poets and artists emerge expressing the newer realities of their time.[17]

Chapter 5

Carmen Pursifull
Dancing from New York
to Anglo-Illinois

···

To the memory of Otto Pikaza and Sammy Medina (RIP)

Illinois has been a site of Puerto Rican writing for the past several years, primarily because of the mass migration to the Chicago area during the last half-century. In chapter 4, I have written about Chicago Puerto Rican writers. Here I wish to discuss the first Puerto Rican writer to emerge in Illinois outside the Chicago metropolitan area, the first indeed of what may become a larger group of non-Chicago-based Illinois Puerto Rican writers, if only because the urban population base is now moving into suburban areas and because currently growing numbers of island- and U.S.-based Puerto Rican professionals, including, it may be surmised, some who are or may become writers, are finding employment in every part of the United States. In this sense, our writer, Carmen M. Pursifull, the virtually unknown but not unimportant subject of this essay, may well be a harbinger of a new generation of Midwest Puerto Rican writers, and may well tell us where Midwest Puerto Rican writing is going, even more so than where it has been.

Pursifull, by virtue of never having rooted in the Second City, may be the Illinois-based Puerto Rican writer most representing New York qualities, even as she has come to express a nonurban, downstate sensibility. Furthermore, Pursifull is probably the most prolific resident Illinois Puerto Rican woman writer, only surpassed on the published page by Chicago's Clementina Souchet (see chapter 4). But unlike Souchet, who did some newspaper writing in Chicago, Carmen Pursifull views herself as a professional creative writer—the author of several books now, only the first of which was self-published, and a writer whose work has appeared in *The Americas Review* and several other Latino and non-Latino journals since the 1970s.

Intense, erotic, ironic, sometimes embarrassingly direct, flat, uneven, at times evocative and haunting, Pursifull's poetry portrays the full range of her life. That life starts with her childhood in New York (she is of the same generation as Nicholasa Mohr); her life continues with her youthful years as a ballroom dancer and sometime partner to dance king Killer Joe Piro in New York's 1950s Manhattan nightclub scene; it goes on to her many marriages and divorces, her many jobs in and outside the show business world (she was also a forklift driver, factory worker, and waitress); it includes her many travels and returns, her problems with parents and husbands, lovers and children—until settling down with an Anglo sailor and, with great difficulty, accepting midwestern Anglo life and her own personal aging process in Champaign, Illinois; and her life culminates, finally, with her rebirth and career as a poet and a woman who gradually becomes aware of her feminism, her Latina identity, her political convictions, and finally (and most fully, as the years have gone by) her spirituality.

Looking at Pursifull's life and work, this chapter primarily emphasizes Latino/a and Puerto Rican dimensions. It is a contribution to understanding Midwest and U.S. Latino/a writers and their experience.

Pursifull's's Life, Her Views

Carmen Pursifull was born in New York during the early years of the Great Depression. Though we have no reference to the surname of her Spanish mother, her Puerto Rican father was Pedro C. Padilla. Her poems indicate that her parents were primarily Spanish-speaking at home; they were also conservative and strict, although she sometimes (though not always) portrays them as warm and loving. Writing of her childhood and family, she notes: "Our economic situation in New York City was probably considered lower middle-class. My father was a truck-driver with the Department of Sanitation for twenty-two years. He retired and received a pension until he died of a massive hemorrhage. He suffered from emphysema [and] was an invalid for twenty years. I never went hungry or went to school looking poor, but there were times, [like when] Papa put cardboard in my shoes in between paychecks, before he could afford to buy me a new pair."[1]

Although she did well in school and was "an achiever," Carmen was "raised very strictly and was spanked quite a lot by [her] parents and brothers." She rebelled early against family discipline and her situation as a Latin woman whose life role was to find a male protector. At age fifteen she married a Latino sailor and had two children by the time she was eighteen, only to get divorced and become part of the glittery show-business world of the New York club scene at age twenty. Early in the game, she teamed up with famed Italian American Latin dance teacher Joe Piro (later doubly famed as the inspiration for a Benny Golson song, best rendered by Horace Silver, "Killer Joe"), demonstrating and teaching the latest mambo and cha-cha moves to eager Latino dance fans. Then she became an interpretive dancer with an Afro-Cuban troupe making the rounds in New York, New Jersey, and Connecticut. Gravitating toward the New York jazz scene at the moment of the great Caribbean-Harlem jazz fusion, Carmen married a drummer and became a band singer, going with the Ray Almo band on a tour that took her to the Caribe Hilton in Puerto Rico, and then on to the Virgin Islands and the Dominican Republic. The whole giddy spiral leveled out at age twenty-four, however, when, guilt-ridden about leaving her children in her parents' care, she tried to leave her show-business work behind her.

Supporting her children led to some more dancing around, it is true; she became a bartender and traveled once again to San Juan, St. Thomas, Florida, and California, divorcing her second husband (a heroin user), marrying again (this time to a wife beater), divorcing again, and in flight from spouse number three, who followed her to Florida, finally meeting and marrying her current husband of many years, John Pursifull, a career Navy man, who took her to live in California. Apparently the only stable male in her life after her father, Pursifull adopted Carmen's children. After some years in Jacksonville Beach, Florida, in 1970 she and Pursifull moved to Champaign to be near her son, who was attending the University of Illinois and was apparently having emotional problems. The son turned hippie, changed his name to Rajiam, and left the state—but the Pursifulls stayed on.

In her new environment, Pursifull worked six and a half years for Kraft Inc., first in production, then as a forklift driver, and then as a sanitation worker. In 1974, after going through a considerable amount of surgery and experiencing a series of emotional and spiritual problems, she joined the Rosicrucians, learning "how to modulate [her] behavior and . . . thinking." This apparent crisis also led her to writing as a means of dealing with a life that seemed drained of meaning and direction. In the beginning, at least, "writing," she says, "was a therapeutic way to purge negative feelings from my mind":

> It was also a way to "see" the secrets of my unconscious, by automatic writing. I meditate and often wake up to find inspired notes on my writing pad. I have had psychic experiences, and they plagued me for many years until I learned how to block unwelcomed "channels." I was led to writing to release the swell within me of pain and frustrations. This could only be done by destructive acts or creative acts. I chose the creative route and found to my delight and relief that the pain within me eased and that I became more spiritual and aware that the world didn't center on me. When I came to that point in my life, I became a better person and a better poet.

Within a few years, she started to consider her writing in a more public manner as she began participating with the Red Herring Poetry Workshop, a group of primarily Anglo English professors and part-time writers from the University of Illinois and the local community.[2] Apparently the effect of this group in part parallels that of the Iowa Writers School on Chicago Chicana superstar writer Sandra Cisneros. On the one hand, Pursifull says, "through their patient guidance I eventually developed my own style." On the other hand, the guidance was often indirect. While she accepted many of the group's criticisms, she used them to modify her style as it emerged. So she writes of her early days with the group:

> No! I didn't get much guidance at the Herring Workshop for years, because I had a different voice. So I made my own markets and earned their grudging respect. They were amazed I got published and frankly, so was I. No, I didn't think my being a Latina interfered with my progress at the workshop; it was because I was a city poet in Champaign/Urbana. They were using flowers and vegetables and farm imagery while I was using blood and guts. They were turned off by my intensity and my images. They could not relate to my eroticism or my street-wise themes. I hung in there but I had the sense to moderate my images so my audience wouldn't be limited. The intensity and passion is still there, but more controlled.

Since 1975, Pursifull, a compulsive, prolific poet, has published widely in Illinois, midwestern, and national publications, including a few poems in the literary magazine of the University of Illinois' La Casa Cultural Latina, the campus Latino student center, of which she became a kind of local poet laureate and matriarch. She also published in *Raza Cósmica* and what was for several years the prime Latino literary journal, *Revista Chicano-Riqueña* and its successor, *Americas Review*. In 1982, she also self-published the largest volume of poetry by any Illinois Puerto Rican poet, *Carmen by Moonlight*. Since then, she has added several small volumes to her published opus and has worked on other texts, including a novel. Her last two poetry volumes are texts cowritten with Dr. Edward L. Smith.[3]

Nevertheless, in spite of her long Illinois residency and literary connections, and in spite of her clear Latino roots, she is somewhat difficult to place as a Midwest Latina or Puerto Rican writer. First, to the degree she is Latina in her work, she expresses more of a New York voice and orientation, but one that has been clearly displaced by her own life experience and choices. Thus, although Carmen speaks with a diluted New York accent, the Latino/a referent, at least in its overt representations, is rather infrequent and weak. Carmen does not often express herself overtly as a "Latina" writer; her work has not been affected directly by

Chicano/a or Puerto Rican cultural nationalism. One could say the same about the early work of Sandra Cisneros, but a major difference is that Cisneros wrote clearly out of her sociocultural, if not political, experience as a Latina. Pursifull comes to her writing as a mature woman who has drifted very far from her Latino/a roots, into a jazz and then Anglo ambiance. Even when she uses Spanish, or writes of her Latino/a family childhood or of trips to Puerto Rico and so forth, the ethnic cultural reference is vague, unsettled.

So at best she would seem to express and represent the situation of those transplanted New York–area Puerto Ricans who have distanced themselves from their ethnic and national dilemmas and contradictions and have cultivated gardens in which there are only seemingly slight and superficial tropical implantations. At least some of her own direct words on the question bear this out. First, as cited above, she believes that the difference in her writing did not stem from her Latin but from her city identity. A pre–Operation Bootstrap Puerto Rican whose New York family roots go back to the period prior to the large-scale Puerto Rican diaspora (here the parallel to Nicholasa Mohr), with closer ties, apparently, with her Spanish mother than with her Puerto Rican father, she apparently has seen herself as a New Yorker more than anything—a New Yorker whose voice has been modified, it goes without saying, by Spanish–Puerto Rican roots and by her long midwestern residence:

> Being born and raised in New York City definitely influenced the way I write. In fact, they call me a city poet around town. It seems that living in the Midwest has only affected my writing slightly. I tend to be more blunt, more open than Illinois poets I have read. But in their way, they are very open and honest. I guess what I'm trying to say is, we say it differently. The only way I can honestly say that living in Illinois has affected my writing is that I'm more gentle in my language even though the emotion is intense. . . . I have maintained my rhythms and themes, but in how I present them, I've noticed a subtle change. . . . The change I have noticed in my writing is language. . . . I hope it's for the better. I have more control, I believe. . . . I guess time and age and geography have made me sensitive to the constraints of the Midwesterner.

As for the differences of Latino/a writers from the city and her identification with Latino/a ethnic writing, she remarks:

> The city has a hard reality, a street-wise sophistication, a cynicism more acute. . . . I have no idea if Illinois [Latino] writers have more or less opportunities to publish/grow than their counterparts in the U.S. But . . . I . . . guess . . . they might be limiting themselves to only Latin American publications. We are Lati-

nos. We should all be proud of our heritage, but we are also Americans. We should keep our heritage in our hearts and in our writing; we must share that heritage, in language more universal, the Latino experience. That would expand the markets for Latino writers. That is my belief. When I write, I only speak for myself. I cannot be presumptuous and speak for others. I see myself as a writer who happens to be a Latina and proud of it! When I write about passion or pain, I tend to feel like a Latina. The difference was in my strict upbringing and macho mentality of the Latino male. As I have traveled a lot and seen the world, showbiz, bartending, four marriages and lovers in between marriages, I've come to the conclusion that *most* men suffer from this machismo myth. It is not their fault. It is the throwback from the father who raised them or their peers. I do not feel trapped by my feelings of being Latin. In fact, I believe it enhances my ability to bring to the reader the multitudinous range of emotions, because of background and history, understanding of the Latin experience and why we are what we are.

In spite of these specific thoughts about Latin identity, stirred by the questions posed for this study, Pursifull insists on not being limited to Latino questions. So, she says:

Poetry . . . enables me to say what is in my heart, my mind, my fears and unconscious. It is therapeutic . . . it releases the occasional bouts with the anger that still resides within me. It also releases the imagination. I can fly! I can travel through space! I can create worlds and I can articulate more fully and with more sensitivity, what I mean to say to others. . . . I have written poetry about passion, hate, resentment, frustration, pain, joy, love, society, politics—almost the entire range of human emotion and circumstance. . . . I tend to also write about life and truth, as I perceive it to be. I write about the Soul, Self, reincarnation, death, life, rebirth, science, politics and events. . . . Writing poetry is essential to my well-being. Writing poetry is a constant source for renewal. It is the prod I need to enlarge my . . . construct. The larger my paradigm, the more in control I can become of my destiny and the more compassionate I become.

Indeed, in the 1980s, Pursifull became politically involved, serving as a delegate on Jesse Jackson's Democratic Party Convention slate of 1988, and thus directly involved, like other Latino poets, in the "Rainbow Coalition." Some of her poetry during the late 1980s exhibited more Latino touches, as well as political emphases (including a poem on the unlikely subject of the Supreme Court nomination of Judge Robert Bork—although of an earlier generation, is she not in some way the wise Latina woman poetic voice corresponding to Sonia Sotomayor?). Nevertheless, she is concerned about work that is specifically and (to her mind stereotypically) "Latino," and makes no bones about her ultimately integrationist stance:

I . . . became published because I made a serious attempt to be articulate and not rant or rage on the laments of the Latinos. Few publishers appreciate self-pity. On the other hand, circumstance presented in metaphor and original imagery, motivate a publisher to give the poet an opportunity to have an audience. . . . I believe America has no choice but to accept Latinos. We are many and growing. The trick is not to make non-Latinos feel threatened or they will shut the door in our faces. It is very important for Latinos to write and study their historical background to get a sense of who they are and then integrate into our society, never losing the fact of their mixed heritage. That adds spice. The chip on the shoulder should be thrown away and hard work, study, and integrating into American society will vastly help young writers. After they can get an audience, they can occasionally interject a long poem as a vehicle of historical research on the background of the Latino, and it will have a better chance of being taken seriously because of the controlled voice and fact. . . . Only through understanding will the non-Latinos (fellow Americans) accept us as a viable creative force. We will be taken seriously if we are conscientious, research thoroughly and are aware of our audience. The only way to gain respect is through our determination to learn and integrate without losing on the way, our Latino heritage or our compassion towards others.

While many Latino/a writers would take issue with integrationist and other aspects of Pursifull's statements, there is no doubt but that she also represents many other Latinos and U.S.-based Puerto Ricans in her views. The question in the context of this study is: how do her Latina or Puerto Rican and Illinois or Midwest dimensions come together in her writing? Isolated from her Nuyorican past and ambiance, writing mainly from her southern Illinois home while also painting, gardening, crocheting, and attending to varied interests in Rosicrucianism (she became a high-degree member), particle physics, and the like, to what degree was she going to maintain that dimension of her background that might be ascribed to her Latino/a or Puerto Rican roots? And is not her reference to "Latino" a negation of Puerto Rican specificity, and perhaps a reflection of a generalized identity emphasizing her mother's Spanish background over her father's Puerto Rican roots? In struggling for her place as a Latina in an Anglo-centered world, does she not erase another conflict involving Puerto Rican coloniality as a marked distinction in relation to other Latinos?

These questions became especially acute after a serious and disabling car accident in 1979 left her with physical and emotional pain and an inability to carry on sustained physical work. Even her most Latino/a-centered poems, the recognition she received in 1986 and over the years from the University of Illinois' Casa Cultural, and even the fact that she can deliver a talk on "Growing Up Puerto Rican in New York," do not of themselves dispel the questions. The answers must be found in the poetry itself. What follows, then, is not a careful study of her work in all its detail, but a brief survey, highlighting the specifically regional and ethnic coordinates of her "paradigm"—and this through a study focused mainly on her more specifically Latino/a-inflected work. Finally, in relation to these broader questions, I offer some suggestions about a more specifically gendered interpretation of Pursifull's life work—her movement from dance to poetry as a logical development within the sphere of U.S. Latina feminine performance, as a frame for relative self-actualization and achievement.

Ethnic Markings in *Carmen by Moonlight*

Summarizing the contents of *Carmen by Moonlight*,[4] *Champaign-Urbana News-Gazette* staff writer Nina Rubel comments:

> The subjects of her poems range from her early years as a dance instructor, performer in a dance troupe, band singer and barmaid to the contentment she has found in her enduring marriage of 20 years to her fourth husband, John. They include remembrances of her Spanish mother and Puerto Rican father and her childhood in a Hispanic section of New York City as well as appreciations of the strength and stability of Maple Street [Champaign] and the Midwest. Among the poems are outpourings of love for her daughter and son, works of high erotic intensity, explorations of the inner mind as well as of particle physics and quantum mechanics, and a group of works about [her] near-fatal auto accident . . . and [her] struggles of recuperation. (*Champaign-Urbana News-Gazette,* October 3, 1982)

Indeed, these are among the topics covered in this volume, although the erotic element and strong subjective emotion pervade all the poetry, sometimes heightening, sometimes disturbing the poetic texture, the objective power of the work. If this criticism seems similar to that which Pursifull imputes to her Red Herring writing group, then perhaps we are touching upon those elements in her work that have not been fully acculturated or tamed by her midwestern and non-Latina experience. Nor are they a simple matter of "New York." "As a New Yorker," Rubel reports her saying, "I'm a hugger and a lot of people in the Midwest don't like that. They feel you are intruding on their space when you hug them. So I restrain myself. But I'm still a hugger." And, perceptively if discretely (that is, without making a specific, overt Latino/a connection), Rubel associates the hugging not with New York but the "Hispanic" heritage of Pursifull's mother: "Pursifull grew up as the youngest of five children. She evokes her parents in the poem, 'Remembering You,' in which she writes about her mother: 'You'd gossip with your daughters, / your sons' wives hugging all crying / tears mingling with the spices of your ancestry' (*Champaign-Urbana News-Gazette,* October 3, 1982).

The strong emotions and ultimately the erotic pull of her work are hardly matters she seeks to deny. Indeed, characterizing her own verse, Pursifull writes: "No matter what theme I write about, it tends to be written erotically. I use erotic images because I guess I am erotic, or was, when I was young. Ha!" (ibid.)

There is no doubt that her subject matter and style at their best express a sensuous eroticism that is as direct and scandalous as anything found in Sandra Cisneros or Ana Castillo. Like these writers, too, the eroticism is portrayed as rebellion against family and familial culture: "My father said I had 'big balls.' He said I should have been born a boy. I guess I was a feminist before it was popular to be one. I cannot be bullied, restrained or constrained. Many husbands and lovers and family have tried and they failed. My fourth husband . . . succeeded. The trick was to give me my space and I would not dishonor him but I'm not a possession or a thing. I'm a person, and I expect to be treated as such. Of course, I reciprocate the courtesy."

Her directness in discursive writing is only outmatched in her poetry. So, referring to her relation with her mother, she can write:

> My Spanish mother
> wrapped me in her skirts
> smelling of guilt and musk.
> . . .
> I learned survival in a world
> tilted by the weight of balls.
> I grew mine large
> heavy with the weight of pain.
>
> Hardened by the dripping
> in my blood.
>
> I shamed her in those years.
> Her oaths of anger
> struck like a snake
> spread venom in my flesh
> and I became
> her prediction.
> (*CBM,* 7)

Much of *Carmen by Moonlight* charts the author's rebellions and her sexual and imaginative adventures through the different phases of her life. As in poems by

Cisneros and other Latinas, the autobiographical impulse is overwhelming. At least in this initial collection, there is no poem that is decentered from the writer, and there seems little capacity for getting beyond personal history. Indeed the very intent of the text would seem to be to project the poet-protagonist beyond ethnic-familial origins into an individuated U.S. life. Though each of the eight sections of the book has a title in Spanish and some poems have Spanish titles, English by far predominates in the collection, with only a few key words and phrases in Spanish, usually ones that conjure up conventional cultural attitudes or feelings: "Vieja, cuando vamos a comer?" asks our tyrannical father (*CBM*, 1). "Adios, mi viejo," says the mother as her husband dies (*CBM*, 4).

The first poems take us through memories of her parents, beginning with a portrait of the loving mother in relation to a wheezing, emphysemic, tyrannical, and *machista* father. We have thoughts meditating on her parents' death, what they have given. Then, we move through her conceiving of her daughter to a man she doesn't love; we explore her attitudes toward her children, and so forth. Inevitably, family is both motive and inhibition, cause of, as well as limit to, life orientations and possibilities. However, the section is not ordered to chart the protagonist's step-by-step rebellion, but seems to explore the chronology of family attitudes (especially maturing wifely ones) throughout the protagonist's life. Above all, they foreshadow her fundamental departure from a Latino/a world, her painful, reluctant, and gradual acceptance of "a subtleness alien to me," her acceptance of "differences" and her merging with a rhythm that is not naturally hers (*CBM*, 21–22). Next, in "Aspectos," we have extended metaphors of sexual desire, masturbation, coitus, and orgasm; we see a leveling of flamenco dancer and "señorita" through sexual desire. But the Cinderella fantasy comes crashing down in the section's final poem. The dream of the perfect romantic love seems to die. Section 3, "El Sabor de Amor," is a series of directly sexual poems, portraying coitus, oral sex, and a series of sexual emotions often through extended metaphors once again, some fresh, some less so.

The pattern continues in section 4, "Caras de Nueva York," only here, as in section 1, the poems are more narrative, directly and concretely autobiographical. The intelligent, repressed city Latina breaks out of her parents' world and out beyond her unhappy marriage and a family that binds her even as she finds maternal love. We pass on to her efforts to get beyond the circle of family, as she breaks into a New York nightlife world of commercialized glamour, of sex and danger. The poems deal with Pursifull's show-business career, her mambo teaching and dancing, her sexual encounters and rather bizarre imagined ones of toothless, spaghetti-eating, and castrating hookers, of serial killers. One poem especially relevant to this study portrays the poet walking through the park, receiving "verbal flowers" from the "macho men," but they fall "to the ground, / walked over / by high heels / clicking like / castanets" (*CBM*, 59). The Latin lovers are left behind, and so are other New York scenes and types. Before we know it, we are in "Campiña, Illinois," remembering back to New York, to some times in California, to Florida, and even (though in not very memorable terms) to Puerto Rico. In "Mutations," she considers her midwestern fate:

> clinging to identity
> amidst
>
> the quiet mannered
> trapped in mid center
> like a cob in a husk
> a decade in the grip of reticence
> has slowed my New York cadence
>
> a hybrid human
> too tame for the city
> too street wise for the gentle
> folks in the garden.
> (*CBM*, 75–76)

Section 6, "El Accidente," details the grim story of Pursifull's accident and recovery with her characteristically macabre (and strained) humor: the traction unit compared to a lover—embarrassing stuff, at least for this timid commentator. Some of her better, more meditative efforts appear in her section 7, "Mundos interiores," alongside other, perhaps more questionable, full moon forays. In "Hauntings," we read:

> I've seen a woman
> Latin-in-lace
>
> struggling for expression.
> (*CBM*, 100)

In another poem she writes:

> I write of dreams
> of travels into different
> depths.
> (*CBM*, 102)

And in still another:

> My nest is on
> the mountain
> and after flights of
> thoughtful freedom
> I'm pulled against my will
> to melt into the landscape
> that I carved.
>
> I have become the occupant
> of my creation.
> (*CBM,* 105)

Doppelgangers emerge, there are images of death of decline:

> I see your face
> in mirrors
> your curious expression
>   reflected
>   in my eyes.
>
> My voice is dim
> I'm shrinking bit by bit.
> I'm an intruder in a
> spector hotel where
> matter matters not.
> (*CBM,* 114)
>
> The hotel is holding my
> reservation waiting to
> claim my dream.
> Then I will cease to exist.
> (*CBM,* 117)

This poem and the volume as a whole is the spectral dance of Pursifull "determined to ward off / the horror of her death" (*CBM,* vi); and this process of dying would seem to begin as the character leaves behind her world and adjusts to a life rhythm and pattern leading toward loss of being and desire. The life journey out of a Latino/a New York world seems pointed toward the decline and fall of all such projects in the cold midwestern world of Champaign, Illinois. But the final section, "Mundos exteriores," holds out some sense of hope in its image of life as an undated journey toward a death that is no more than a "transition," a movement to another state of being. The narrator has traveled "through a space with many faces / to find a planet green and blue / where the air is sweet / where the earth bears fruit" (*CBM,* 120). Later on she says:

> I am
> exploding with the knowledge
> that the person that I was
> is no more
> torn apart by forces strong enough
> to separate and scatter
> the matter that was I
> then like a sock turned inside out
> space curved into herself
> pushing me through a door of time
> so I could be
> again.
> (*CBM,* 122)

Finally, as if she is making a resolution that transcends the solitude she has lived, she says:

> I ride no ship
> nor have a body to call mine
>
> only awareness of
> who we are
> (*CBM,* 123)

Manhattan Memories

Since her strange, evocative, and uneven first volume, the work of a poet of disturbing lyrical gifts and lapses, Pursifull went on to write the poems that would appear in subsequent volumes.[5] Among the books important to this study are *Manhattan Memories* (1989), *The Twenty-four Hour Wake* (1989), *Elsewhere in a Parallel Universe* (1992), and *The Many Faces of Passion* (1996). *Manhattan Memories* is a Puerto Rican woman's *Mambo Kings Play Songs of Love* in verse, where the poems tell a story and where the final text in fact becomes a narrative without stanzas. Pursifull now focuses on one dimension of her first book: her life as nightclub dancer and partner of Killer Joe Piro during the New York Latin music craze of the 1950s. With a matter-of-factness and lack of poetic transformation that marks a decline, I believe, from *Carmen by Moonlight,* many of the poems go into more graphic detail about phases of her life already treated in the earlier work. Indeed, they could as readily have been used to expand and deepen the existing sections of her first book than as to provide a new text. And yet there is also a potential larger work only faintly expressed in these poems and only glimpsed when the poems are seen as raw material for that work—the novel we might well wish Pursifull had written, a Nuyorican woman's take on this remarkable time in music culture and Latino/a transformations that we mainly know through Cuban and African American eyes and ears. But the opportunity, if it existed, is lost; and what we get are these detailed fragments of a world requiring a fuller, more coherent and Puerto Rican exploration.

More concretely than in *Carmen by Moonlight,* we experience the young girl's break from family, and the story of her first husband (*MM,* 1–3). Then we see her working at the Palladium, dancing to Afro-Cuban beats, going to New Jersey and dancing there (*MM,* 4). Next we see her back in New York, dancing with Killer Joe for the tourists, then returning home to be with her children (*MM,* 6). Next it's "Birdland and the 50s Jazz Scene" where she "snapped [her] fingers / to a pulse alien to [her] Latin veins," and gets an offer to sing "in a band . . . play maracas / travel leave my nest of twigs and leaves"—her children accepting this last flight (*MM,* 10). Still another poem portrays her work in the Ray Almo band (*MM,* 10–11), her encounter with the man who would be her second husband ("He was a charmer laid back super cool./ I shrugged my shoulders, / thought 'what the hell, why not'?" [(*MM,* 11–12)]), her discovery that Prince Charming was a drug user (*MM,* 12), and then, once again, her traveling to Puerto Rico, this time told with greater clarity:

> San Juan in Nineteen Fifty-Three
> taught me the meaning of intolerance.
> I watched manipulation of local Puerto Ricans
>
> in their land by "Continentals."
> This was my father's land, his people—
> and I (a Nuyorican) could not
> tolerate injustice.
> (*MM,* 12)

In another poem "Double-Split," the poet evokes the "wild . . . days of [her] unleashing" (*MM,* 14), and then her finally going home, the prodigal daughter, soon to divorce her addict mate and to be mother and father to her children: "'Mama nunca voy a dejar los niños.' / 'Gracias a Dios hija mía'" (*MM,* 15). But of course

Pursifull could not stay home, and her restless journey was to carry her to distant spaces, as she moved her dancing from nightclub floors to the printed page.

More Recent Work

The subsequent work of Pursifull has generally involved a distancing from overtly Latino/a and ethnic themes and a development of the more metaphysical and mystical sides of her opus. Published in the same year as *Manhattan Memories*, *The Twenty-four Hour Wake* is an interesting formal experiment constituted by a series of poems tracing the hours of the day seen as life phases. The poems deal with such themes as time, space and energy, desire, hope, resignation, and death. Above all, they show the influence of quantum theory and mysticism on a woman whose Nuyorican roots and rhythms are here overlaid (if not overwhelmed) by midwestern Anglo life. Following in a similar vein, *Elsewhere in a Parallel Universe* is a book of memories and meditations, imaginings and speculations, quantum physics and mystic revelations. It is a book centered on subliminal communications with a "parallel universe," on calls and responses—with much family and personal musing, some politics, and a few, though very few, Latino references (for example, "Elsewhere/Wave #3"). The introduction by Dimitri Mihalas, a University of Illinois astronomy professor, urges we see the poems in function of relativity, indeterminacy, and those dimensions of modern physics from which we may generalize about our unfixed, undulating world.

How, we might ask, have "Manhattan Memories" led to the mystical volumes? But instead of seeing these universalistic concerns as Latino/a and Puerto Rican "evasions" and "displacements," perhaps we would be wise to consider them as some kind of return from U.S.-imposed identity wars to the kinds of writing that we might find in indigenous documents or the writings of San Juan de la Cruz. The questions of quantum physics are not far from those Antonio Benítez Rojo (1999) has seen as central to the form and rhythm of Caribbean literature. And of course, such concerns are obsessions in the poetry of a Nicaraguan revolutionary like Ernesto Cardenal, or in the feminist writings of Lorena Dos Santos of Mayaguez, Puerto Rico. In phone conversations and at poetry readings in one place or another during the 1990s, this critic tried to point out some of these relations to Pursifull herself, just as I suggested that she read and see herself as part of a line of U.S. Puerto Rican writers that included Julia de Burgos and William Carlos Williams, Sandra María Esteves, Judith Ortiz Cofer, Esmeralda Santiago, or, to mention another midwestern Puerto Rican woman isolated from Latino/a worlds,

Sandra Benítez of Edina, Minnesota. I tried to point to her affinities with younger Illinois feminist Latinas like Ana Castillo and Sandra Cisneros; I pointed to her familial, ethnic, and generational affinities with Nicholasa Mohr; I urged her to read these and other Latin American, Latino, Latina, and U.S. Puerto Rican writers. But during the many years I indeed talked with her from time to time (she sometimes called to see when or if I was ever going to publish an earlier version of this work), I found that she had skillfully evaded all my suggestions, continuing to read and relate to Anglo midwestern writers such as Red Herring poet Olivia Diamond and her recent poetry partner, Dr. Edward L. Smith, far more than to the Latin Americans, Latinos, or Latinas I constantly mentioned. Perhaps this has been Pursifull's way to avoid contamination, her way of transcending what she may well consider the limitations imposed on Latina writers by their ethnic and gender inscription in U.S. society. Indeed, perhaps the signature song of Pursifull's generation (almost as important in Latin America as in the United States and a corollary to his New York song) was Frank Sinatra's rendition of Paul Anka's cheesy classic, "My Way." Also, like many Puerto Rican women of her generation, Pursifull has taken what she has considered the road to personal, as opposed to political, independence.[6]

Carmen Padilla did it her way by inscribing herself in the Latina stereotype, first erasing Padilla to become pure Carmen the partner and subordinate in the symbolic/commodity representation of Latina (as opposed to specifically U.S. Puerto Rican) identity in the New York club scene, then leaving New York and that inscribed identity, to become Pursifull, the Americanized woman who could then achieve in poetry a dance in which at first she has no partner but is able to create her own identity, her own way. The intensity and vivacity of her verse perhaps corresponds and struggles against the ebbing of other life energies. The fact that she lived in the Midwest led her to imagine and create a wider world. That she can no longer dance has led to her dancing on paper and even to her intent to understand the dance and energy of the stars. It is through this cosmic dance that she has lately found a new partner in her trips across the printed page.

Of course, some might well see Pursifull trapped as the exotic, token Latina in the Red Herring Anglo writers' group. But those who know her doubt that this feisty, New York–talking woman could be a pushover for anyone. And as if to bear this out, some of her poems, like "Encore" and "Ninth Wave," bespeak a more directly articulated sociopolitical consciousness, while "The Alien" expresses her sense of estrangement in the Midwest "prison of repose . . . away from the New York sights and sounds." A long-unpublished poem, "Papa," which finally appeared in *The Many Faces of Passion* (1996), captures her ambivalent ties to her Puerto Rican father with whom (she tells us) she fought violently when she was twenty, but whose memory points toward complex relations with her creative work:

> Finally—he is clay.
> Fear has died with him.
>
> I plant red blossoms in my garden
> using his soil
> & Puerto Rican blood as fertilizer.
>
> In summer, heat will answer questions
> I asked him in my youth.
> When petals open—the bee will bear
> his message & when the first frost
> kisses my petals I'll understand.
> (*MFP*, 39)

Finally, in "The Death of Innocence," (an occasional *Latinidad* poem, almost begged for by her University of Illinois Latino students and friends of the campus Casa Latina—*Carmen please write us a Latino poem!*, which also appears in *The Many Faces of Passion* [27]), we have words that perhaps present Pursifull's most suggestive portrayal of Latino problems in the Midwest:

Cafe Con Leche

The perfect tint
an inbred tan
and eyes which spark
a static tension
search the flatlands
for a friendly face.

the threshold of capitulation.
And granting that your eyes
were blurred
your vision is restored
but altered
by a different point of view.

Your arm is raised.
Your fist is clenched
in the familiar pose
of the oppressed
but underneath the stone

of your expression
lies the broken heart
of the apprentice.
Digame!
Have you felt the space
you cannot enter undisturbed?
Although the door is open
which you view with optimism
you hesitate to cross

Welcome to reality, Amigo!
(*MFP*, 27)

Actively working away at her poems, admittedly compulsive in her writing as in her political and mystical awakenings, still attempting to grow as a poet and human being, even as she paints, quilts, crochets, knits, gardens, and cans, Carmen Pursifull represents those of her generation who sought to leave the problems of Puerto Rican and Latino/a identity behind and to integrate as best she could (and on her own terms) into U.S. society. Without giving up her belief in integration, without ever grasping or articulating the colonial dimension of Puerto Rican difference, she has honestly confronted and written of her continuing internal alienation, and she has responded in her poetry and life to the fact that things have not been nor are equal in the land of opportunity. Transplanted from New York, attempting to adjust gracefully to the Midwest and all that life brings, she has written a body of poetry that, while sometimes uneven, rough, sentimental, trite, ecstatic, strained, or exaggerated, is an often haunting testimony to one kind of Latino/a and human response to our times. Perhaps *The Many Faces of Passion* most succeeds in bringing her Latina, erotic, and metaphysical concerns together in a single text. Her subsequent writing with Smith brings forth still newer dimensions. For her story, for her dedication, persistence, and industry in attempting to forge a poetic universe and make sense of her experience, she has more than earned inclusion in any account of U.S. Latino/a literature as well as any account of Puerto Rican diasporic writing and identity.

Chapter 6

Cuban–Puerto Rican Relations and Final Projections

....

To the memory of Lorenzo Soler (Lolo) from Puerto Rico and Francisco Genaro Sánchez (El Viejo) from Cuba (RIP)

In closing this book, I thought I would share with readers a reflection on the negative treatment of Puerto Ricans in Cuban American and other Latino writing, leading to the briefest comments on the future of U.S. Puerto Rican culture, literature, and life. With regard to the first matter, I draw on my previously unpublished study of Miguel Barnet's *La vida real* (1986), a long testimonial narrative seeking to answer Oscar Lewis's negative treatment of the marginalization of the poor in Castro's Cuba (Lewis, Lewis, and Rigdon 1977), but to do so by means of a Caribbean *indirecto*—that is, by posing a positive Cuban American life in contrast to that of the sordid culture of poverty life portrayed in Lewis's *La Vida* (1966).

I see Barnet's portrayal of his protagonist Julián Mesa as an effort by the famed Cuban testimonial editor of *The Autobiography of a Runaway Slave* (1973) to ingratiate himself with the revolution by taking on an anthropologist whose work had previously fascinated him but whose negative portrayal of growing "marginality" in revolutionary Cuba had led to Lewis being expelled from the country by the Castro regime. By contrasting the attitudes of Julián Mesa with those of the characters in *La Vida,* Barnet seeks to refute Lewis and show how New York's poor Latinos can live lives of dignity and value. Julian Mesa lives an authentic or real life—a life that is in its own way royal. Indeed, Barnet goes on to imply, such are the lives of many dissident and *independentista* Puerto Ricans whose example repudiates the ideas of Lewis.

The only problem with this approach is that it leaves unanswered questions about Lewis's contention of an emergent "marginality" not unrelated to questions of race and to the "culture of poverty" thesis, and most important, not as something previous to the revolution but as a product of it. This matter is treated with complexity in Sara Gómez's film, *De cierta manera;* it comes to the fore in the Mariel exodus of 1980 and, in a smaller but symptomatic way, it is implicit in the oblivion of prerevolutionary musicians as portrayed in the film *Buena Vista Social Club*. In this sense, Mesa's attitude toward Puerto Ricans separates the exceptional *independentista* supporters from the mass of Puerto Ricans whom he indeed sees as marginal or lumpen sectors and as subject to Lewis's thesis after all. And why not? Because Barnet seeks to refute Lewis by contrasting the enriched possibilities in Cuba with the worst dimensions of problems induced by a capitalist and racist society and coming to bear on susceptible, colonized Puerto Rican victims.

Barnet on Oscar Lewis

There is no doubt that the young Barnet was taken by Lewis and saw the anthropologist's work in terms that he will come to apply to his own—first in Lewis's "search for new resources and new techniques of ethnological investigation" and second Lewis's "ethnographic realism," which involves creating a "story" that draws on "elements of fiction without doing damage to the book's core scientific value" (Barnet 1983, 62).[1]

Praising Lewis's method of involving himself with the people he studies in the fashion of a novelist, Barnet asserts that Lewis's *The Children of Sánchez* is "a contribution to modern ethnography . . . because . . . Lewis constructs the chosen environment, the community or object of study, and describes in minute detail every aspect of material culture. With this approach, Lewis provides the reader with an intimate vision of the object of study where the most subtle and valuable aspects of the relations, in this case familial and personal ones, are discovered" (1983, 63). It is "a singular book that, nevertheless, does not run the risk of losing its relevance. . . . The book will endure because it expresses the naked truth of its time" (ibid., 63–64).

Years later, with the appearance of *La Vida* and the growing criticism of Lewis among varying liberal and left sectors, Barnet's view of Lewis went through an evolution charted in Elzbieta Sklodowska's account (1992). Probably the most definitive statement he makes is the following: "The fundamental aspect of language in the testimonial novel is that it is supported in spoken language. Only in this way does it possess life. But it's a distilled spoken language. I would never write a book faithfully reproducing what the tape recorder dictates to me. From the tape recorder, I would take the tone of the language and anecdote. The rest, the style, the details, would always remain my contribution. Because this simplistic and trite literature, which is the byproduct of transcription, doesn't go anywhere" (1979, 29). And then as if by example, he adds:

A book like Oscar Lewis' *La vida*, a great contribution to the psychology and sociology of the marginal masses, . . . is not literature; it's simply and plainly *I write
what you tell me*. This road doesn't have much to do with the testimonial novel
that I am practicing. Because the literary imagination should go hand in hand with
the sociological imagination. And the author of the testimonial novel should not
accept limits but should give full rein to his imagination when it doesn't under-
mine the character of his protagonist or betray his language. The only way that
the author can gain the greatest profit from a phenomenon is by applying his
fantasy, inventing within a real essence (1979, 29–30).

Sklodowska cites damning offhand comments of Barnet that indeed feed the
growing negative critique of Lewis: "If you're not an artist, then what happens to
you is like what happened to Oscar Lewis who wrote a book like *La vida*, which is
a huge bore that no one reads, because although it makes a contribution through
its language and, perhaps, its psychology, it is tremendously monotonous. I want
a work that always has this human thing, this human element" (first quoted in
Bejel 1981, cited in Sklodowska 1992, 20).

Politicized discourse often finds aesthetic reasons for rejecting ideologically discordant matters. And this may well be what's behind another passage Sklodowska
cites, when she notes how Barnet portrays Lewis as "a paternalistic author who,
from a train station and with a little notebook . . . has claimed to arrive at the
last word on the human condition on the basis of dogmatic anthropological pre-
suppositions" (in Sklodowska 1992, 40).

In "Encuentro con Miguel Barnet," an interview conducted and edited by Edna
Acosta-Belén and Jean-Philippe Abraham (1992), Barnet speaks about the relation of *La vida real* to his previous work and its relation to *La Vida*:

I had already dealt with the lives of immigrants in Cuba. . . . Now I wanted to
present the Cuban outside his home environment. I wanted to know how Cubans
behaved in the immigration process. I was curious about the behavior of Cubans
outside their context—their behavior, their attitudes. And I've discovered . . .
that for the Cubans, Cuba isn't a country but a person, a human being; . . . that
they live in a state of inconsolable nostalgia; and that . . . Cubans can't adapt
to living outside their country. The . . . things I've discovered are present in *La
vida real*. I've learned that the people of the culture of poverty, as opposed to
what the anthropologist Oscar Lewis thought, can do many positive things; they
can also achieve their goals, even when these lives are anchored in an oppressive
marginality. These lives have a constructive human vision that is not necessarily
decadent or pessimistic (Acosta-Belén and Abraham 1992, 112).

When asked point-blank if "his novel is therefore a response to Oscar Lewis's *La
Vida*, Barnet comments at length:

In reality, I didn't write *La vida real* with the exclusive purpose of responding to any one. But when I entered the Latino neighborhoods of New York, and above all El Barrio, I became aware . . . that together with people who lived marginalized on very depressing levels, with very simple lives without verticality, there lived many people making the good fight—people with very open and progressive mentalities. Among them I interviewed women above all because Oscar Lewis mainly deals with Puerto Rican women and shows them in a bad light. They all seem like women obsessed with sexual desire, subject to the manipulation of men who in their turn are manipulated as well. And therefore I thought always with my perspective of not seeking only the dark or positive sides. And I realized that there were people who had a vision different from Lewis's, . . . that there were many people with a constructive vision of life with desires to excel in spite of living in a difficult, hostile environment that all but swallows them, that discriminates against them and segregates them. But . . . *La vida real* is not exactly an answer to Oscar Lewis' *La vida*, even though . . . I chose the title with every intention of evoking the comparison, because I had worked with him . . . some six or seven months and I could perceive [his] inclination . . . for the most morbid and depressing themes and [his] obsession . . . with always finding . . . the ugly side of life—the incapacity to act, the lack of initiative, the lack of a will to live, the lack of any notion of country or nation. Then I discovered that in New York there are many Puerto Ricans with a great nationalist tradition who want the Puerto Rican situation to change, so that Puerto Rico does not continue being a sad and obscure colony. Because what's more, I have been in Puerto Rico and I admire the fact that even with its being a colony of the United Status, the people have maintained their popular culture so alive, so rooted, so strong. And I'm not talking about *bomba* and *plena* but rather a way of acting, a way of moving, of gesturing and using language (1986, 112–13).

Praising contemporary Puerto Rican island literary elites (Edgardo Rodríguez Juliá, Luis Rafael Sánchez, and so forth) in their efforts to portray Puerto Rico's continuing identity struggles, Barnet notes:

I recognize and admire all this; but nothing of this is found in [*La Vida*] . . ., where we find a Puerto Rico of "slums," a marginal Puerto Rico of mafia, drugs, prostitution, and it's just not like this. There is some of this, unfortunately, but it requires a little bit more to trace the causes explaining why these other desolating things exist. And so the feminine character in my book, and in the last chapter about immigration, is a Puerto Rican woman, who without having a militant attitude, has an open, progressive mentality that encourages her husband who is a Cuban and has passed forty years without returning to his country. She encourages him to return. Finally, she's a woman who understood the struggle of Albizu Campos as did many other women I interviewed—above all, the old nationalist women from the Albizu Campos era; and I was impressed with how they maintained this living spirit of revolution and justice (1986, 113–14).

Mesa's Narrative and Cuban/Rican Contrasts

In one sense, Barnet's book presents to us a Cuban *vida* different from Oscar Lewis's Puerto Rican account, and one that relates most directly to and follows such U.S. Puerto Rican classics as the *Memorias de Bernardo Vega* and Jesús Colón's *A Puerto Rican in New York*—both of which Julián refers to. It is also a book that must be seen in obvious contrast to the literature of the pre-1959 Cuban migration like Oscar Hijuelos's *Our House in the Last World* (published in 1983, but dealing with events that took place much earlier) and also in relation to such post-1959–based narratives as Iván Acosta's *El Super* and Hijuelos's *The Mambo Kings Play Songs of Love* (1989). And like this last volume, it is one that is especially notable for its treatment of a very touchy matter—not U.S.-Cuban relations so much as ones between Cubans and Puerto Ricans—that is, we have a Cuban view of Cuban–Puerto Rican relations.

In the introduction to *La vida real,* Barnet immediately raises the issue of thematic selection and sets off a series of questions that can only plague his text:

> All human lives are important. Nevertheless, certain lives possess more outstandingly representative traits than do others. The life of the Hispanic immigrants in New York is a case in point. Up to now I have not known a single work that presents the feelings of pain and dissatisfaction of Cuban immigrants in the North. Overly abstract cultural patterns and stereotyped ways of life have, unfortunately, been the most common indicators for describing the life of the Hispanic immigrants in general. Not at all convinced by these generalizations, I opted to write a book that could show the heart of this human conglomerate . . . (1986, iv)

With this statement, with its slides between Cuban and "Hispanic immigration," Barnet not only criticizes the immigration literature of his compatriots but also Puerto Ricans and others who have written about the immigration experience. Puerto Rican Generation of 1940 writers like René Marqués, Pedro Juan Soto and José Luis González, whom Lewis had consulted and given thanks in *La Vida,* had already written their savage anti-New York texts; Piri Thomas, Nicholasa Mohr, Eduardo Rivera, Ed Vega and countless other Nuyoricans had written prose works portraying life in the city. Indeed, Hijuelos's first book had already appeared. Was Barnet being fair? Perhaps instead of focusing on these matters properly, perhaps for relative ignorance of the growing body of Nuyorican literature, he was in effect influenced first by Oscar Lewis's conflict with the Revolution, as well as the conflict of various Cuban-American writers who were his contemporaries. It was the Mariel of 1980 that sent from the island thousands who seemed to confirm

Lewis's view of the revolution in not only failing to eliminate but also generating its own marginal sectors and representatives of the culture of poverty.

These matters may explain why Barnet immediately hedges his view by disclaiming that he can in any way present a definitive portrait even of Cuban immigration in the '40s and '50s. But he claims to have chosen a figure who represents a significant part of that history, and whose life story responds to a silence on the printed page for at least one sector of those who "bourgeois historiography" has designated as "people without history." Inscribing Mesa among those who have abandoned their island "in search of a better way of life," Barnet underlines Julián's "conjugal tie with a woman of Puerto Rican origin, her social permeability, the forms of expression acquired by means of readings and the clash with a new cultural environment"—all this in the course of indicating how these factors fail to distance his Cuban protagonist from his "patriotic roots." He expresses his hope "of having shown with this book that the life of men of the so-called culture of poverty does not always lack a will to be and a historical consciousness. And that even if this is anchored in a feeling of marginality, the flame of life incites a turn towards the future."

In effect, the book goes beyond a mere answer to Lewis's treatment of Puerto Ricans, but it is also (without acknowledgment) an answer to the Mariel experience that seemed to confirm Lewis's views of Cuba. To carry out his purpose, Barnet apparently hung around the center for progressive Cubans, Casa de las Américas, on 14th Street in New York and cultivated a friendship with Julián Mesa, a pre-Castro emigrant, a man almost organically "revolutionary" and perhaps even exceptional among the Casa group. But this leads to a certain disappointment, perhaps, for the reader, who is faced with the good fellow traveler, whose views are too guided by *The Daily World* or *Granma* issues he receives and whose independence of mind seems somewhat compromised.

Indeed, the book is a disappointment for one wishing to explore the immigrant question, because so much of the story takes place in Cuba. But in the course of telling us about Cuban life in the '40s and '50s, Julián is showing how history had given the Cubans such a strong sense of self and nation that it could help them stand against submission to poverty and the worst ills of immigration. Presumably, Puerto Rican workers, because of the island's colonial status, and its lack of a strong national, creolized bourgeoisie along with the socioeconomic development this entails—matters explored by José Luis González (1980) and others—had less of this sure history and sense of nationhood and *patria,* and were so engulfed by the U.S. system that they had no adequately firm defense against the U.S.-powered modernization. The Cuban/Puerto Rican contrasts multiply throughout the book.

Cubans and Ricans in *La vida real*

One of the first Cuban–Puerto Rican contrasts Julián makes is when he poses his own life story as richer than much fiction. And here it turns out that his Puerto Rican wife's life is a history worthy of radio novels, while his own life is more like novels meant to be read. So, making reference to the programs presented to a predominantly Puerto Rican audience in New York, Julián, while comparing his own life with a novel, sees the *telenovelas* his wife watches as *case histories*, noting that "No one has told my story, nor even anything at all similar. They present matrimonial conflicts, cases of adolescent sex, or of female sterility" (280), but presumably nothing nearly as important as his epic Cuban narrative.

The clinical cases Celia watches may somehow be equivalent to Oscar Lewis narratives but can't capture Julián's "real life"—his own Manhattan experience. In his New York retrospective view, he describes himself as a man who has gone where the wind has taken him in a life of "*ir y venir*." He has learned from life and hunger not to live by fear, but by hope and efforts. In keeping with Barnet's schema, this is Julián's book of fire. Fire has followed Julián all his life. Fire was fever and heat in the cane fields and hovels; fire was Julián's heated will to live and transcend his impoverished *guajiro* life through a series of events that lead him to the United States. And fire is precisely what he will find lacking (though not among Puerto Rican women in bed) in many of the Puerto Ricans he comes to know in New York.

His first references to the Puerto Rican world are set in Cuba as Julián, in New York, recalls how Havana went crazy for singer Bobby Capó, the fiery Puerto Rican "Bolero superstar" after the attempt on Harry Truman's life in Blair House and the arrest of *independentista* leader Pedro Albizu Campos ("a great patriot and not a crazy man, as they say of him") for complicity in an attack on the San Juan fort (193). Julián's growing political awareness, his extension from Cuban to a broader sense of nationalism, only make his growing discontent with Havana and his need to travel all the more intense. So he decides to leave, explaining that "Life in Havana was getting out of one problem to enter another. I couldn't raise my head. And I wasn't [Puerto Rican singer] Daniel Santos, nor did I have the makings of a gigolo or a hired gun" (206).

Julián tells of his first days in New York, including his interactions with other Cubans, with Puerto Ricans, and Italians, who see him as black even though he is not "coal-dark" but "a light-skinned mulatto with wavy hair." However, it is the Cuban/Puerto Rican relationship that is central to our look here. So, responding to the racial discrimination he faces in New York, Julián notes that "Whoever has black blood is black, no matter how well it's hidden and how hard it is to tell.

They've even put *black* on the ration cards of white and blonde Puerto Ricans" (217). Nevertheless, Julián lives in function of a "color edge" as well as his "will to live," which he believes distinguishes at least lighter Cubans and that enables him to "get ahead" with complete "fearlessness." In a telling passage, he articulates this distinction in a contradictory way that requires the analysis of a Caribbean specialist but, in my eye, contrasts with the worlds of Oscar Lewis and perhaps casts a shadow on his subsequent Puerto Rican connections:

> Us Cubans . . . crossed Niagara on a bicycle and later we forgot about it. So people think we're just a bunch of winners. We always look like we're riding high and eating the world. And it's better that way, don't you think? It's bad if they see some of us down in the dirt moaning away under a banana leaf. We don't want to give any one the pleasure of seeing us like that. . . . I spend my life telling my wife . . . because Celia is real good, as are all the Boricua women, but they lack that vital spark. She always seems to me like she's going to die tomorrow. I don't know, maybe it's because her blood's made of horchata (215).

In spite of this view reminiscent of René Marqués's pronouncements on Puerto Rican docility (and perhaps seeing it as a feature of Puerto Rican phenotypical whiteness from the perspective of a mulatto Cuban), Julián is very well aware of the feistiness of Puerto Ricans in the job competitions among poor Caribbeans, especially in a place where the Puerto Ricans are the vast majority. So speaking of his first and longtime job as a busboy, he says: "The bus-boy was a common servant, nothing else. Sometimes they had me wash plates in the kitchen or clean up the restaurant. And I couldn't even say, hey this mouth is mine because there were always lines of Puerto Rican waiting for those restaurants" (239).

This passage points to how, contrary to the myth, Puerto Ricans indeed struggled to get even the worst jobs in the 1950s. It can remind us of how the busboy was important to the Guatemalan/Chicano struggle presented in Gregory Nava's *El Norte*; but it is also important in one of the more successful filmic looks at Puerto Rican poverty struggles and Puerto Rican/Cuban relations, the film *Popi* (1969), which presents a Puerto Rican sometime-busboy father who does not run away or enter the world of drugs and who in fact realizes how better his sons' possibilities would be if they were Cuban (see Acuña, n.d.). It is perhaps unconscious that Julián virtually produces a busboy/dishwashing-related pun in his discussion of the Puerto Rican situation when he says, "They've dished out a lot of dirty plates to Puerto Ricans in this country" (236).[2] This, then, is a significant theme in this Cuban text that points to contrasts with Oscar Lewis's views of Puerto Rican aspirations. But the Puerto Ricans pay almost as big a price in this narrative as in Lewis's.

More on the Puerto Rican Dimension

In recounting his first days in New York, Julián compares Cubans and Puerto Ricans:

> Cubans are more open, more conversational, and more risk-taking. Although they may seem similar to the Cubans, Boricuas are more closed, they speak less. They're a little head-down, I'd say. The Cubans don't take things to heart, the Puerto Rican become hotheaded about some minor matter. Though we're two peoples with a lot in common, you can sense the difference. But of course, you shouldn't plant yucca in dry land. And you have to take into account the fact that they are oppressed. Almost the whole Puerto Rican working class migrated to the United Status to work. This has drained the people's blood, it's divided them. There's a lot of confusion in this country, though the number of *independentistas* grows every day—at least that's what I hope (225).

This perspective may seem politically "progressive" and preferable to some of the ignorant and terrible things said and thought in la Calle 8 and other charming spots in Miami and elsewhere, but they still smack of condescension and schematic self-justification. This problem persists in the text. So at one point Julián comments: "The Americans are dry and go right to point. Us Hispanics give a lot of spin to things, we stir the pot wherever we can. . . . The Boricuas invented the hothead, who's always ready to fight, and the Cubans invented the wise guy who's a big mouth no one can shut up (253–54). . . . Many Puerto Ricans born in the United States speak Spanish with a special accent. Once in a while they stick in English words. And when they get mad, they shout in English, with curse words that are common to New Yorkers. Most of them feel more Puerto Rican than North American" (275).

He describes the tensions mounting in the barrio during a heat wave—the growing aggressiveness and obscenity of the people (262). In the midst of it all, the barbershop is the Barrio UN (263). Although a lot of sellouts and opportunists come there, "in general the majority are progressive people" (268). And it is a progressive history of Puerto Rico that the progressive Puerto Ricans recount and Julián learns to piece together:

> Many workers had arrived from San Juan—tobacco workers, anarchists and peasants. Some of them were arrested on arrival, accused of a plot to murder President Wilson. That's why they arrested so many Puerto Ricans. Here they never wanted to see a Hispanic liberal press develop. So the upshot was the confiscation of newspapers like *El Corsario* and the mechanization of the tobacco industry. This led to the rise of hundreds of lowlifes all over the Barrio. . . . That's what they talked about in the barbershop. That and the presence of nationalist leaders and

their benefactors and their opportunistic yes-men. . . . There's still plenty of discussion of these political matters. The nationalists go off one way, the socialists another—a regular "mess" or "*revolú*" as they themselves call it. The oldtimers very much remember Jesús Colón and Bernardo Vega, the founder of the newspaper, *Gráfico* from the 1920s—those they think of as the spokesmen of justice for the boricuas. And what should we say about Vito Marcantonio, the most beloved congressman of the Puerto Ricans? Because Vito always favored Puerto Rican independence (264–65).

The contrast to this recounting of New York Puerto Rican historical highlights is Julián's view of how 116th Street came to bear the name of Luis Muñoz Marín, whom he sees as a traitor to the Puerto Rican people:

He built hotels and highways, but left the poor unemployed and in unhealthy neighborhoods. That's why the working class is where it's at in Spanish Harlem, in the most deplorable conditions (262). . . . The Barrio filled up with low life petty criminals. Many arrived from Latin American countries. They did their misdeeds there and . . . gave the Puerto Ricans a bad name. . . . The Barrio seemed like a streetfair. It still gives this impression today. But it's a fair without joy. The people teem in the street because they're unemployed. They enter and leave the bars, the herb shops and the cafes; they walk around lost, with their gaze on the horizon, badly dressed—it's a shame to see so many human beings this way. Religious consolation, really the only consolation of the poor in this country, has made it so that every day more herb shops emerge in the Barrio. But they don't sell much, because the people don't have anything (265–66).

Julián's views about the poverty and colonial situation of Puerto Ricans may explain but cannot quite excuse his comments about his Puerto Rican marriage and wife. First, the relationship should be seen in the context of an appreciation of family. Julián notes the similar dependence of Cubans and Puerto Ricans on family structure. Unlike Oscar Lewis, he still sees that structure at work, even though threatened (304). It is his treatment of Celia herself that is so striking, especially in view of the treatment of Puerto Rican women in *La Vida*:

When I met Celia, she was without purpose, an orphan without father or mother (278). . . . Since she lived in the Barrio, she had Boricua customs. She dressed, ate—she did everything in the Latino way. And she spoke of her country, the country of her parents, as Cubans speak of Cuba or Mexicans speak of Mexico. I would have preferred a Cuban wife, but today, after thirty years of matrimony, I don't regret anything, because Celia turned out pure gold (275). . . . My home filled with artificial flowers and ceramic ornaments according to her taste. Everything changed in my life. Not since then have I sewed a button, or fried a banana. I have a model wife, for sure (281–82).

Later in the text, he contrasts Celia's Puerto Rican attitude to his Cuban one: "I still had hopes of lifting myself up. . . . The Cuban is that way. Not her, she was resigned and conformist" (292).

The question of his attitude toward Puerto Rican women continues, much in the vein of *La vida,* when he comments that "Boricua women [are] hotter than Cuban women" (252). They are also good for collecting monies to help the revolution, so much so that 135th to 145th streets became known as El Escambray "because of the money that came out of there for the mountains" (334). Indeed "the majority of the Puerto Ricans felt the triumph of the Revolution as something that belonged to them too. Even those born in New York, like my wife" (336). But even with their support of the revolution, these women lack fire, except in the bedroom.

Some Final Puerto Rican Projections in *La vida real*

Thinking over his experience, Julián reflects that "the life of an immigrant is the most solitary in the world" (290). Living in El Barrio and then Red Hook, two of the worst New York Puerto Rican neighborhoods, watching the life of *bomba, plena, rumba, salsa,* and *cha-cha-cha* (to say nothing of break dance and drugs), he still has hopes for himself and his fellow Latinos.

Julián lives his solitude among the Puerto Ricans at the barbershop, but also among the small group of progressive Cubans at the Casa de las Américas on 14th Street, who provide a link with Cuba and the revolution and who are the nucleus of what Cuban immigration might have been. Thinking of his life, Julián can say, "I've never really left Cuba" (318).

Oscar Lewis and his crew did leave in 1970. But they left with lingering fears about a possibly growing marginalization process within the revolution—a process with racial and political implications that would be the subject of Sara Gómez's *En cierta manera,* a process crucial in understanding the Mariel exodus of 1980. Posing his work against Lewis's view of Puerto Rican and Cuban poverty, Barnet less overtly poses his work against the refugees of 1959 and 1980. He had sought a figure who would provide an alternative subjectivity and an alternative history reminding us of José Martí and Fernando Ortiz, but also Albizu Campos, Bernardo Vega, Jesús Colón, and all those he might learn about from the Centro de Estudios Puertorriqueños, where he did some of the research for this book. Through Julián, he seeks to vindicate Cuban and Puerto Rican migrations and Cuban–Puerto Rican relations, so deeply damaged in recent years; he thereby points to the possibility of positive, progressive Latino identifications, interactions, and actions for future times.

It is true that much of recent New York and Cuban history remains blurred in the final pages of Barnet's work; it is true that the writing is often putative, projecting characters and situations without presenting them in sufficient complexity. This is far from a fulfilled novel in conventional terms or even in comparison with Barnet's earlier efforts. But it is a book that relates to and anticipates such full novelistic accounts—a book looking to the pre-Castroite exodus as a way of imagining an alternative Cuban and Puerto Rican history in the United States— including Puerto Rican and Cuban progressive participation in their enclaved U.S. life. Placing his narrative in relation to those by Vega and Colón, Barnet has extended beyond his Cuban trilogy and his initial testimonial/ethnographical texts to contribute to the elaboration of a U.S. Cuban literature that can relate to the contemporary U.S. Latino literary scene and its implications for past, present, and future. His story has the virtue of leaping the bounds of its foreseeable standing vis-à-vis Latin American *testimonio* and Oscar Lewis's *La Vida*. Portraying Julián's life as a busboy, Barnet evokes not only *El Norte* but, again, some of the best moments of other works of Latino literature involving restaurant slavery. By portraying Julián's declining years as a "super" completely the slave of tenants and "boila," he not only points to the situation of Roberto in Acosta's play but may well remind the reader of the heating problems in Piri Thomas's *Down These Mean Streets.* The super motif and the sad story of Julián's *socio* Miguelito anticipate the tragicomedy of lost American dream at the heart of Hijuelos's *Mambo Kings;* the trip to Cuba projected at the end of the book anticipates the final section of Cristina García's *Dreaming in Cuban.*

The portrait Barnet paints through Julián is of no perfect being; he's no perfect social realist or Lukácsian typical hero, no harmonious Cuban–Puerto Rican instance of Hispanic unity. Like the sad sacks of *The Mambo Kings,* Julián is sexist and melancholic, drowning in nostalgia and not fully aware of his limitations, his prejudices, or the process in which he is involved. Like the Mambo Kings, he is not fully able to live in the United States but is trapped in memories of his island. However, unlike them, he has a sense of a political agenda, a political reading of the problems he and other Latinos must face—even if a trip to Cuba is not necessarily what most might see that future involving. Through Julián, Barnet points to a time beyond present polemics and impositions against Cuba and against Latin American immigrants to the United States. In the midst of it all, Barnet presents a character whose overt progressive politics don't prevent him from reproducing the "gunk" of Cuban–Puerto Rican relations. But this reproduction in itself is symptomatic of those relations, at least since 1959, so that even in the midst of a seemingly uncritical portrait, Barnet points to problems and issues that will lead to future confrontations and, it is hoped, future identifications important for the struggles to be faced in the new century and era in which we live.

Coda: Cuban American Images, Puerto Rican Answers

In Iván Acosta's play, *El Super,* there is a fine debate about the relative importance of Cubans and Puerto Ricans, in which Acosta is able to show how Cubans see Puerto Ricans and their problems as less important than their own. This work and other examples aside, there is no doubt that Barnet's book shares in the negative view of Puerto Ricans common in Cuban American literature. In Oscar Hijuelos's *Mambo Kings,* our musical heroes can only succeed by weaving their way through a Puerto Rican music mafia (see the comments of Juan Flores 2001). In Cristina García's *Dreaming in Cuban,* Lourdes portrays Puerto Rican women as low-class thieves. In Achy Obejas's *Memory Mambo,* the most seamy and sexist dimensions of Puerto Rican barrio life come to the fore.

In spite of the many positive qualities of *La vida real,* its negative portrayal of Puerto Ricans in no way contradicts the Cuban American model, even as Barnet's text purports to be sympathetic to Puerto Rican problems and the falsification of their reality by Oscar Lewis. This is a negativity shared in Jewish American representations (*The Pawnbroker, West Side Story,* or *Capeman,* not to mention the notorious Seinfeld episode or the negative foray by Earl Shorris). It is a negativity I have also mentioned in relation to Juan Bruce-Novoa and Linda Chavez. It is one that prevents a truer, deeper portrayal of U.S. Puerto Rican cultural realities such as we may find them in the work of Juan Flores, Edna Acosta-Belén, Frances Aparicio, Arlene Dávila, and Agustín Laó-Montes—indeed, two successive generations of U.S. Puerto Rican specialists.

This new view of course parallels transformations in Puerto Rican migration patterns and indeed Puerto Rican life, as processes of gentrification, upward mobility, and educational development have meant new possibilities and even a reactive reassertion of Puerto Rican identities spurred on by the confrontation over Vieques and other recent concerns. In the years to come, more of the U.S. Puerto Rican artists, writers, and cultural performers may be college-bred and focused on issues far different from Oscar Lewis's and Piri Thomas's worlds. But the question of ethnic, gender, and other identifications will become even more crucial in a highly complex, high-tech, multicultural, and multiracial world marked by patterns of globalization and its effects.

It is true that older views still circulate. So in a recent piece commissioned and published by the Council on Hemispheric Affairs (COHA), Arienna Grody (2009) cites Manuel Maldonado-Denis's 60s-style *independentista* view that Puerto Ricans have not yet achieved "a true 'decolonization,' either in the political or in the psychological sense of the word." And Grody cites Pedro Malavet (2004, 75) to argue that Puerto Ricans on the island and elsewhere suffer from a "U.S.-imposed inferiority complex" that hinders their every move toward creative freedom.

Recent Puerto Rican writers have sought to contest such views, and Grody at least cites Jorge Duany's take, that U.S. Puerto Ricans "perceive themselves as Puerto Ricans first, Americans second" and that "the vast majority of Puerto Ricans imagine themselves as distinct from Americans as well as from other Latin American and Caribbean peoples." In fact, migration "has produced an affirmation of *puertorriqueñismo* as a nationality in the continental U.S. . . . [where] Puerto Ricans . . . continue to exhibit a strong sense of cultural identity." In this light, Edna Acosta-Belén and Carlos E. Santiago end their book about Puerto Ricans in the United States with the following assessment:

> Regardless of . . . [their many] political and social differences, there is among U.S. Puerto Ricans . . . a strong affirmation of cultural identity and a fervent sense of affiliation with Puerto Rico. [And] there is also a panethnic identification with the shared experiences and struggles of other U.S. Latinos. Some old stereotypes and misconceptions . . . are being eradicated, [as many] Puerto Rican[s] . . . work tirelessly to improve the[ir] socioeconomic and political status. The invisibility and marginality of the past are gradually waning, and new generations . . . are growing up . . . with more opportunities to learn about their heritage and develop a consciousness of the issues and obstacles impeding their . . . progress. Old assimilation models . . . proved to be elusive . . . [because of] racial discrimination. [So] Puerto Ricans' affirmation of their cultural identity [in literature and the arts] fulfills important social, political and psychological functions [as] . . . part of a process that empowers them and helps to counteract their experiences of marginality and exclusion (2006, 228–29).

Given the rather gloomy views reinforced in the writings of Cuban Americans and others (and yes, of Puerto Ricans as well), I believe it is fitting that we close this consideration of U.S. Puerto Rican culture and literature by citing still another vignette by Chicago's Leonardo Rodríguez (1988), in which a young boy can't believe that a Puerto Rican was the chief architect of a major skyline building. "A Puerto Rican did that?" he asks in disbelief. "Are you sure?" he asks, doubting his informant, unable to believe what he hears. "Of course we have ballplayers, boxers, writers, artists and singers," a student once told me, "But nothing else." So goes the Puerto Rican lament, the colonial difference in its clear, self-negating form— so that Puerto Rican achievements are effaced or doubted, or at least qualified in ways that withhold any major sense of pride. No matter what field in which a Puerto Rican excels, the achievement or even the field itself becomes questionable. This is precisely what is being contested by contemporary U.S. Puerto Rican writers, artists, actors, and film directors—and what is contested by the people themselves. In spite of Anglo, Jewish American, Latino, Cuban, and Puerto Rican naysayers, U.S. Puerto Ricans look toward performances that are ever richer and better and best express the potentialities of a people that has suffered but has endured. Puerto Ricans have lived through the *apagón* of the diaspora, and again and again have become—as if they'd ever ceased to be—*gente;* the *carreta* continues making its u-turn; the *gua-gua aerea* goes back and forth in transnational gyrations creating ever more complex and globalized identities.

Indeed, Puerto Ricans are on the move beyond Hawaii—and can be found doing everyday and remarkable things all over the globe, affirming, mixing, and transforming their identities in ways that only nomadic postmodern theories can begin to capture. U.S. Puerto Ricans today seek to forge works of literature and art, of drama, film, and performance that correlate with and transform the richest dimensions of their diasporic experience.

Notes

Introduction

1. Thanks to Ben Pacheco for some details here.
2. *Claridad* is Puerto Rico's most read *independentista* newspaper.
3. In an e-mail note dated June 1, 2010, Adal Maldonado wrote me the following:

In your text . . . you mention that Pedro and Papoleto presented you with a passport to Loisaida [Manhattan's Lower East Side]. They may have articulated it to you in that way . . ., but the passport is a document that represents "El Spirit Republic de Puerto Rico" [which] could be seen as a metaphor for Loisaida, but . . . to stay in the spirit of the concept that distinction needs to be made clear. I remember you from Viequethon of course and am grateful to all of the poets and musicians who collaborated in the effort. But you may not have been aware of some of the behind the scenes stuff that made El Viequethon possible. [In fact,] the Viequethon idea was brought to El Puerto Rican Embassy by Ricardo Leon Peña Villa, who was our Ambassador of Journalism Without Border; and the steering committee of El Puerto Rican Embassy—Rev. Pedro Pietri, Adal Maldonado, Jesus Papoleto Meléndez, Sheila Candelario, and Alma Ville-gas—made it happen. Also, I personally was able to get from then Governor of Puerto Rico, Sila Calderón, a Proclamation proclaiming Vieques 'La Isla de los Poetas.'"

4. For a take on gay performance, primarily by U.S. Puerto Ricans, see Larry La Fountain-Stokes, *Queer Ricans: Cultures and Sexualities in the Diaspora* (2009), with chapters on Luis Rafael Sánchez, Manuel Ramos Otero, Luz María Umpierre, Frances Negrón-Muntaner, Rose Troche, Erika Lopez, Arthur Aviles, and Elizabeth Marrero. This book came out too recently for me to review in relation to my final draft. This is also the case with another recent take on Puerto Rican life and literature, Ramón Soto-Crespo's *Mainland Passage* (2010). It would be interesting to note how this book reinforces or contradicts mine.

5. For a recent effort to relate Díaz-Quiñones's *arte de bregar* to contemporary Latin American cultural studies theory and then apply the concept to cultural politics under Muñoz-Marín, see Catherine Marsh Kennedy, 2009.

6. For a pioneering effort to evaluate Jewish–Puerto Rican relations and attitudes, see Jesús Colón, "The Jewish People and Us," in Colón 1993, 65–66.

Chapter 1. Puerto Rican and Chicano Crossovers
in Latino Film and Music Culture

1. Another recent take on Lopez and Selena, including the Afro-colonial question underlined earlier in Rodríguez Juliá, is found in Negrón-Muntaner's *Boricua Pop* (2004), 228–46.

2. On a related note, just as Marc Anthony was touted as the Rican Sinatra, Hector Lavoe's professional name is a Boricua version of Sinatra's nickname, "The Voice"—though clearly the "colonial difference" (and the "coloniality of power"—see note 6, below) must ultimately mitigate against overplaying any Italian-Rican connections, unless we wish to get into Sicily's role as an Italian colony. Still, on some levels, as I've noted, "Latin" once referred to both Italians and Puerto Ricans—though clearly the African American connection was to be key (see further on in this essay and in subsequent notes).

3. Even though some Mexican males may seek Puerto Rican women in the quest for legalization or welfare benefits, I would venture that the number of lasting marriages between U.S.-based Puerto Rican men and Mexican women is much higher. When confronted with Latinos of mixed national origins, researchers frequently ask about the nationality of the mother, to determine the stronger identity. In Chicago, a Mexirican answer to my purposely mumbled, almost inaudible question is eight times out of ten, "*¿mande?*" Now if that isn't erasing the Puerto Rican, what is?

4. For a study of Mexican–Puerto Rican relations in Chicago, treated in terms of Chicago's initial Rican settlement, see Elena Padilla's dissertation of 1947; for later developments, see Félix Padilla (1985), and the recent book by Nick De Genova and Ana Y. Ramos-Zayas (2003). A book edited by Mérida Rua centering on Padilla was published by the University of Illinois Press in 2010.

5. See Laó-Montes, "Introduction: Mambo Montage," and above all, his essay, "Niuyol" in Laó-Montes and Dávila, ed., 2001—above all 120–22, and notes 9–10. See also his essay in Bedoya, Belpoliti, and Zimmerman, eds., 2008, 52–61. Laó-Montes refers to the contemporary postcolonial condition affecting "Diasporicans" in New York and other cities as "global coloniality," which is in turn subject to a particular version of what he calls an "urban regime"—a form of urban governance or "governmentality" with particular effects for colonial, racialized groups such as Puerto Ricans. For coloniality of power, which I tend to conflate with a "colonial difference" separating Puerto Ricans and Latinos (but even here there are specific Rican differences stemming from their unique colonial status) from even the most oppressed Euro-immigrants, in spite of similarities, see Quijano 1992 and Mignolo 2000. The term "Diasporicans" seems to have been coined by Adam Pagán (1997) and is used especially by Lisa Sánchez González (2001) and Wilson Valentín Escobar, again in Laó-Montes and Dávila, ed. 2001. Finally, in "Niuyol," (2009) Laó-Montes characterizes Puerto Rican resistance in terms of a struggle for radical democratization and a politics involving "the decolonization of power"; it becomes a dominant term also in Torres-Padilla (2008). This resistance can be seen in terms of social movements, or, I would suggest, in terms of particular forms of individual and symbolic action—for example in the realm of the arts, though again I note that the key text for understanding Puerto Rican action would probably be Díaz-Quiñonez's *Arte de bregar* (2000).

6. Note also how the film *Nothing like the Holidays* has a mixed cast, but a Chicano di-

rector and Mexican writer who present our Chicago Ricans hardly without the colonial or Afro-Caribbean dimensions so crucial to many U.S. Ricans, and indeed playing out Latino more than specifically Puerto Rican roles. A redeeming matter is the portrayal of a Puerto Rican son who has returned from Iraq. At press time, I've yet to see the performance of J. Edward Olmos in Sonia Fritz's film version of Esmeralda Santiago's *América*. But judging by his wooden Trujillo in the film version of Julia Álvaréz's *In the Time of the Butterflies*, I doubt there's much hope for *América* being one of his more successful efforts.

7. The well-known Hollywood star is the nephew of Ferrer's wife, singer Rosemary Clooney.

8. I'm poking malicious fun here. For a more balanced view, see my comments in chapter 3.

9. Acosta-Belén and Santiago point to the improved socioeconomic situation of U.S. Ricans throughout the 1990s (2006, 137), although I believe statistics will show downward trends at least since the general economic crisis of 2008.

10. For examples of island production, see Rivera Nieves and Gil, eds. (1995); for examples from the island and U.S. communities, see Negrón-Muntaner and Grosfoguel (1997) and my edited volume with Luis Felipe Díaz (2001). Indeed, Díaz is the only professor I know of at the University of Puerto Rico brought up in a U.S. barrio—in this case, Chicago. Among other academics brought up in the Chicago barrio are the late Rane Arroyo and critic Israel Reyes. Perhaps it's not insignificant to note that all three of these intellectuals are gay.

Chapter 2. The Flag and Three Rican Artists

As noted in the introduction, this essay is a recent rewrite of an article originally published in *Que Ondee Sola* (vol. 26, no. 4–5, 14–32), written to accompany Puerto Rico '98, an art exhibit at Chicago's Puerto Rican Cultural Center and then at the Chicago Art Institute, featuring a series of ironic references to the U.S. flag and *la bandera puertorriqueña*. To improve this version, and also to pay special homage to my friend and collaborator, Michael Piazza, who died suddenly in his artistic and personal prime, I have incorporated descriptions of different art works appearing here from his article in the same journal issue, "Three visions of a CENTENNIAL." I hope the accompanying images from the exhibit, along with Michael's descriptions, will help the reader to understand the text. Thanks again to the editors of *Que Ondee Sola* and the artists for the images.

1. The reference here is to an iconoclastic article by Carlos Pabón that appears as chapter 1 in his book (2002), and involves a mocking portrayal of Puerto Rican nationalism and above all of the *independentista* leader and founder of Nationalist Party, who spent years in prison for his opposition to Governor Muñoz Marín's concoction of Puerto Rico's Estado Libre Asociado status.

2. See the introduction for a brief discussion of some of the key Puerto Rican postmodern texts, though here we should add the names and works of Juan Gelpí, Irma Rivera Nieves, Carlos Gil, and others from the island. For more recent takes on some of the issues involved, see the excellent review articles (and books reviewed) in Emilio Pantojas-García (2005) and Jorge Duany (2005). Perhaps the U.S. Puerto Rican artist who most expresses the globalized, postmodern trend in New York was Jean-Michel Basquiat, born

of a Haitian father and a Puerto Rican mother, whose art reaches out from a mainly African American view of New York City to the world, the Caribbean included. See Negrón Muntaner's essay in *Boricua Pop* (2004) and note 1 in chapter 3 of this book.

3. "A *vejigante* is a clown-like character in Puerto Rican festival celebrations (mainly seen in Carnival time). . . . Today, vejigantes wear brightly colored, ornate masks of all colors and a costume with bat-like wings. The term vejigante derives from the word *vejiga* (bladder) and *gigante* (giant), due to custom of blowing up and painting cow bladders. Bystanders are often tapped with the bladders during the processional. The masks are often linked to many festivals that continue today, especially in Loíza and Ponce. . . . In Loíza, vejigante masks are made from coconut, whose cortex has been carved out to allow a human face. The eyes and mouth are carved out of the coconut with an addition of bamboo teeth. The costume is made of 'a jumper' that has a lot of extra fabric at the arms to simulate wings. . . . In Ponce vejigante masks are made from papier mache, and usually contain many horns." From http://en.wikipedia.org/wiki/Vejigante.

4. It is true that of the three, only Juan Sánchez remains in the United States, while López and Escobar currently live in Puerto Rico—as do Antonio Martorell, Arnaldo Roché Rabell, and other contemporary artists like Nick Quintano, Rafael Trelles, Marta Pérez García, and so forth. In an earlier epoch, island artists like Lorenzo Homar and Rafael Tufiño, along with Rafael Palacios and Olga Albizu, came to New York to develop their work. From the 1950s into the 70s, many island artists came to "teach and learn" through the efforts of Amalia Guerrero working for Los Amigos de Puerto Rico (Acosta-Belén and Santiago 2006, 208). Meanwhile, New York muralists like Johnny Vásquez and Millito López, Manuel Vega, Nitza Tufiño (daughter of Rafael), Marina Gutiérrez, and Rafael Ferrer (brother of José Ferrer) developed *costumbrista* and modernist murals portraying island and New York images; as did other artists like Pedro Villarini, Ralph Ortiz, Martha Vega, Ernesto Ramos-Nieves, Marcos Dimas, Carlos Osorio, Manuel Otero, Armando Soto, Adrián García, and Martín Rubio (ibid., 208–12) and to just name a few of many recent New York examples, Adal Maldonado, Eduardo Figueroa, Soraida Martínez, Dennis Mario, and Pepón Osorio. For Chicago Rican artists, Acosta-Belén and Santiago (2006, 215) cite Marinar Benítez (1988) to mention the presence of artist Rufino Silva, who "made his mark in Chicago, where he was on the faculty of the [School of] the Art Institute for many years." Acosta-Belén and Santiago also describe Roché Rabell's years in Chicago and his winning of the Illinois Governor's Lincoln Medal for "his artistic contributions" to the state (ibid., 215); the authors also discuss and show an example of the work of Gamaliel Ramírez (ibid., 213–14); they speak well of Bibiana Suárez (ibid., 216). For a further sample of Ramírez's work, see chapter 4. In addition, the reader may wish to Google materials about such other artists as Raúl Ortiz, Jorge Félix, Oscar Martínez, or Sonia Baéz Hernández, the latter now relocated to Fort Lauderdale.

5. Leonardo Rodríguez, "The Flag and the Cap of Andrés," in *They Have to be Puerto Ricans* (1988), 1.

6. In relation to these themes, see "Sacar la Bandera" and "El syndrome puertorriqeño" in Jorge Duany's *La nación en vaivén* (2010, 30–31 and 52–54). Duany cites Roberto Lewis-Fernández (2003).

7. The biography that follows is based on Goldman (1994, 435–36), and Marysol Nieves in *Rican/Structions*, 5–10.

8. As chapter 4 will indicate, the Young Lords were born in Chicago, but it was the New York branch that grew in the popular imagination.

9. This passage and indeed many of the biographical details that follow come from the back cover of the manual written by López himself (1988). See Ramón López, "La cajita roja de Vincent Van Gogh," in López 1995, 37–38.

10. For López on Puerto Rican and U.S. flags, see his *Tapices puertorriqueños* 1988, 11–13; see also his *Pupil's Works* (1998), 5 and elsewhere. For questions of *santería*, in itself and in a struggle against *espiritismo* and the powerful evangelical movement (above all, Pentacostalism) that has so enveloped Puerto Rican communities (especially among the poor) in the United States as well as on the island, see the many books of Migene González-Wippler—for example, *Santería: The Religion, Faith, Rites, Magic*, 1994. For a rich consideration of Puerto Rican religiosity and its images, see Quintero-Rivera, ed., 1998. It is constantly debated whether *santería* has deep roots in Puerto Rican society, with most agreeing that it is primarily a Cuban import into U.S. Rican communities and then more directly into Puerto Rico through the exile community that took root on the island. The syncretism between Yoruba-based and other African practices rooted in Puerto Rico makes the matter one of great difficulty and controversy. López claims he came to *santería* on the island, which after years in the United States, has become his home again. In his notes about the first draft of this text, and particularly about López and Sánchez in this essay, Ben Pacheco rails against what he considers to be my uncritical adoption of *santería* as Puerto Rican. Pacheco, like many others, considers this an imposition, a result of Cuban hegemony and inaccurate ideas about "true" Puerto Rican identity. He specifically targets Ramón López, pointing to the *independentista* artist's "acceptance of another colonizer [Cubans]." One might suggest that Pacheco overdoes his attack, taking on a form of Pedreira's *insularismo* by seeming to argue that anything African is foreign to true Puerto Rican identity. At one point, Pacheco labels López's *santería* as a case of cultural confusion or ignorance, asking "what's the relationship of this Cuban esoteric belief to Puerto Rico?" and crying out, "Ay, madre melancólica, que ya no somos nosotros!" Surely African religious practices are deeply imbedded in Puerto Rico, even if the Yoruba presence central to *santería* is not what it is in Cuba. In the "liquid modernity" we know today, those older elements may have helped *santería* to become an intensified aspect of Boricua culture with special ties among performers and indeed among sectors involved in the Puerto Rican informal economy.

11. In part, this treatment of Escobar draws upon materials I drafted with Michael Piazza for the introduction to our edited volume, *New World (Dis)Orders* (1998). Since his release from prison, Escobar has gone through many creative transformations not discussed in this essay, originally drafted while he was still locked up in Oklahoma.

12. Biographical details here have mainly followed and updated the "biography" presented in *Elizam Escobar: Art as an Act of Liberation* (Chicago: n.p., n.d., 31).

13. Places of publication include the anthologies edited by Escobar 1991; Silén 1991; O'Brien and Little 1994; Rivera Nieves and Gil 1995; and Piazza and Zimmerman 1998.

Chapter 3. U.S. Puerto Rican Literature

1. Basquiat might be an example of this position in art. In the retrospective brought to Houston in 2005–2006 by the Brooklyn Museum, Basquiat, a New York Haitian-Rican, makes reference to the Caribbean and, in a few isolated cases, to Puerto Rico—most specifically to Juan Tizol, the Ellington valve trombonist and composer of "Perdido"—virtually the theme song for Luis Valdez's *Zoot Suit,* and "Caravan," a Puerto Rican dessert fantasy, and perhaps, in a subtle, ambiguous way, to Tito (Puente, Rojas, Trinidad, or other—it is not clear). However, his Caribbean map shows Cuba and Haiti while leaving out Puerto Rico, even though he attended a year of high school on the island and apparently visited fairly often. My speculation is that his relative exclusion of Puerto Rican references is a result of his phenotypically Afro-Caribbean features, which may have led him to having negative experiences on the island. In the United States, racialization trumps ethnic identification. As one Chicago Rican exclaimed to his daughter after jazz saxophonist David Sánchez, short and Black, came out to perform at a "Latino" concert, "¡Ay! Y yo pensaba que era puertorriqueño." "Oh! And here I thought he was Puerto Rican." For a Rican-centered essay on Basquiat, see the chapter in Negrón-Muntaner's *Boricua Pop* (2004).

2. Flores 1988, 39–44. His phases are an extension and refinement of those found in Eugene Mohr 1982. As noted in the introduction, for a summary of Sánchez González's critique (2001) of Flores and Mohr, see Torres-Padilla and Rivera 2008, 12–13.

3. For a recent treatment of the New York Antillean community and its representatives in the nineteenth century, see Mirabal, in Laó-Montes and Dávila, eds., 2001. Drawing on several researchers, Acosta-Belén and Santiago (2006, 171–76) provide an excellent quick survey of pre-phase writers as well as vivid summaries of Muñoz Marín, Vega, Colón, Capetillo, Armiño, and Belpré. For more detailed treatments of early-twentieth-century writers Juan Labarthe, Arturo Alfonso Schomburg, Bernardo Vega, and Jesús Colón, see Irizarry Rodríguez; for Capetillo, see Sánchez-González; for Belpré and Graciany Miranda Archilla as well as Colón, see Torres-Padilla—all three articles in Torres-Padilla and Rivera, eds., 2008.

4. See Capetillo 1992 and 2004. Acosta-Belén and Santiago (2006, 217–18) list several studies of her work, including Sánchez González 2001, 16–41.

5. Many of these figures are mentioned in a note to me outlining some of her dissertation research, from María Teresa Rojas-Vera, then a University of Houston graduate student involved with the Recovering Hispanic Literary Heritage project, and developing her now completed dissertation on Betances. Citing the research of Altagracia Ortiz (1996), Rojas-Vera also mentions titles for Pedro Juan Labarthe that go beyond my list of works cited. For more on these matters, see Sánchez González 2001 and Flores, ed., 2003; on the specific question of women, see also Roy-Fequière 2004. Kanellos's coedited anthologies *Herencia* (2002a) and *En otra voz* (2002b) contain work by and/or information about Erasmo Vando, Américo Meana, Wilfredo Braschi, and Tomás R. Gares. The two volumes also include Bernardo Vega's first-hand accounts of early Puerto Rican theater in New York and of Capetillo's life and work (including the role of the tobacco factory readers); Vega also refers to newspapers like *Cultura Proletaria* and *La Prensa,* which preceded *El Gráfico* as the main outlet for New York Puerto Rican writers; and he points to additional early

writers such as Gabriel Blanco and Muñoz Marín (Kanellos, ed., 2002b, 249–55). Juan Flores has observed that parts of *El negocio* and *Los redentores*, the later novels of Manuel Zeno Gandía, a canonical island writer, take place in the United States; and frequent bibliographical reference is made to still another unpublished novel by Zeno Gandía entitled *Hubo un escándalo* (or *En Nueva York*), though it has not yet been possible to study that manuscript. José de Diego Padró, an interesting but neglected writer active between 1910 and 1930, set much of his long, bizarre novel *En Babia* in New York, as did the dramatist Fernando Sierra Berdecía in his comedy *Esta noche juega el jóker*. But for Flores, these are "random and rare exceptions and still do not indicate any inclusion of emigrant experience in the thematic preoccupations of the national literature" (1988, 42).

6. See Cruz-Malavé, 1988, a major source for what follows here on Nuyorican poetry. For a look at the left political connections of New York Puerto Rican writing, see Hickman 2008, 143–61; for an updating of recent developments of Nuyorican poetry in terms of Sánchez González's diasporican point of view, see William Burgos's essay (2008), 125–42.

7. See William Luis's *Dance Between Two Cultures* (1997) for a more detailed look at the Young Lords–Nuyorican poetry connection.

8. In the detailed description of texts and trends that follows, Chicago materials are mainly left out in view of the matters covered in chapter 4. Also left out is a treatment of Philadelphia writers—see Negrón-Muntaner, ed., 1994. Many of the descriptions of texts are based on entries in Zimmerman 1992, the main sources for which were: Acosta-Belén 1988, 56-62; Foster, ed., 1983; Lindstrom in Foster, ed., 1982, 221-45. I also had frequent recourse to reviews and articles appearing in the two leading Latino literary/cultural journals, *Américas Review* and *The Bilingual Review*, and more recent bibliographical efforts—for example that of Marisol Ortiz (2000), which updates my own listings (1992). I have attempted to bring things up to date as of 2009, drawing on Kanellos's recent *Greenwood Encyclopedia of Latino Literature* (2008), Roberto Márquez's volume *Puerto Rican Poetry* (2007), and other sources.

9. For a recent treatment of this writer, see Betsy A. Sandlin's essay (2008). See also the articles by Arnaldo Cruz-Malavé (1993) and Juan Gelpí (2001).

10. For some provocative thoughts on Ferré (and Victor Hernández Cruz), see Frances Aparicio's essay, "Las migraciones de la escritura" in Díaz and Zimmerman, eds., 2001, 291–313.

11. See Gordills 1988, 54; and her source, Marzán, 1986; also see Kutzinski 1987, 37 and 258. For a perhaps self-serving negative critique of Gordills, see Sánchez González 2008, 54–56.

12. For work on Pietri, see Israel Reyes (2005) and Víctor Figueroa (2008).

13. For good work on Laviera, see William Luis's recent introduction to *Mixturao and Other Poems* (2008); see also John Waldron's article in Torres-Padilla and Rivera, eds., 2008.

14. Apparently Arte Público Press has additional work, including two chapbooks, by Esteves in the press' archives.

15. Zavala's creative work rarely centers on the immigrant or New York experience, though she lived and taught in New York for some years, before relocating to the Netherlands and elsewhere. N. Kanellos informs that his Arte Público archives contain one

manuscript by her, *El gran mamut,* that should be scrutinized in relation to this book's predominant themes.

16. Umpierre's book *The Margarita Poems* (1987) "is a courageous and moving bilingual collection about women in love" (Acosta-Belén and Santiago 2006, 195); her most recent collection continues in this vein. For recent work on Levins Morales, see Ferdá Asya 2008, 107–24.

17. For a brief discussion of Escobar's poetry in relation to his essays, see García Cuevas 2006, 199–204, especially 200.

18. Roberto Márquez recently told me about how Espada acknowledged that his reading of Márquez's classic anthology, *Latin American Revolutionary Poetry* (1974) confirmed for the young poet the path he should take in his own writing.

19. For a discussion of recent transformations of the Nuyorican Poets' Café and its writer base, see Hickman's essay (2008, 149–54). Hickman points to the importance of Algarín's "The Sidewalk of High Art" and the introduction to the anthology *Aloud* (1994), ed. Algarín and Holman, as symptomatic of the many changes affecting Nuyorican poets and the café itself.

20. For a recent essay on Thomas, see Santiago-Díaz (2009).

21. For an analysis of Pietri's story, see Juan Carlos Quintero Herencia's essay (2009).

22. For a treatment of this work, see Antonia Miguela's essay (2008).

23. For an interesting critique of this novel, see Joanna Barszewska Marshall's essay (2008).

24. Cited in *American Literature: A Journal of Literary History, Criticism and Bibliography* (Durham, N.C.: Duke University Press, 2004), 407–9. For a more recent discussion of Ambert and Santiago, see Suero-Elliott (2008).

25. For a treatment of Quiñónez, see Domínguez-Miguela, in Torres-Padilla and Rivera, 2008, 173–77; see also Arlene Dávila's interesting interpretation (2004, 27–28).

26. See the discussion of their work in Enrique Morales-Díaz's essay (2008). La Fountain's book of short fiction, *Uñas pintadas de azul/Blue Fingernails* (2009) includes fourteen stories centered on gay Puerto Rican characters, and sometimes incorporating elements of science fiction and fantasy.

27. For a discussion of Morales's work, representative of Hawaii's community of more than thirty thousand Puerto Ricans who first began settling the island to work in the sugar cane fields after the hurricane of 1899, see Maritza Stanchich (2008).

28. For a remarkable treatment of *West Side Story* with a significant commentary on *Capeman* and the problems of Jewish representations of Puerto Ricans, see Frances Negrón-Muntaner's "Sitting Pretty" chapter in *Boricua Pop* (2004).

29. For a brief and telling critique of the film, see the unsigned *Time Magazine* article, "The Children's Minute," at http://www.time.com/time/magazine/article/0,9171,941706,00.html.

30. Unfortunately at press time, I have yet to see a more recent film, *Héctor Lavoe: The Untold Story* (2011), which I understand is rather weak, though with a portrayal of Lavoe that rivals Marc Anthony's.

31. As noted in chapter 1, that moment may have indeed come with the release on

December 27, 2005, of *Chicago Boricua* and other Chicago films—see our brief discussion at the end of chapter 4.

Chapter 4. Puerto Rican Poets in Chicago

Research for the first draft of this chapter was supported by a Harold Washington Chicago Studies grant from the Office of Social Science Research of the University of Illinois at Chicago. I wish to acknowledge the invaluable participation of Carlos Cumpián of El Movimiento Artístico Chicano (MARCH); also, University of Illinois at Chicago students Monica Winter, Dalia Tapia, Dalia Sabaliaushas, José Resto, Vírgen López, Mario Gamboa, and Andrea Barrientos. Unless otherwise noted, quotes and biographical details relating to David Hernández and Salima Rivera are derived from their responses to my written questionnaire, dated February 1988. Thanks to Gamaliel Ramírez for help in modifying some details. Nicolás Kanellos's comments on the penultimate version of this text are designated by "NK."

1. Significantly enough, in relation to the theme of this study, Matías's poem appeared not in a specifically Puerto Rican publication, but in two very differently conceived vehicles: first, in *Revista Chicano-Riqueña*'s special issue, *Nosotros* (1977), 37; and then in the second and final issue of the Chicago-based journal of MARCH, *Abrazo* 1979, 10.

2. Of Cuban and Mexican parents, Morton writes that a friend "was trying to be a soul brother and I a puertorican"; also that his "neighborhood was a multicolored rainbow of nationalities," including "sultry rice eaters from an island once fair" (4–5). Morton was a friend of David Hernández in the early 1970s. He would later write about Puerto Rican theater in New York, though his primary work would be as a Chicano playwright in the U.S. Southwest.

3. Under my supervision, preliminary research conducted by Cumpián through a Discovering Hispanic Heritage Recovery Project grant revealed no definitively pre-1970s Chicago Rican writing—partially because we could not verify if the few pieces found were actually written or merely published in Chicago.

4. For Act I of *Carnicería Rodríguez*, see Casuso, Obejas, and Zayas 1983—with an introductory note (Zimmerman 1983).

5. Says Wikipedia: The United States Capitol shooting incident . . . was an attack on March 1, 1954, by four Puerto Rican nationalists who shot 30 rounds using automatic pistols from . . . a balcony for visitors [in] the House of Representatives chamber. . . . Lolita Lebrón, Rafael Cancel Miranda, Andres Figueroa Cordero, and Irving Flores Rodríguez unfurled a Puerto Rican flag and began shooting at the 240 Representatives of the 83rd Congress who were on the floor during debate over an immigration bill. Five representatives [and two pages] were shot in the attack. The attackers were immediately arrested. All the attackers were given minimum sentences of 70 years in prison. From http://en.wikipedia.org/wiki/United_States_Capitol_shooting_incident_(1954).

Followers of nationalist Pedro Albizu Campos, and themselves icons of anticolonialist struggle, the prisoners were released in 1981 after twenty-five years, and were celebrated and honored in many Puerto Rican communities in the United States and on the island. In fact, this writer met the woman who would become his third wife at a special party honoring Cancel Miranda on his visit to Chicago to celebrate the Grito de Lares, a special event commemorating a nineteenth-century anticolonial uprising in rural Puerto Rico.

6. I have recently become aware of another volume of island memories, written by the mother of Chicago Puerto Rican professor and performer Samuel Betances, of Northeastern University—a work that I believe remains unpublished. There is also Columbia College Professor Tony Del Valle's novel of Chicago Puerto Rican life, parts of which have appeared over the years (including one part nominated for the Pushcart Prize), as have some of his poems and creative nonfiction.

7. Barillas also adds a bibliographical note that merits quoting:

Commentary on Rane Arroyo's poetry includes Glenn Sheldon's entry on the writer in David William Wallace's *Latin American Writers on Gay and Lesbian Themes: A Bio-Critical Sourcebook* (1994): 43–46; Leslie Naton's notice of *Pale Ramón* in *Ohioana Quarterly* 54 (Winter 2000): 316–17; and Rigoberto González's review of *Home Movies of Narcissus,* "Expounding on Myth," in *El Paso Times,* September 29, 2002. In "The Already Browned Skin of 'American' Modernism: Rane Arroyo's *Pale Ramón*" (in *Midwestern Miscellany* 30 [Fall 2002]: xx–xxi), María DeGuzmán argues that Arroyo revises the New World consciousness of Wallace Stevens and other Modernists. Arroyo's papers are held at El Centro de Estudios Puertorriqueños at Hunter College.

Since Barillas drafted his commentary, Arroyo has published at least two other collections (2005a and 2005b). He may indeed be the most prolific and most important of the Chicago Puerto Rican poets.

8. Serious research on Chicago's Puerto Rican community begins with the work of Elena Padilla in the 1940s and the books of Félix Padilla in the 1980s and 90s. For crucial treatments of recent community developments, see *The Journal of the Centro de Estudios Puertorriqueños* special issue on Chicago, 13.2 (Fall 2001), with scholarly and personal essays, photographs, and poetry by several representatives of a new generation of Puerto Rican Chicago studies scholars (the full text is available online at http://www.centropr.org/journal/jrnal24.html). Important also are the two books published in 2002 by Nilda Flores and Tony Del Valle on Roberto Clemente High School—though here, in keeping with Pérez's book, we should note the demographic transformations that mean that what was founded as the primary Puerto Rican high school in the city now has many Mexican and African American students. Ana Y. Ramos-Zayas's *National Performances* (2003), Nicholas De Genova and Ana Y. Ramos-Zayas's *Latino Crossings* (2003), and Gina Pérez's *The Near Northwest Side Story* (2004) are crucial not only for understanding the 1966 uprising but also recent transformations in Chicago Puerto Rican life, including continuing gentrification struggles. On Chicago Puerto Rican resistance to gentrification, see also Michael Rodríguez Muñiz in Bedoya, Belpoliti, and Zimmerman, eds. 2008, 223–42. On Chicago Latino gangs, see Darrel Enck-Wanzer, ed., *The Young Lords: A Reader* (2010), which, according to the book blurb, "shows how this group originated as a Chicago street gang fighting gentrification and unfair evictions in Puerto Rican neighborhoods, and then . . . became a part of a national movement with headquarters in New York City and other [urban] centers." See also Cha Cha Jiménez (2002).

9. Nicolás Kanellos notes that New Mexican Juanita Jaramillo played a part in *Nosotros,* and adds that "Ana Castillo had a lot to do with the production of this anthology, although her work does not appear in it. In fact, I think she was going with Chico Rivera at the time" (NK). But Gamaliel Ramírez, reading this note, says that the Rivera going with Castillo (and married to her) was Chico's brother, Kenny. Chico and Kenny were brothers of Salima Rivera, who once told me that Castillo's breakup with Kenny eventually led to a definitive falling out between the two women. In fact, I would argue that with the exception of David Hernández and Frank Varela in their relation to the Chicano writers of MARCH, the falling out of Castillo with the Riveras was decisive in deepening a divide between Chicago Chicano and Rican writers (MZ).

10. Frustrated with my conjectures on this and other points, Kanellos suggests I call Noboa and ask him about the issues in question (NK). But as a student of Lucien Goldmann and other, anti-intentional theorists, I don't believe the telephone call would resolve anything of significance in relation to my point; indeed, while I respect empirical work greatly, I firmly believe, as a scholar-theorist, in the power and necessity of creative extrapolation and, yes, conjecture (MZ).

11. For example, Hernández is the one Chicago Puerto Rican poet represented in Barradas and Rodríguez, ed., 1981, 86–89.

12. The comments by Hernández stem from his written answers in 1985 to my questionnaire of the same year.

13. Commenting on this passage, Kanellos himself reveals the power and value of conjecture based on years of work and commitment in words applicable to many (but clearly not all) of the Nuyorican and writers as well: "I think what really happens to self-taught community poets is that their lack of reading and study does not let them grow, so that they stay at one level and become repetitive but cannot go on to experiment and develop further. It is very much the folkloric syndrome, where there is one genre, one set of themes, one function in the community, but no need to explore new form and aesthetics, because ultimately it is not about esthetic experimentation; it more about communication and saying things that others in the community cannot say" (NK).

14. Biographical details and comments by Rivera stem from her answers to a questionnaire I sent and she answered in 1985.

15. For a discussion of Puerto Rican trauma induced by the participation of Puerto Ricans in U.S. wars, as well as by participation in the U.S. military's occupation of the island, see the essay by Juan Carlos Rodríguez in Duchesne Winter, ed., 2009, 1139–74.

16. For an eight-minute film clip from *Chicago's Puerto Rican Story,* see http://www .youtube.com/watch?v=OuwbJRz1hqk.

17. Also in 2008, Chicago Puerto Rican resident artist José Pellot and Chicago Brazilian Henrique Cirne-Lima codirected a short film, *Rice, Blood and Hot Sauce,* about the daily life of some retired Puerto Ricans, who pass their days playing dominoes next to one of the iron flags in Humboldt Park. Two years later, the same filmmakers completed a film, *I'm the queen,* on Chicago Rican transgender queen contestants, which has been shown at the University of Chicago and at El Local in Santurce, Puerto Rico, as well as at the Chicago Latino Film Festival in April 2011 (Baerga 2011).

Chapter 5. Carmen Pursifull:
Dancing from New York to Anglo-Illinois

1. Pursifull, in her answers to the questionnaire I sent and she answered in 1985. Unless otherwise indicated, quotations of Pursifull are from this source.

2. In existence for several years before Pursifull joined in the late 1970s, the group is somehow affiliated with the Channing-Murray Foundation of the Unitarian-Universalist Campus Center at UIUC. For further information, the reader may e-mail channing-murray@ prairienet.org. The group holds Monday evening poetry readings at the Campus Center and also is affiliated with a vegetarian restaurant.

3. Since her partnership with Dr. Smith, Pursifull has cowritten fifty-six of her more than 550 poems that have been published in Great Britain and the United States. The poems written with Smith have been published in two volumes by Hawk Productions Press, which she and he seem to run. The first volume, *Brimmed Hat with Flowers,* a collection of "free verse," appeared in 2000; the second, *World of Wet,* appeared in 2002. This coproduction with Smith stands outside the scope of this chapter, which has been updated many times since its initial drafting in 1988.

4. In some of my comments on specific poems, I have drawn on a letter to Pursifull written by Red Herring author Olivia Diamond on August 4, 1986. All poems in this section of the paper are from *Carmen by Moonlight,* referred to as *CBM.*

5. Throughout this section, page numbers refer to Pursifull's *Manhattan Memories,* indicated as *MM.*

6. See my comments on Clementina Souchet in chapter 4. In turning in her husband, Souchet also did it "her way." This Italianate Sinatra theme, the personal dimension of *El arte de bregar,* is sometimes seen as the quintessential New York world view, but in this book must be seen in relation to the diasporican version of the coloniality of power (see notes 2 and 5 above). A sexist joke current in Chicago's Puerto Rican community, which I'm sometimes credited or rather slandered as fabricating, goes something like this: Question: "Why haven't Puerto Ricans won their independence?" Answer: "Because their women have won it house by house, day by day." The joke of course refers to Puerto Rican women's assertiveness and feistiness, but also to wounded male egos. The sad side of things is that even among that small sector of women who have found and did it their way, the results have not led to a dispelling of overall Puerto Rican problematics.

Chapter 6. Cuban–Puerto Rican Relations
and Final Projections

1. Throughout this essay, citations from Barnet and his *La vida real* are my translations from the original Spanish.

2. Literally, "Al puertorriqueño se han hecho muchas trastadas en este país."

Bibliography

Acosta, Iván. *El Super: Tragi-comedia.* Miami: Ediciones Universal, 1982.

Acosta-Belén, Edna. "Conversations with Nicholasa Mohr." In *Revista Chicano-Riqueña* 8.2 (1980): 35–41.

———. "The Literature of the Puerto Rican Minority in the United States." *ADE Bulletin* no. 91 (Winter 1988): 56–62. Updated version of an article with same name published in *Bilingual Review/Revista bilingüe* 5.1–2 (1978): 107–16. Republished with revisions in A. LaVonne Brown Ruoff and Jerry W. Ward, eds., *Redefining American Literary History* (New York: MLA, 1990), 373–78.

———. "Beyond Island Boundaries: Ethnicity, Gender, and Cultural Revitalization in Nuyorican Literature." In *Callaloo* 15 (1992): 979–98.

———. "The Building of a Community: Puerto Rican Writers and Activists in New York City (1890–1960)." In Gutiérrez and Padilla, eds., 1994, 179–95.

——— and Jean-Philippe Abraham, eds. "Encuentro con Miguel Barnet." In *Hispanofila* 35, no. 2 (1992): 101–12.

——— and Carlos E. Santiago. "Merging Borders: The Remapping of America." In *Latino Review of Books* 1 (1995): 1–12.

——— and Carlos E. Santiago. *Puerto Ricans in the United States: A Contemporary Portrait.* Boulder, Colo.: Lynne Rienner Publishers, 2006.

Acuña, Rodolfo. *Popi.* Review of film in *La Voz de Aztlán,* vol. 3, issue 10. www.aztlan .com. n.d.

Agüeros, Jack. *Correspondence between the Stonehaulers.* Brooklyn, N.Y.: Hanging Loose Press, 1991.

———. *"Dominoes" and Other Stories from the Puerto Rican.* Willimantic, Conn.: Curbstone, 1993.

———. *Sonnets from the Puerto Rican.* Brooklyn, N.Y.: Hanging Loose Press, 1996.

———. *Lord, Is This a Psalm?* Brooklyn, N.Y.: Hanging Loose Press, 2002.

Alarcón, Norma. "An Interview with Miguel Piñero." In *Revista Chicano-Riqueña* 2.4 (1974): 55–57.

Algarín, Miguel. "Introduction." In Algarín and Piñero, eds., 1975.

———. *Mongo Affair.* Houston: Arte Público Press, 1978.

———. *On Call*. Houston: Arte Público Press, 1980.

———. "Nuyorican Literature." In *MELUS* 8.2 (1981): 89–92.

———. *Body Bee Calling from the Twenty-first Century*. Houston: Arte Público Press, 1982.

———. *Time's Now/Ya es tiempo*. Houston: Arte Público Press, 1985.

———. *Love is Hard Work: Memorias de Loisaida/Poems*. New York: Simon and Shuster, 1997.

——— and Tato Laviera. *Olú Clemente*. In Kanellos and Huerta, eds., 1979, 151–71.

——— and Miguel Piñero, eds. *Nuyorican Poetry: An Anthology of Puerto Rican Words and Feelings*. New York: William Morrow, 1975.

——— and Lois Griffith, eds. *Action: the Nuyorican Poets Cafe Theater Festival*. New York: H. Holt, 1994.

——— and Bob Holman, eds. *Aloud: Voices from the Nuyorican Poets Café*. New York: Simon & Schuster, 1997.

Álvaréz, Julia. *In the Time of the Butterflies*. Chapel Hill, N.C.: Algonquin Books, 1994.

Ambert, Alba. *A Perfect Silence*. Houston: Arte Público Press, 1995. Trans. as *Porque hay silencio*. Arte Público, 2005–2006.

———. *The Eighth Continent and Other Stories*. Houston: Arte Público Press, 1997.

———. *Alphabets of Seeds*. London: Mango Publishing, 2002.

Antush, John, ed. *Recent Puerto Rican Theater: Five Plays from New York*. Houston: Arte Público Press, 1991.

———, ed. *Nuestro New York: An Anthology of Puerto Rican Plays*. New York: Mentor, 1994.

Aparicio, Frances. "Tato Laviera y Miguel Algarín: Hacia una poética bilingüe." In *Centro de Estudios Puertorriqueños Bulletin* 2.3. (1988a): 7–13, 86–96.

———. "*La Vida es un Spanglish Disparatero*: Bilinguism in Nuyorican Poetry." In Fabre, ed., 1988b, 43–58.

———. "Salsa, Maracas, and Baile: Latin Popular Music in the Poetry of Victor Hernández Cruz." In *MELUS* 16.1 (1989–90): 43–58.

———. "Language on Language: Metalinguistic Discourse in the Betrayal of US Latinos." In *Latino Studies Journal* 2.2 (1991): 58–74.

———. *Listening to Salsa: Gender, Latin Popular Music, and Puerto Rican Cultures*. Middleton, Conn.: Wesleyan University Press, 1998.

———. "Las migraciones de la escritura. Los espacios de la literatura puertorriqueña estadounidense." In Díaz and Zimmerman 2001, 291–315.

———. "Jennifer as Selena: Rethinking Latinidad in Media and Popular Culture." In *Latino Studies* 1, no. 1 (March 2003): 90–105.

——— and Susana Chávez-Silverman, eds. *Tropicalizations: Transcultural Representations of Latinidad*. Hanover, New Hampshire: Dartmouth College Press/ University Press of New England, 1997.

Arocho, Eduardo. *Poems Behind the Máscara*. Chicago, self-published, 2002.

———. *Paseo Boricua Renaissance*. Chicago, self-published, 2003.

———. *The Fourth Tassel*. Chicago, self-published, 2006.

Arrarás, María Celeste. *Selena's Secret: The Revealing Story Behind Her Tragic Death*. New York: Simon & Schuster, 1997.

Arrillaga, María. *Mañana Valentina*. San Juan: Instituto de Cultura Puertorriqueña, 1996.

Arroyo, Rane. *The Singing Shark*. Tempe, Ariz.: Bilingual Press, 1996.

———. "USA: A Writer of Color Rethinks the Chicago Renaissance." Ph.D. diss., University of Pittsburgh, 1997.

———. *Pale Ramón*. Cambridge, Mass.: Zoland Books, 1998.

———. *Home Movies of Narcissus: Poems*. Tucson: University of Arizona Press, 2002.

———. *How to Name a Hurricane*. Tucson: University of Arizona Press, 2005a.

———. *The Portable Famine: Poetry*. Kansas City: BkMk Press, 2005b.

Asya, Ferdâ. "Anarchism in the Work of Aurora Levins Morales." In Torres-Padilla and Rivera, eds., 2008, 107–24.

Augenbraum, Harold, ed. *Latinos in English: A Selected Bibliography of Latino Fiction Writers of the United States*. New York: Mercantile Lib., 1992.

——— and Ilan Stavans, ed. *Growing Up Latino: Memories and Stories*. Boston: Houghton, 1993.

Ayala, César, and Rafael Bernabe. *Puerto Rico in the American Century. A History since 1898*. Chapel Hill: University of North Carolina Press, 2007.

Ayala, Naomi. *Wild Animals on the Moon*. Willimantic, Conn.: Curbstone Press, 1997.

Babín, María Teresa. *Panorama de la cultura puertorriqueña*. New York: Las Américas, 1958.

———. "The Path and the Voice." In Babín and Steiner 1974, xi–xvi.

——— and Stan Steiner, eds. *Borinquen: An Anthology of Puerto Rican Literature*. New York: Knopf, 1974.

Baerga, Vanesa. "Documentan a las reinas del Paseo Boricua." *Claridad* 3 (9 de marzo, 2011): 15a.

Barillas, William. *Midwest Latino Writers*. Urbana: University of Illinois Press, forthcoming.

Barnet, Miguel. "La novela testimonio: socio-literatura" (1969). In Barnet 1979, 25–50.

———. *La canción de Rachel*. Barcelona: Editorial Laia, 1979.

———. *La fuente viva*. La Habana: Editorial Letras Cubanas, 1983.

———. *La vida real: novela*. La Habana: Editorial Letras Cubanas, 1986.

———. *Afro-Cuban Religions*. Princeton, N.J.: Markus Wiener Publishers/Kingston Jamaica: Ian Randle Publishers, 2001.

———, ed. *The Autobiography of a Runaway Slave, Esteban Montejo*. New York: Vintage Books, 1973.

Barradas, Efraín. Review of *Street Poetry and Other Poems*, by Jesús Papoleto Meléndez. In *Sin nombre* 5.1 (1974): 85–87.

———. "De lejos en sueños verla . . . : Visión mítica de Puerto Rico en la poesía neoyorrican." In *Revista Chicano-Riqueña* 7.3 (1979a): 46–56.

———. "Puerto Rico acá, Puerto Rico allá." In *Revista Chicano-Riqueña* 8.2 (1980): 43–49.

———. "Introducción." In Barradas and Rodríguez, eds., 1981, 11–30.

———. "Pedro Pietri, narrador." In *Revista Chicano-Riqueña* 9.4 (1981): 66–70.

———. "Conciencia feminina, conciencia social: La voz poética de Sandra María Esteves." In *Third Woman* 1.2 (1982b): 31–34.

———. Review of *The Nuyorican Experience: Literature of the Puerto Rican Minority*, by Eugene Mohr. In *Revista Chicano-Riqueña* 12.1 (1984): 76–78.

———. "Literatura puertorriqueña en los Estados Unidos o cómo, con un poco de voluntad hasta Shakespeare puede llegar a ser boricua." In *Brújula/Compass: Boletín del Instituto de Escritores Latinoamericanos* 7–8 (1990): 20–22.

———. "Mira, mira, mira: Julio Sánchez, pintor neorrican." In *Plástica* (September 1993): 37–49.

———. "How to Read Bernardo Vega." In Torre, Rodríguez Vecchini, and Burgos 1994, 313–28.

———. *Partes de un todo: Ensayos y notas sobre literatura puertorriqueña en los Estados Unidos.* San Juan: Editorial de la Universidad de Puerto Rico, 1998.

——— and Rafael Rodríguez, eds. *Herejes y mitificadores: Muestra de poesía puertorriqueña en los Estados Unidos.* Río Piedras, P.R.: Huracán, 1981.

Barreto, Lefty (Manuel). *Nobody's Hero.* New York: New American Library, 1977.

Barry, John, ed. *Voces en el viento: Nuevas ficciones desde Chicago.* Chicago: Editorial Esperante, 1999.

Barszewska Marshall, Joanna. "Translating 'Home' in the Work of Judith Ortiz Cofer." In Torres-Padilla and Rivera, eds., 2008, 256–73.

Bauman, Zygmunt. *Liquid Modernity.* Cambridge, U.K.: Polity Press, 2000.

Becker, Carol, ed. *The Subversive Imagination: Artists, Society, and Social Responsibility.* New York: Routledge, 1994.

Bedoya, Cardenio, Flavia Belpoliti, and Marc Zimmerman, eds. *Orbis/Urbis Latino: Los "Hispanos" en las ciudades de los estados unidos.* Houston: LACASA, 2008.

Bejel, Emilio: "Miguel Barnet." In *Hispanoamérica* 29 (1981): 41–47.

Belpré, Pura. *Firefly Summer.* Houston: Arte Público Press, 1996.

Benítez, Sandra. *A Place Where the Sea Remembers.* New York: Simon & Schuster, 1993.

———. *Bitter Grounds.* New York: Hyperion, 1997.

———. *The Weight of All Things.* New York: Hyperion, 2000.

———. *The Night of the Radishes.* New York: Theia, 2003.

———. *Bag Lady: A Memoir of Illness and Recovery.* Forthcoming.

Benítez-Rojo, Antonio. *The Repeating Island.* Durham, N.C.: Duke University Press, 1999. New version of *La isla que se repite.* Hanover, N.H.: Ediciones del Norte, 1989.

Benmayor, Rina. "Getting Home Alive: The Politics of Multiple Identity." In *Americas Review* 17.3–4 (1989): 10–17.

Bergmann, Emilie, and Paul Julian Smith, eds. *Queer Readings, Hispanic Writings.* Durham, N.C.: Duke University Press, 1995.

Beverley, John. *Against Literature.* Minneapolis: University of Minnesota Press, 1993.

Binder, Wolfgang. "An Interview with Piri Thomas." In *Minority Voices* 4.1 (1980): 63–78.

———. "'A Midnight Reality': Puerto Rican Poetry in New York, a Poetry of Dreams." In Fabre, ed., 1988, 22–32.

Black, Timothy. *When a Heart Turns Rock Solid: The Lives of Three Puerto Rican Brothers on and off the Streets.* New York: Pantheon Books, 2009.

Bourgois, Philippe. *In Search of Respect: Selling Crack in El Barrio.* New York: Cambridge University Press, 1995.

Braschi, Giannina. *The Empire of Dreams.* Introduction by Alice Ostriker. New Haven,

Conn.: Yale University Press, 1994. Trans. of *El imperio de los sueños*. Barcelona: Anthropos, 1988.

———. *Yo-Yo Boing!* Introduction by Doris Sommer. Pittsburgh: Latin American Literary Review Press, 1998.

Bruce-Novoa, Juan. *RetroSpace*. Houston: Arte Público Press, 1990.

———. "Judith Ortiz Cofer's Ritual of Movement." In *Americas Review* 19.3–4 (1991): 88–100.

Burgos, Julia de. *Song of the Simple Truth: obra completa poética/The Complete Poems*. Willimantic, Conn.: Curbstone Press, 1997.

Burgos, William. "Puerto Rican Literature in a New Clave: *Notes on the Emergence of DiaspoRican*." In Torres-Padilla and Rivera, eds., 2008, 125–42.

Caballero, Pedro. *Paca antillana: Novela pedagógica puertorriqueña*. New York: F. Mayans, 1931.

Cañas, Dionisio. *El Poeta y la Ciudad. Nueva York y los escritores hispanos*. Madrid: Editorial Cátedra, 1994.

Capetillo, Luisa. *Amor y anarquía: Los escritos de Luisa Capetillo*, ed. Julio Ramos. Río Piedras, P.R.: Ediciones Huracán, 1992.

———. *A Nation of Women: An Early Feminist Speaks Out/Mi opinión sobre las libertades, derechos y deberes de la mujer*. Introduction by Félix V. Matos Rodríguez. Houston: Arte Público Press, 2004.

Cárdenas, Brenda, and Johanny Vásquez, eds. *Between the Heart and the Land/Entre el corazón y la tierra: Women Poets from the Midwest*. Chicago: MARCH/Abrazo Press, 2001.

Carrero, Jaime. *Jet Neorriqueño: Neo-Rican Jet Liner*. San Germán, P.R.: Universidad Interamericana, 1964.

———. *Flag Inside, Capitan F4C, Pipo subway no save reir, El caballo de ward*. Río Piedras, P.R.: Ediciones Puerto Rico, 1966.

———. *Raquel no tiene un mensaje*. Río Piedras, P.R.: Ediciones, 1970.

———. *Los nombres*. Río Piedras, P.R.: Editorial Universitaria, Universidad de Puerto Rico, 1972.

———. *El hombre que no sudaba*. Houston: Arte Público Press, 1982.

——— and Robert F. Muckley. *Notes on Neorican Seminar*. San Germán, P.R.: Interamerican University, 1972.

Castillo, Ana. *My Father was a Toltec*. Goleta, Calif.: West End Press, 1988.

Casuso, Jorge, Achy Obejas, and Billy Zayas. *Carnicería Rodríguez*, Act I. In *Ecos: A Latino Journal of People's Culture and Literature*. Chicago: University of Illinois Press, 1983, 29–40.

Centro del Estudios puertorriqueños 1, no. 2 (Fall 2001). http://www.centropr.org/journal/jrnal24.html.

Certeau, Michel de. *The Practice of Everyday Life*. Berkeley: University of California Press, 1984.

Chavez, Linda. *Out of the Barrio: Toward a New Politics of Hispanic Assimilation*. New York: Basic Books, 1991.

Chevigny, Bell G., and Gari Laguardia, eds. *Latin American Literature: Reinventing the Americas*. New York: Cambridge University Press, 1986.

Cintrón, Humberto. *Frankie Cristo*. New York: Taino, 1972.

Cintrón, Ralph. *Angel's Town: Chero Ways, Gang Life, and Rhetorics of the Everyday*. Boston: Beacon Press, 1997.

Cirne-Lima, Henrique, and José Pellot. *I'm the Queen* (film). 2010.

———. *Rice, Blood and Hot Sauce*, described by Baerga, 2011, 15.

Cisneros, Sandra. *My Wicked, Wicked Ways*. Bloomington, Ind.: Third Woman Press, 1987.

———. *The House on Mango Street*. Houston: Arte Público Press, 1988.

Clarke, Gerard P. Review of *La Carreta Made a U-Turn*, by Tato Laviera. In *MELUS* 8.1 (1981): 80–81.

Colón, Adolfo. *Cantos de Seboruco*. Chicago: Editorial El Coquí, 1989.

Colón, Jesús. *A Puerto Rican in New York and Other Sketches*. New York: Mainstream Publishers, 1961. Reprint, New York: International Publishers, 1982.

———. *"The Way It Was" and Other Writings*. Edna Acosta-Belén and Virginia Sánchez Korrol, eds. Houston: Arte Público Press, 1993.

———. *Lo que el pueblo me dice: Crónicas de la colonia puertorriqueña en Nueva York*. Houston: Arte Público Press, 2001.

Colón López, Joaquín. *Pioneros Puertorriqueños en Nueva York: 1917–1947*. Houston: Arte Público Press, 2002.

Cortés, Felix, Angel Falcón, and Juan Flores. "The Cultural Expression of Puerto Ricans in New York City: A Theoretical Perspective and Critical Review." In *Latin American Perspectives* 3.3 (1976): 117–50.

Cortés, Lydia. *Lust for Lust*. New York: Ten Pell Books, 2002.

Cortina, Rodolfo, and Alberto Moncada, eds. *Hispanos en los Estados Unidos*. Madrid: Instituto de Cooperación Iberoamericana, 1988.

Costa, Marithelma, "¿Y qué dicen los escritores neorriqueños sobre el idioma, la literatura y la identidad nacional?" In *La revista del Centro de Estudios Avanzados de Puerto Rico y el Caribe* 9 (1989): 69–73.

Cotto Thorner, Guillermo. *Trópico en Manhattan*. New York: Americas, 1959.

Cruz, Migdalia. *"Telling Tales": A Study Guide from Gale's "Drama for Students" (vol. 19, chapter 11)*. Electronic book text 10.1223/GALFSDFS0000286. Detroit: Gale, 2004.

Cruz, Nicky. *The Lonely Now*. Plainfield, N.J.: Logos, 1971.

——— and Jamie Buckingham. *Run, Baby, Run*. Plainfield, N.J.: Logos, 1968.

Cruz-Malavé, Arnaldo. "Teaching Puerto Rican Authors: Identity and Modernization in Nuyorican Texts." In *Multicultural Literature: Part IV*. *ADE Bulletin* no. 91 (Winter 1988): 45–51.

———. "Para virar el macho: La autobiografía como subversión en la cuentística de Manuel Ramos Otero." In *Revista iberoamericana* 162–63 (1993): 239–63.

———. "'What a Tangled Web . . . !': Masculinidad y abyección en la literaura puertorriqueña de los Estados Unidos." In *Postdata* (1995): 76–83.

———. "Towards an Art of Transvestism: Colonialism and Homosexuality in Puerto Rican Literature.¿Entiendes?" In Bergmann and Smith, eds., 1995, 137–67.

Daly-Heyck, Denis Lynn, ed. *Barrios and Borderlands: Culture of Latinos and Latinas in the U.S.* New York: Routledge, 1994.

Dávila, Arlene. *Sponsored Identities: Cultural Politics in Puerto Rico.* Philadelphia: Temple University Press, 1997.

———. *Latinos, Inc.: The Marketing and Making of a People.* Berkeley: University of California Press, 2001.

———. *Barrio Dreams: Puerto Ricans, Latinos, and the Neoliberal City.* Berkeley: University of California Press, 2004.

Daydí-Tolson, Santiago. *"Tropicalization:* In Search of Poetic Language." In *Bilingual Review/Revista bilingüe* 7.1 (1979): 94–96.

———. "The Right to Belong: A Critic's View of Puerto Rican Poetry in the United States." In *Bilingual Review/Revista bilingüe* 10.1 (1983): 81–86.

De Genova, Nicholas. *Working the Boundaries: Race, Space, and "Illegality" in Mexican Chicago.* Durham, N.C.: Duke University Press, 2005.

——— and Ana Y. Ramos-Zayas. *Latino Crossings: Mexicans, Puerto Ricans, and the Politics of Race and Citizenship.* New York: Routledge, 2003.

DeGuzmán, María. "The Already Browned Skin Of 'American' Modernism: Rane Arroyo's *Pale Ramón." Midwestern Miscellany* 30 (Fall 2002): xx.

de la Campa, Román. "En la utopía redentora del lenguaje: Pedro Pietri y Miguel Algarín." In *Americas Review* 16.2 (1988): 49–67.

de Monteflores, Carmen. *Singing Softly/Cantando bajito.* San Francisco: Spinsters/Aunt Lute, 1989.

Del Valle, Tony. "Voices." In *West Side Stories,* ed. George Bailey. Chicago: City Stoop Press, 1992, 11–22.

———. *Written Literacy Features of Three Puerto Rican Family Networks in Chicago: An Ethnographic Study.* Lewiston, N.Y.: E. Mellen Press, 2002.

———. "Cadenas," and "Cuatro de Julio 2002." In *Contratiempo,* ed. Febronio Zataraín, vol. 41, 2006, 18.

———. "Letter" and "Cathedral." *The Poetry Magazine,* 25th Anniversary Edition. Ed. Juanita Torrence-Thompson, in *Mobius* 22 (2007): 6 and 13.

———. "Sugarcane: a Prose Poem." *South Loop Review* (2009): 70–72.

Diamond, Olivia. Letter to Carmen Pursifull. August 4, 1986.

Díaz, Luis Felipe, and Marc Zimmerman. *Globalización, Nación, Postmodernidad (Estudios culturales puertorriqueños).* San Juan: LACASA, 2001.

Díaz Quiñones, Arcadio. *La memoria rota.* Río Piedras, P.R.: Huracán, 1993.

———. *El arte de bregar.* San Juan: Ediciones Callejón, 2000.

Díaz Valcárcel, Emilio. *Schemes in the Month of March.* New York: Bilingual, 1979a.

———. *Harlem todos los días.* Río Piedras, P.R.: Huracán, 1979b.

Domínguez Miguela, Antonia. "Literary Tropicalizations of the Barrio: Ernesto Quinonez's *Bodega Dreams* and Ed Vega's *Mendoza's Dreams."* In Torres-Padilla and Rivera, eds., 2008, 165–83.

Duany, Jorge. *The Puerto Rican Nation on the Move. Identities on the Island and in the United States.* Chapel Hill: University of North Carolina Press, 2004.

———. "The Rough Edges of Puerto Rican Identities." In *Latin American Research Review* 40, no. 3 (2005): 177–90.

————. *La nación en vaivén*. San Juan: Ediciones Callejón, 2010.

Duchesne Winter, Juan, ed. "Puerto Rico Caribe: Zonas poéticas del trauma." *Revista Iberoamericana* (University of Pittsburgh), vol. 5, no. 229 (October-December 2009).

Enck-Wanzer, Darrel, ed. *The Young Lords: A Reader*. New York: New York University Press, 2010.

Escobar, Elizam. *Discurso a la noche y Sonia Semenovna*. New York, 1985.

————. "Havana Biennial and Art in Latin America." In *Panic* 3 (1988): 25–38.

————. "The Feigned Battle: The Echo-Narcissism of Transfixion." In Piazza and Zimmerman, eds., 1998, 191–213.

————. *Los ensayos del artificiero: más allá de lo político-directo y el post-modernismo. (1983–1993)*. Cayey / San Juan: Sopas de Letras Editores / Isla Negra Editores, 1999.

————. *Elizam Escobar: Paisajes y pasajes del regreso. Views and Passages of the Return*. Ponce, P.R.: Museo de Arte de Ponce, 2002a.

————. *Dobles de Elizam Escobar: con un interensayo por Joserramón Melendes*. Santurce, P.R.: Libros Libres, 2002b.

————. "Biography." In Escobar, ed., n.p., n.d., 311.

————, ed. *Elizam Escobar: Art as an Act of Liberation*. Chicago: n.p., n.d.

————, et al., eds. *Disparities and Connections: The Excluded on Postmodernism*. Chicago: Axe Street Gallery, 1991.

Espada, Martín. *The Immigrant Iceboy's Bolero*. Madison, Wisc.: GhostPony Press, 1987.

————. *Trumpets from the Islands of their Eviction*. Tempe, Ariz.: Bilingual Press/Editorial Bilingüe. Expanded Edition, 1988.

————. *Rebellion Is the Circle of a Lover's Hands / Rebelión es el giro de manos del amante*. Willimantic, Conn.: Curbstone Press, 1990.

————. *City of Coughing and Dead Radiators*. New York: W.W. Norton, 1993.

————. *Imagine the Angels of Bread: Poems*. New York: W.W. Norton, 1996.

————. *Zapata's Disciple: Essays*. Cambridge, Mass.: South End Press, 1998.

————. *Alabanza: New and Selected Poems, 1982–2002*. New York: W.W. Norton, 2003.

Esteves, Sandra María. *Yerba Buena*. New York: Greenfield Review, 1982.

————. *Tropical Rains: A Bilingual Downpour*. Houston: Arte Público Press, 1984.

————. *Bluestown Mockingbird Mambo*. Houston: Arte Público Press, 1990.

Fabre, Genvieve, ed. *European Perspectives on Hispanic Literature of the United States*. Houston: Arte Público Press, 1988.

Fernández, Carole. *Sleep of the Innocents*. Houston: Arte Público Press, 1991.

Fernández, Roberta, ed. In *Other Words: Literature by Latinas of the United States*. Houston: Arte Público Press, 1994.

Fernández Fragoso, Victor. *Ser islas/Being Islands*. New York: Viaje, 1976.

Fernández Olmos, Margarite. "From the Metropolis: Puerto Rican Women Poets and the Immigration Experience." In *Third Woman* 1.2 (1982): 40–51.

————. *Sobre la literatura puertorriqueña de aquí y de allá: aproximaciones feministas*. Santo Domingo: Editora Alfa y Omega, 1989.

————. "Growing Up *Puertorriqueñas:* The Feminist Bildungsroman and the Novels of Nicholasa Mohr and Magali García Ramis." In *Centro de Estudios Puertorriqueños Bulletin* 2.7 (1989–1990): 56–73.

Ferré, Rosario. *The House on the Lagoon*. New York: Harper, 1995.

Fiet, Lowell, and Janette Becerra. *Caribe 2000: Definiciones, identidades y culturas regionales y/o nacionales*. San Juan: Universidad de Puerto Rico, 1997.

Figueroa, José Angel. *East One Hundredth Street*. Detroit: Broadside, 1973.

———. *Unknown Poets from the Full-Time Jungle*. New York: Noo Jork, 1975.

———. *Noo Jork*. San Juan: Instituto de Cultura Puertorriqueña, 1981.

Figueroa, Víctor. "Discordant Differences: Stratregic Puerto Ricanness in Pedro Pietri's *Puerto Rican Obituary*." In Padilla and Rivera, eds., 2008, 184–200.

Flores, Juan. "Back down These Mean Streets: Introducing Nicholasa Mohr and Louis Reyes Rivera." In *Revista Chicano-Riqueña* 8.2 (1980): 51–56.

———. "Puerto Rican Literature in the United States: Stages and Perspectives." In *ADE Bulletin* no. 91 (Winter 1988.): 39–44.

———. *Divided Borders: Essays on Puerto Rican Identity*. Houston: Arte Público Press, 1993.

———. *From Bomba to Hip-hop: Puerto Rican culture and Latino identity*. New York: Columbia University Press, 2000.

———. "Life off the Hyphen." In Laó-Montes and Dávila, eds., 2001, 185–206.

———, John Attinasi, and Pedro Pedraza. "*La Carreta Made a U-Turn*: Puerto Rican Language and Culture in the United States." In *Daedalus* 110.2 (1982): 193–213.

———, ed. *Divided Arrival: Narratives of the Puerto Rican Migration, 1920–1950*. Princeton, N.J.: Markus Wiener Publishers, 2003.

Flores-González, Nilda. *School Kids/Street Kids: Identity Development in Latino Students*. New York: Teachers College Press, 2002.

Foster, David, ed. *Sourcebook of Hispanic Culture in the United States*. Chicago: American Library Association, 1982.

———, ed. *U.S. Puerto Rican Literature: A Bibliography of Secondary Sources*. Westport, Conn.: Greenwood, 1983.

Fritz, Sonia. *América* (film). 2011.

Fusco, Coco. "Signs of Transition: 80's Art From Cuba." In Fusco, ed., 1988, 1.

———, ed. *Signs of Transition Exhibition Catalogue*. New York: Museum of Contemporary Hispanic Art, 1988.

Gallardo, Edward. *Simpson Street and Other Plays*. Houston: Arte Público Press, 1990.

García, Cristina. *Dreaming in Cuban*. New York: Knopf, 1992.

García Cuevas, Eugenio de J. *Lengua en tiempo: sabores buenos, malos y feos*. San Juan and Hato Rey, P.R.: Isla Negra, 2006.

Gavin, Larry. "The World of Piri Thomas." In *Crisis* 82.6 (1975): 196–203.

Geertz, Clifford. *The Interpretation of Cultures: Selected Essays*. New York: Basic Books, 1973.

Gelpí, Juan. "Historia y literatura en *Página en blanco y staccato* de Manuel Ramos Otero." In Díaz and Zimmerman 2001, 281–90.

Gil, Carlos. "Elizam Escobar o la pérdida de la utopía (Reflexiones en torno a un sentimiento plano)." In Rivera Nieves and Gil, eds., 1995, 228–41.

Glasser, Ruth. *My Music Is My Flag: Puerto Rican Musicians and their New York Communities, 1917–1940*. Berkeley: University of California Press, 1995.

Goldman, Shifra M. "Living on the Fifth Floor of the Four-Floor Country." In Goldman 1994, 433–34.

————. *Dimensions of the Americas: Art and Social Change in Latin America and the United States*. Chicago: University of Chicago Press, 1994.

González, José Luis. *Paisa, un relato de la emigración*. D.F., Mexico: Fondo de Cultura, 1950.

————. *Mambrú se fue a la guerra*. D.F., México: Editorial Joaquín Mortiz, S.A., 1972.

————. *En Nueva York y otras desgracias*. D.F., México: Siglo XXI, 1973.

————. *Literatura y sociedad en PR: de los cronistas de indias a la generación del 98*. D.F., México: Fondo de Cultura Económica, 1976.

————. *El país de cuatro pisos y otros ensayos*. Río Piedras, P.R.: Ediciones Huracán, 1980.

González, Rigoberto. Review of Rane Arroyo, *Home Movies of Narcissus,* "Expounding on Myth." *El Paso Times,* September 29, 2002.

González Echevarría, Roberto: "*Biografía de un cimarrón* and the Novel of the Cuban Revolution." In *Novel: A Forum on Fiction* 3 (1980): 249–63.

González-Wippler, Migene. *Santería: The Religion, Faith, Rites, Magic*. St. Paul, Minn.: Llewellyn Publications, 1994.

Gordills, Yanis. "Island and Continental Puerto Rican Literature: Cross-Cultural and Intertextual Considerations." *Multicultural Literature,* in *ADE Bulletin* 91 (Winter 1988), 52–55.

Grody, Arienna. "Puerto Rican Nationalism and the Drift Towards Statehood." *Council on Hemispheric Affairs (COHA)*. At http://www.coha.org/2009/07/puerto-rican-nationalism-and-the-drift-towards-statehood/, August 2009.

Grosfoguel, Ramón. *Colonial Subjects: Puerto Ricans in a Global Perspective*. Berkeley: University of California Press, 2003.

———— and Chloé S. Geras. "Latino Caribbean Diasporas in New York." In Laó and Dávila, eds., 2001, 97–118.

Gugelberger, Georg M., ed. *The Real thing: Testimonial Discourse and Latin America*. Durham, N.C.: Duke University Press, 1996.

Gutiérrez, Ramón, and Genaro Padilla, eds. *Recovering the US Hispanic Heritage*. Houston: Arte Público Press, 1994.

Haslip-Viera, Gabriel, Félix V. Matos Rodríguez, and Angelo Falcón, eds. *Boricuas in Gotham: Puerto Ricans in the Making of New York City*. Princeton, N.J.: M. Wiener Publishers, 2004.

Hernández, Carmen Dolores. *Puerto Rican Voices in English. Interviews with Writers*. Westport, Conn. and London: Praeger, 1997.

Hernández, David. *Despertando*. Chicago: Self-published, 1971.

————. *Collected Words for a Dusty Shelf*. Chicago: Self-published, 1973.

————. *Satin-City Lullaby*. Chicago: Self-published, 1987.

————. *Roof Top Piper*. Chicago: Tía Chucha Press, 1991.

————. *Elvis Is Dead But At Least He's Not Gaining Any Weight*. Chicago: Self-published, 1995.

————. *The Urban Poems*. Chicago: Fractal Edge Press, 2004.

———— and the Street Sounds. *Liquid Thoughts* (vol. 1), and *Immigrants* (vol. 2). Chicago: Street Sounds Poetry/Music Workshop. Cassette tapes. 1988.

Hernández Cruz, Víctor. *Papo got his gun!* New York: Calle Once Publications, 1966.

————. *Snaps*. New York: Random House, 1968.

————. *Mainland*. New York: Random House, 1973.

————. *Tropicalization*. New York: Canon, 1976.

————. *By Lingual Wholes*. San Francisco: Momo's, 1982.

————. *Rhythm, Content, and Flavor: New and Selected Poems*. Houston: Arte Público Press, 1989.

————. *Red Beans*. Minneapolis: Coffee House Press, 1991.

————. *Panoramas*. Minneapolis: Coffee House Press, 1997.

————. *Maracas: New and Selected Poems, 1966–2000*. Minneapolis: Coffee House Press, 2001.

Hickman, Trenton. "The Political Left and the Development of Nurorican Poetry." In Torres-Padilla and Rivera, eds., 2008, 143–61.

Hijuelos, Oscar. *Our House in the Last World*. New York: Persea Books, 1983.

————. *The Mambo Kings Play Songs of Love*. New York: Farrar, Straus, Giroux, 1989.

Hoffer, Bates L. "Sociology by Value Systems: Explication and Some Implications of Two Studies on the Folklore of the Hispanics in the United States." In *Bilingual Review/Revista bilingüe* 9.2 (1982): 172–77.

Horno-Delgado, Asunción, et al., eds. *Breaking Boundaries: Latina Writing and Critical Readings*. Amherst: University of Massachusetts Press, 1989.

Husband, Bertha. "Deep Sea Diver in the Phantom(ly) Country." In Escobar, ed. n.p., n.d.: 22.

Huyke, Juan Bernardo. *Vida escolar: novela*. San Juan: Cantero, Fernández, 1925.

Iglesias, Andreu César, ed. *Memorias de Bernardo Vega*. Rio Piedras, P.R.: Huracán, 1977.

————, ed. *Memoirs of Bernardo Vega*. New York: Monthly Review, 1984.

Irizarry Rodríguez, José M. "Evolving Identities: Early Puerto Rican Writing in the United States and the Search for a New Puertorriqueñidad." In Torres-Padilla and Rivera, eds., 2008, 31–51.

Jiménez, Cha Cha. "The Origins of Puerto Rican Gangs in Chicago," excerpted from an interview by Ralph Cintrón and Erika Rodríguez (June 2002), at http://www.gangresearch.net/ChicagoGangs/younglords/chacha.htm.

Kanellos, Nicolás. "La literatura hispana de los EEUU y el género autobiográfico," *Hispanos en los Estado Unidos*. In Cortina and Moncada, eds., 1988, 219–30.

————. *A History of Hispanic Theatre in the United States: Origins to 1940*. Austin: University of Texas Press, 1990.

————. *The Hispanic American Almanac: A Reference Work on Hispanics in the United States. Second edition*. Detroit: Gale, 1997.

————. *Hispanic Literature in the United States: A Comprehensive Reference*. Westport, Conn.: Greenwood Press, 2005.

———— and Jorge Huerta. "Nuevos Pasos: Chicano and Puerto Rican Drama." In *Revista Chicano-Riqueña* 7.1 (1989): 151–71.

————, ed. *Hispanic Theatre in the United States*. Houston: Arte Público Press, 1984.

————, ed. *Bibliographical Dictionary of Hispanic Literature in the United States: The Literature of Puerto Ricans, Cuban Americans, and Other Hispanic Writers*. New York: Greenwood Press, 1989.

————, ed. *Short Stories by Hispanic Writers of the United States*. Houston: Arte Público Press, 1993.

————and Luis Dávila, eds. "A Decade of Hispanic Literature." In *Revista Chicano-Riqueña* 10.1–2 (1982).

———— and Jorge Huerta, eds. *Nuevos pasos: Chicano and Puerto Rican Drama*. Houston: Arte Público Press, 1989.

————et al., eds. *En otra voz*. Houston: Arte Público Press, 2002a.

————et al., eds. *Herencia: The Anthology of Hispanic Literature of the United States*. Oxford: Oxford University Press, 2002b.

————, ed. *The Greenwood Encyclopedia of Latino Literature*. 3 vols. Westport, Conn. Greenwood Press, 2008.

Keller, Gary, and Francisco Jiménez, eds. *Hispanics in the United States: An Anthology of Creative Literature*. 2 vols. *Bilingual Review*, 1980–82.

Khader, Jamil. "Decolonizing the Commonwealth: A Postcolonial reading of Gloria Vando's *Promesas: Geography of the Impossible*." In *College Literature*, Fall 2003.

Kutzinski, Vera. *Against the American Grain: Myth and History in William Carlos Williams, Jay Wright, and Nicolás Guillén*. Baltimore: Johns Hopkins University Press, 1987.

Labarthe, Pedro Juan. *The Son of Two Nations: The Private Life of a Columbia Student*. New York: Carranza, 1931.

La Fountain-Stokes, Larry. "My Name, Multitudinous Mass." In Manrique with Dorris, ed., 1999, 61–67.

————. *Queer Ricans: Cultures and Sexualities in the Diaspora*. Minneapolis: University of Minnesota Press, 2009.

————. *Uñas pintadas de azul/Blue Fingernails*. Tempe, Ariz.: Bilingual Press/Editorial Bilingüe, 2009.

Laguardia, Gari. "The Can and the Air-Conditioner: Modern Puerto Rican Poetry." In *Bilingual Review/Revista bilingüe* 9.2 (1982): 178–81.

Laguerre, Enrique. *El Laberinto*. New York: Américas, 1959. Trans. *The Labyrinth*. New York: Americas, 1960.

Lane, James B. "Beating the Barrio: Piri Thomas and *Down These Mean Streets*." In *English Journal* 61 (1972): 814–23.

Laó-Montes, Agustín, "Mambo Montage: The Latinization of New York City." In Laó and Dávila, eds., 2001, 1–52.

————. "Niuyol: Urban Regime, Latino Social Movements and Ideologies of Latinidad." In Laó and Dávila, 2001, 119–57.

———— and Arlene Dávila, eds. *Mambo Montage: The Latinization of New York*. New York: Columbia University Press, 2001.

Laviera, Tato. *La Carreta Made a U-Turn*. Gary, Ind.: Arte Público Press, 1979.

————. *Enclave*. Houston: Arte Público Press, 1981.

————. *AmeRican*. Houston: Arte Público Press, 1985.

————. *Mainstream Ethics*. Houston: Arte Público Press, 1988.

————. *Mixturao and Other Poems*. Houston: Arte Público Press, 2008.

Levins Morales, Aurora, and Rosario Morales. *Getting Home Alive*. Ithaca, N.Y.: Firebrand Books, 1986.

————. *Medicine Stories: History, Culture, and the Politics of Integrity*. Cambridge, Mass.: South End Press, 1998a.

————. *Remedios: Stories of Earth and Iron from the History of Puertorriqueñas*. Boston: Beacon Press, 1998b.

Lewis, Oscar. *Five Families; Mexican Case Studies in the Culture of Poverty*. New York: Basic Books, 1959.

————. *The Children of Sánchez, Autobiography of a Mexican Family*. New York: Random House, 1961.

————. *La Vida: A Puerto Rican Family in the Culture of Poverty—San Juan and New York*. New York: Random House, 1966.

————, K. S. Karol, and Carlos Fuentes. *La cultura de la pobreza: Pobreza, burguesía y revolución*. Barcelona: Anagrama, 1972.

————, Ruth M. Lewis, and Susan M. Rigdon. *Living the Revolution: An Oral History of Contemporary Cuba*. Urbana: University of Illinois Press, 1977.

Lewis-Fernández, Roberto. *The Puerto Rican Syndrome*. New York: Other Press, 2003.

Lindstrom, Naomi E. "Cuban and Continental Puerto Rican Literature." In Foster, ed., 1982, 221-45.

Lippard, Lucy R. "On the Horns of Contradiction." In Escobar, ed., n.d., 8–16.

López, Ramón. *Tapices puertorriqueños de Ramón López*. San Juan: Gráfica Metropolitana, 1988.

————. "La cajita roja de Vincent Van Gogh." In López, ed., 1995, 37–38.

————. "Juan Sánchez: La construcción de otra creencia." In *Rican/Structions: Puerto Rican Prisoners of War: Laser Prints by Juan Sánchez*. *Que Ondee Sola* 25, no. 4 (April 1997): 3–4.

————. *Pupil's Works: El proyecto colonial en la escuela pública 1898–1903*. Chicago: n.p., 1998.

————. *Puerto Rico, USA: Historia de un país imaginario y otros ensayos*. Río Piedras, P.R.: Ediciones Huracán, 2000.

————. *El valor histórico de la artesanía puertorriqueña*. San Juan: Instituto de Cultura Puertorriqueña, 2001.

————. *La cultura popular puertorriqueña en Estados Unidos*. San Juan: Instituto de Cultura Puertorriqueña, 2002.

————, ed. *Los tapices de Ramón López*. Chicago: n.p., 1995.

López-Adorno, Pedro, ed. *Papiros de Babel: Antología de la poesía puertorriqueña en Nueva York*. Río Piedras: University of Puerto Rico Press, 1991.

López Torregrosa, Luisita. *The Noise of Infinite Longing: A Memoir of a Family and an Island*. New York: HarperCollins, 2004.

Lugo López, Lourdes. *Poemas que me desnudan y me definan*. Chicago: Editorial El Coquí Publishers, 1992.

Lugo de Puig, Isabel C. "Immigration and Writing: A Woman's Perspective." In *Revista de estudios generales* 10 (1995–96): 87–98.

Luis, William. "The Politics of Memory and Miguel Barnet's *The Autobiography of a Runaway Slave*." In *MLN* 2 (March 1989): 475–91.

————. *Literary Bondage: Slavery in Cuban Narrative*. Austin: University of Texas Press, 1990.

————. *Dance between Two Cultures: Latino Caribbean Literature Written in the United States*. Nashville: Vanderbilt University Press, 1997.

———. *Lunes de Revolución: Literatura y cultura en los primeros años de la Revolución Cubana*. Madrid: Editorial Verbum, 2003.

Maciel, Olivia, ed. *Shards of Light/Astillas de luz*. Chicago: Tía Chucha Press, 1998.

Malavet, Pedro. *America's Colony: The Political and Cultural Conflict between the United States and Puerto Rico*. New York: New York University Press, 2004.

Maldonado-Denis, Manuel. *The Emigration Dialectic: Puerto Rico and the U.S.* New York: International Publishers, 1980.

Manrique, Jaime, with Jesse Dorris, eds. *Bésame Mucho: New Gay Latino Fiction*. New York: Painted Leaf Press, 1999.

Manrique, Manuel. *Island in Harlem*. New York: Day, 1966.

Manrique Cabrera, Francisco. *Historia de la literatura puertorriqueña*. Río Piedras, P.R.: Editorial Cultural, 1969.

Mariposa (Maria Teresa Fernández de Rosario). *Born Broxeña: Poems of Identity, Survival, Love and Freedom*. New York: Bronxeña Books, 2001.

Marqués, René. *La Carreta*. Río Piedras, P.R.: Editorial Cultural, 1955. Trans. *The Oxcart*. New York: Scribner's, 1972.

———. *El puertorriqueño dócil y otros ensayos, 1953–1971*. San Juan: Editorial Cultural, 1993.

Márquez, Roberto. "De Boricuas, jíbara(o)s y jibaristas: Memory, Memoir, and Mimicry." In *Latino Review* 2, no. 1 (Spring 1996): 112–18.

———, ed. *Latin. American. Revolutionary. Poetry/Poesía Revolucionaria. Latinoamericana*. New York: Monthly Review Press, 1974.

———, ed. *Puerto Rican Poetry: An Anthology from Aboriginal to Contemporary Times*. Amherst and Boston: University of Massachusetts Press, 2007.

Marsh Kennedy, Catherine. *Negociaciones culturales: Los intelectuales y el proyecto pedagógica del estado muñocista*. San Juan: Ediciones Callejón, 2009.

Marzán, Julio. *Translations without Originals*. New York: Reed Books, 1986.

———. "Mrs. Williams's William Carlos." In Chevigny and Laguardia, eds., *Latin American Literature: Reinventing the Americas*. New York: Cambridge University Press, 1986, 106-21.

———. *Puerta de Tierra*. San Juan: Editorial de la Universidad de Puerto Rico, 1998.

———, ed. *Inventing a Word: An Anthology of Twentieth-Century Puerto Rican Poetry*. New York: Columbia University Press, 1980.

Matías, Alfredo. "Where are the Latin Poets?" In *Abrazo. Chicago: Movimiento Artístico Chicano*, vol. 2. Reprinted from the *Nosotoros* issue of *Revista Chicano-Riqueña*, 1979.

Matilla, Alfredo. "The Broken English Dream: Poesía puertorriqueña en Nueva York." In Zavala and Rodríguez, eds., *Libertad y crítica en el ensayo político puertorriqueño*, 1975, 427–43.

———. "Algunos aspectos del teatro de Pedro Pietri." In *Confluencia* 5 (1989): 91–97.

———. "El absurdo de la vida y la muerte del trabajador boricua en los Estados Unidos según Pedro Pietri." In *Exégesis* 3.8 (1989): 2–9.

———. "*Rent-a-Coffin:* Las bases conceptuales del teatro de Pedro Pietri." In *Revista del Instituto de Cultura Puertorriqueña* 98 (1991): 43–46.

——— and Iván Silén, eds. *The Puerto Rican Poets*. New York: Bantam, 1972.

McCracken, Ellen. "Latina Narrative and Politics of Signification: Articulation, Antagonism, and Populist Rupture." In *Crítica* 2.2 (1990): 202–7.

Meléndez, Jesús Papoleto. *Street Poetry and Other Poems*. New York: Barlenmir, 1972.

———. *Concertos on Market Street: Poems*. San Diego: Kemetic Images, 1993.

Méndez Ballester, Manuel. *Encrucijada*. San Juan: n.p., 1958.

Mignolo, Walter. *Local Histories, Global Designs: Coloniality, Subaltern Knowledges and Border Thinking*. Princeton, N.J.: Princeton University Press, 2000.

Miller, John. "Hispanic Theatre in New York, 1965–1977." In *Revista Chicano-Riqueña* 6.1 (1977): 40–59.

———. "The Emigrant and the City: Four Puerto Rican Writers." In *MELUS* 5.3 (1978): 82–99.

———. "Nicholasa Mohr: Neorican Writing in Progress." In *Revista/Review Interamericana* 9.4 (1979–80): 543–49.

———. Review of *Nuevos Pasos: Chicano and Puerto Rican Drama*, Nicolas Kanellos and Jorge Huerta, eds. In *MELUS* 6.3 (1979): 99–100.

Mirabel, Nancy Raquel. "No Country But the One We Must Fight For: The Emergence of an Antillean Nation and Community in New York City, 1860–1901." In Laó-Montes and Dávila, eds., 2001, 57–72.

Mohn, Eugene. *The Nuyorican Experience. Literature of the Puerto Rican Minority*. Westport, Conn. and London: Greenwood Press, 1982.

Mohr, Nicholasa. *Nilda*. New York: Harper, 1973; Houston: Arte Público Press, 1986.

———. *El Bronx Remembered: A Novella and Stories*. New York: Harper and Row, 1975; Houston: Arte Público Press, 1986.

———. *In Nueva York*. New York: Dial, 1977; Houston: Arte Público Press, 1988.

———. *Felita*. New York: Dial, 1979; Houston: Arte Público Press, 1988.

———. *Rituals of Survival: A Woman's Portfolio*. Houston: Arte Público Press, 1985.

———. "On Being Authentic." In *Americas Review* 24.3–4 (1986): 106–9.

———. "Puerto Rican Writers in the US, Puerto Rican Writers in PR: A Separation beyond Language: *Testimonio*." In Horno-Delgado et al., eds., 1989, 111–16.

———. "The Journey towards a Common Ground: Struggle and Identity of Hispanics in the United States." In *Americas Review* 18.1 (1990): 81–85.

———. *Growing Up Inside the Sanctuary of My Imagination*. New York: Messner, 1994.

———. *A Matter of Pride and Other Stories*. Houston: Arte Público Press, 1997.

Monclova, Héctor Iván. "Los hilos de la supervivencia." In López, ed., 1995, 17–25.

Monteflores, Carmen de. *Singing Softly/Cantando bajito*. San Francisco: Spinsters/Aunt Lute Book Company, 1989.

Morales, Rodney. *The Speed of Darkness*. Honolulu: Bamboo Ridge Press, 1988.

———. *When the Shark Bites*. Honolulu: University of Hawai'i Press, 2002.

Morales-Díaz, Enrique. "Identity of the 'Diasporican' Homosexual in the Literary Periphery." In Padilla-Torres and Rivera, eds., 2008, 295–312.

Morton, Carlos. "Social Realism on Aston Place: The Latest Piñero Play." In *Revista Chicano-Riqueña* 2.4 (1974): 33–34.

———. *White Heroin Winter*. El Paso, Tex.: One-Eye Press, 1971.

Myers, John. *Minority Voices: Linking Personal Ethnic History and the Sociological Imagination*. Boston: Pearson, 2005.

Naton, Leslie. "Notice of Rane Arroyo," *Pale Ramón*. In *Ohioana Quarterly* 54 (Winter 2000): 316–17.

Negrón-Muntaner, Frances. *Boricua Pop: Puerto Ricans and the Latinization of American Culture*. New York: New York University Press, 2004.

———. *Anatomy of a Smile and Other Poems*. San Juan and Santo Domingo: Isla Negra, 2006.

———, ed. 1994. *Shouting in a Whisper/Los límites del silencio: Poesía latina en Philadelphia*. Santiago, P.R.: Asterión, 1994.

———, ed. *None of the Above: Puerto Ricans in the Global Era*. London and New York: Palgrave/Macmillan, 2007.

——— and Ramón Grosfoguel, eds. *Puerto Rican Jam: Rethinking Colonialism and Nationalism*. Minneapolis: University of Minnesota Press, 1997.

Nieves, Marysol. "Beneath the Surface: Image, Text and Meaning in the Work of Juan Sánchez." In *Rican/Structions: Puerto Rican Prisoners of War: Laser Prints by Juan Sánchez*. *Que Ondee Sola* 25, no. 4 (April 1997): 5–10.

Nosotros: A Collection of Latino Poetry and Graphics from Chicago. 1977. *Revista Chicano-Riqueña*, 5, no. 1 (Winter). (David Hernández, guest editor.)

Obejas, Achy. *Memory Mambo: A Novel*. Pittsburgh: Cleis Press, 1996.

Oboler, Suzanne. *Ethnic Labels, Latino Lives: Identity and the Politics of (Re)presentation in the United States*. Minneapolis: University of Minnesota Press, 1995.

O'Brien, Mark, and Craig Little. *Reimaging America: The Arts of Social Change*. Philadelphia: New Society Publishers, 1990.

Olivieri Albino, Pablo R. *Cuentos*. Seattle: Rincón Cultural, 1995.

Ortega, Eliana. "Poetic Discourse of the Puerto Rican Women in the U.S.: New Voices of Anacaonian Liberation." In Horno-Delgado, et. al., 1989, 122–35.

———. "Sandra María Esteves' Poetic Work: Demythicizing Puerto Rican Poetry in the United States." In Torre, Rodríguez Vecchini, and Burgos, eds., 1994, 329–42.

Ortiz, Altagracia, ed. *Puerto Rican Women and Work: Bridges in Transnational Labor*. Philadelphia: Temple University Press, 1996.

Ortiz, Fernando. *Ensayos etnográficos*. Selección de Miguel Barnet y Angel L. Fernández. La Habana: Editorial de Ciencias Sociales, 1984.

Ortiz Cofer, Judith. *Peregrina*. Golden, Colo.: Riverstone Press, 1986.

———. *Terms of Survival: Poems*. Houston: Arte Público Press, 1987.

———. *The Line of the Sun*. Athens: University of Georgia Press, 1989.

———. *Silent Dancing: A Partial Remembrance of a Puerto Rican Childhood*. Houston: Arte Público Press, 1990.

———. "Speaking in Puerto Rican: An Interview with Judith Ortiz Cofer," with Rafael Ocasio and Rita Ganey. In *Bilingual Review/La revista bilingüe* 17 (1992): 143–46.

———. *The Latin Deli*. Athens: University of Georgia Press, 1993.

———. "A MELUS Interview: Judith Ortiz Cofer," with Edna Acosta-Belén. In *MELUS* 18.3 (1993): 83–97.

———. "The Infinite Variety of the Puerto Rican Reality: An Interview with Judith Ortiz Cofer," with Rafael Ocasio. In *Callaloo* 17 (1994): 730–42.

————. *Reaching for the Mainland and Selected New Poems*. Tempe, Ariz.: Bilingual Press/ Editorial Bilingüe, 1995a.

————. *An Island like You: Stories of the Barrio*. New York: Orchard, 1995b.

————. *The Year of Our Revolution*. Houston: Arte Público Press, 1998.

————. *Woman in Front of the Sun: On Becoming a Writer*. Athens: University of Georgia Press, 2000.

————. *The Meaning of Consuelo*. New York: Farrar, Straus, and Giroux, 2003.

————. *Call Me Maria: A Novel*. New York: Orchard Books, 2004.

————. *A Love Story Beginning in Spanish*. Athens : University of Georgia Press, 2005.

Ortiz Márquez, Maribel. "'Puerto Rican without Apologies': La narrativa de Abraham Rodríguez, Jr." In *Diálogo* (January 1995): 50–51.

————. "Puerto Rican Literature, 1988–96: An Annotated Bibliography." In *ADFL Bulletin* 28, no. 2 (Winter 1997): 49–54.

Ossers-Cabrera, Manuel A. "Pedro Mir, Pedro Pietri y Nicolás Guillén o hay tres países en el mundo." In *Eme-Eme, Estudios Dominicanos* 19 (1991–92): 33–41, 90–91.

Pabón, Carlos. *Nación post-mortem: La ambigüedad de los tiempos*. San Juan: Ediciones Callejón, 2002.

Pacífico, Patricia. "Piri Thomas Talks at the Inter American University." In *Revista/Review Interamericana* 7.4 (1977–78): 666–73.

Padilla, Elena. *Puerto Rican Immigrants in New York and Chicago: A Study in Comparative Assimilation*. M.A. thesis, University of Chicago, 1947.

Padilla, Félix M. *Latino Ethnic Consciousness: The Case of Mexican Americans and Puerto Ricans in Chicago*. Notre Dame: University of Notre Dame Press, 1985.

————. *Puerto Rican Chicago*. Notre Dame: Notre Dame University Press, 1987.

————. *The Gang as an American Enterprise*. New Brunswick, N.J.: Rutgers University Press, 1992.

———— and Lourdes Santiago. *Outside the Wall: A Puerto Rican Woman's Struggle*. New Brunswick, N.J.: Rutgers University Press, 1993.

————, ed. *Handbook of Hispanic Culture in the United States: Sociology*. Houston: Arte Público Press, 1994.

Pagán, Adam. 1997. "Indestructable: The Young Lords Party and the Cultural Politics of Music in the Construction of Diaspo-Rican Identity." Unpublished paper, cited in Valentín Escobar, 2001, 232.

Pantojas-García, Emilio. "The Puerto Rican Paradox: Colonialism Revisited." In *Latin American Research Review* 40, no. 3 (2005): 163–76.

Pérez, Gina M. "Introduction." Special issue on Chicago of the *Centro de Estudios Puertorriqueños Bulletin*, 13.2 (Fall 2001): 4–5.

————. *The Near Northwest Side Story: Migration, Displacement, and Puerto Rican Families*. Berkeley: University of California Press, 2004.

Pérez, Janet. "The Island and Beyond: Literary Space in Puerto Rican Women's Poetry." In *Revista Canadiense de Estudios Hispánicos* 14 (1990): 473–94.

Piazza, Michael. "Three visions of a CENTENNIAL." *Que Ondee Sola* 26, nos. 4–5 (1998): 6–13.

———— and Marc Zimmerman, eds. *New World [Dis]Orders and Peripheral Strains: Specify-*

ing *Cultural Dimensions of Latin American and Latino Studies*. Chicago: MARCH/Abrazo
   Press, 1998.
Piedra, José. "His and Her Panic." In *Dispositio* 16.41 (1991): 71–93.
Pietri, Pedro. *Puerto Rican Obituary*. New York: Monthly Review Press, 1973.
———. *Lost in the Museum of Natural History/Perdido en el Museo de Historia Natural*.
   Río Piedras, P.R.: Huracán, 1981.
———. *Traffic Violations*. Maplewood, N.J.: Waterfront, 1983.
———. *The Masses Are Asses*. Maplewood, N.J.: Waterfront, 1984.
———. *Illusions of a Revolving Door*. Río Piedras: University of Puerto Rico Press, 1992.
Piñero, Miguel. *Short Eyes*. New York: Hill, 1975.
———. *La Bodega Sold Dreams*. Houston: Arte Público Press, 1980.
———. *The Sun Always Shines for the Cool. Midnight Moon at the Greasy Spoon. Eulogy
   for a Small Time Thief*. Houston: Arte Público Press, 1984.
———. *Outrageous: One Act Plays*. Houston: Arte Público Press, 1986.
Platizky, Roger S. "Human Vision in Miguel Piñero's 'Short Eyes'." In *Americas Review*
   19.1 (1991): 83–91.
Poey, Delia, and Virgil Suárez, eds. *Iguana Dreams: New Latino Fictions*. New York: Harper,
   1992.
Pursifull, Carmen. *Carmen by Moonlight*. Urbana, Ill.: Self-published, 1982.
———. Questionnaire sent by Marc Zimmerman and answered in 1985.
———. *Manhattan Memories*. Barstow, Calif.: Esoterica Press, 1989a.
———. *The Twenty-four Hour Wake*. Urbana, Ill.: Red Herring Press, 1989b.
———. *Elsewhere in a Parallel Universe*. Urbana, Ill.: Red Herring Press, 1992.
———. *The Many Faces of Passion*. Champaign, Ill.: Hawk Productions, 1996.
Quijano, Aníbal. "Colonialidad y modernidad/racionalidad." In *Perú Indígena* 13 no. 29
   (1992): 11–21.
Quintero Herencia, Juan Carlos. "Lost in the Museum of Natural History de Pedro Pietri o la
   mirada imposible: Notes for future referenta." In Duchesne Winter, ed., 2009,1077–94.
Quintero-Rivera, Ángel. *¡Salsa, sabor y control!: sociología de la "música tropical."* D.F.,
   México: Siglo XXI, 1998.
———. *Cuerpo y Cultura: Las músicas y la subersión del baile*. Madrid: Iberoamerican, 2009.
———, ed. *Vírgenes, magos y escapularios: imaginería, etnicidad y religiosidad popular
   en Puerto Rico*. Río Piedras: Centro de Investigaciones Sociales, Universidad de Puerto
   Rico; Santurce: Centro de Investigaciones Académicas, Universidad del Sagrado Corazón;
   San Juan: Fundación Puertorriqueña de las Humanidades, 1998.
Quiñonez, Ernesto. *Bodega Dreams*. New York: Vintage Contemporaries, 2000.
———. *Chango's Fire: A Novel*. New York: Vintage Contemporaries, 2005.
Ramos, Julio. "Migratorias." In *Postdata* (August 1994): 75–79.
Ramos Otero, Manuel. *El libro de la muerte*. Maplewood, N.J./Río Piedras, P.R.: Waterfront
   Press/Editorial Cultural, 1985.
Ramos-Zayas, Ana Y. *National Performances: The Politics of Class, Race, and Space in Puerto
   Rican Chicago*. Chicago: University of Chicago Press, 2003.
Reyes, Israel. *Humor and the Eccentric Text in Puerto Rican Literature*. Gainesville: Uni-
   versity Press of Florida, 2005.

Reyes Rivera, Louis. "Within the Context of a Nuyorican Element: Sandra María Esteves." In *Centro de Estudios Puertorriqueños Bulletin* 2.3 (1988): 50–55.

———. *Scattered Scripture.* New York: Shamal Books, 1996.

———, ed. *Poets in Motion.* New York: Shamal Books, 1976.

———, ed. *Woman Rise.* New York: Shamal Books, 1978.

Rivera, Carmen S. *Kissing the Mango Tree: Puerto Rican Women Rewriting American Literature.* Houston: Arte Público Press, 2002.

Rivera, Edward. *Family Installments: Memories of Growing Up Hispanic.* Hammondsworth, Middlesex, and New York: Penguin Books, 1983.

Rivera, Oswaldo. *Fire and Rain.* New York: Four Windows, Eight Walls, 1990.

Rivera, Raquel Z. *New York Ricans from the Hip Hop Zone.* London: Palgrave MacMillan, 2003.

———, Wayne Marshall, and Deborah Pacini, eds. *Reggaeton.* Durham, N.C.: Duke University Press, 2009.

Rivera, Salima. "The Crazy Women from Plaza Mayo." In *Third Woman* (1982): 25.

Rivera Nieves, Irma, and Carlos Gil, eds. *Polifonía salvaje : ensayos de cultura y política en la Postmodernidad.* San Juan: Editorial Postdata con la colaboración de la Universidad de Puerto Rico. Decanato de Estudios Graduados e Investigación, 1995.

Rivero, Eliana. "Nota sobre las voces femeninas en *Herejes y mitificadores: Muestra de poesía puertorriqueña en los Estados Unidos.*" In *Third Woman* 1.2 (1982): 91–93.

Rodríguez, Abraham, Jr. *The Boy without a Flag.* Milwaukee: Milkweed, 1992.

———. *Spidertown.* New York: Hyperion, 1992.

———. *The Buddha Book.* New York: Picador, 2001.

———. *South by South Bronx.* New York: Akashic Books, 2008.

Rodríguez, Clara. "A Summary of Puerto Rican Migration to the United States." In Romero, Hondagneu-Sotelo, and Ortiz, eds., 1997, 101–13.

Rodríguez, Emma Iris. "Tuley Products." In *The Rican: Journal of Contemporary Puerto Rican Thought.* 1 (May 4, 1974); vol. 2 (October 1, 1974).

Rodríguez, Josefina/Carlos Quiles, *Memorias de Josefina.* Río Piedras, P.R.: Publicaciones Gaviota, 2005.

Rodríguez, Juan Carlos. "Del 'trauma de la literatura' al "relato del trauma': (con)figuraciones de la vergüenza en los relatos sobre la presencia militar norteamericana en Puerto Rico." In Duchesne Winter, ed., 1139–74.

Rodríguez, Leonardo. *They Have to be Puerto Ricans: The Label, the Lie, the Future.* Chicago: Adams Press, 1988.

Rodríguez, Víctor. *Eldorado in East Harlem.* Houston: Arte Público Press, 1992.

Rodríguez de Laguna, Asela, ed. *Images and Identities: The Puerto Rican in a Two World Context.* New Brunswick, N.J.: Transaction Books, 1987.

Rodríguez Juliá, Edgardo. *El entierro de Cortijo: 6 de octubre de 1982.* Río Piedras, P.R.: Editorial Hurucán, 1982.

———. *Una noche con Iris Chacón.* San Juan: Editorial Antillana, 1986.

Rodríguez Muñiz, Michael. "Ejercicios en la Auto-dertminación Boricua: La democracia participativa en el barrio de Humboldt Park." In Bedoya, Belpoliti, and Zimmerman, eds., 2008, 223–42.

Rodríguez Vecchini, Hugo. "Cuando Esmeralda 'era' puertorriqueña: Autobiografía etnográfica y autobiografía neopicaresca." In *Nómada* (April 1995): 145–60.

Romany, Celina. "Neither Here nor There . . . Yet." In *Callaloo* 15 (1992): 103–38.

Romero, Mary, Pierette Hondagneu-Sotelo, and Vilma Ortiz, eds. *Challenging Frontiers: Structuring Latina and Latina Lives in the U.S.* New York: Routledge, 1997.

Rosa, Víctor. "Interview with Víctor Hernández Cruz." In *Bilingual Review/Revista bilingüe* 2.3 (1975): 281–87.

Rosa, William. "Visión humorística del espacio en la poesía de Pedro Pietri." In *Americas Review* 19.1 (1991): 101–10.

Roth, Leonard Q. [pseudonym]. *The Education of H*y*m*a*n K*a*p*l*a*n.* New York: Harcourt, Brace, 1938.

Roy-Fequière, Magali. *Women, Creole Identity and Intellectual Life in Early Twentieth-Century Puerto Rico.* Philadelphia: Temple University Press, 2004.

Rúa, Mérida M., ed. *Latino Urban Ethnography and the Work of Elena Padilla.* Urbana: University of Illinois Press, 2010.

Rubel, Nina. Review of *Carmen by Moonlight.* In *Champaign-Urbana News-Gazette,* October 3, 1982.

Ruíz, Richard. *The Hungry American.* Bend, Ore.: Maverick, 1978.

Ruíz-Cumba, Israel. "Hacia una lectura de *Las memorias de Bernardo Vega.*" In *Inti-Revista de Literatura Hispánica* 31 (1990): 50–66.

San Pedro, Teresa. "La esperpéntica realidad del cuento tradicional en el poema 'Cuento sin hadas' de Luz María Umpierre." In *Americas Review* 19.1 (1991): 92–100.

Sánchez, Reymundo. *My Bloody Life: The Making of a Latin King.* Chicago: Chicago Review Press, 2000.

———. *Once a King, Always a King: The Unmaking of a Latin King.* Chicago: Chicago Review Press, 2004.

Sánchez González, Lisa. *Boricua Literature: A Literary History of the Puerto Rican Diaspora.* New York: New York University Press, 2001.

———. "For the Sake of Love: Luisa Capetillo, Anarchy, and Boricua Literary History." In Torres-Padilla and Rivera, eds., 2008, 52–80.

Sánchez-Korrol, Virginia. *From Colonia to Community. The History of Puerto Ricans in New York City, 1917–1948.* Westport, Conn.: Greenwood Press, 1983.

Sandlin, Betsy A. "Manuel Ramos Otero's Queer Metafictional Resurrection of Julia de Burgos." In Torres-Padilla and Rivera, eds., 2008, 313–31.

Sandoval Sánchez, Alberto. "La identidad especular del alláy el acá: Nuestra propia imagen puertorriqueña en cuestión." In *Centro* 4.2 (1992): 28–43.

———. "*A Chorus Line:* Not Such a 'One Super Sensation' for the Puerto Rican Crossovers." In *Ollantay Theater Magazine* 1.1 (1993): 46–60.

———. "La puesta en escena de la familia immigrante puertorriqueña." *Revista Iberoamericana* 59.162–63 (1993): 345–59.

———. "West Side Story: A Puerto Rican Reading of 'America'." In *Jump Cut* 39 (1994): 59–66.

———. *José, Can You See: Latinos On And Off Broadway.* Madison: University of Wisconsin Press, 1999.

————— and Nancy Saporta Sternbach. *Stages of Life: Transcultural Performance and Identity in U.S. Latina Theater.* Tucson: University of Arizona Press, 2001.

————— and Nancy Saporta Sternbach, eds. *Puro Teatro, A Latina Anthology.* Tucson: University of Arizona Press, 2000.

Santiago-Díaz, Eleurterio e Ilia Rodríguez, "Desde las fronteras raciales de dos casas letradas: habla Piri Thomas." In Duchesne Winter, ed., 2008, 1175–98.

Santiago, Esmeralda. *When I Was Puerto Rican.* Reading, Mass.: Addison-Wesley, 1993.

—————. *América's Dream.* New York: Harper, 1996.

—————. *Almost a Woman.* Reading, Mass.: Perseus Books, 1998.

—————. *The Turkish Lover.* Cambridge, Mass.: Da Capo Press, 2004.

Santiago, Roberto, ed. Boricuas. *Influential Puerto Rican Writings—An Anthology.* New York: Ballatine, 1995.

Scannavini, Anna. *Per una poetica del bilinguismo: Lo spagnolo nella letteratura portoricana in inglese. Studie/ricerche.* Roma: Bulzoni, 1994.

Schmid, Julie M. "A MELUS Interview: David Hernandez, Chicago's Unofficial Poet Laureate." In *MELUS* 25 (2000).

Schomburg, Arturo Alfonso. Schomburg Center Clipping File, 1925–74 [microform]. New York. New York Public Library. [Alexandria, Va.: Chadwyck-Healey, distributor, 1985] 9673 microfiches: ill.; 11X15 cm.

Shorris, Earl. *Latinos: A Biography of the People.* New York: W.W. Norton, 1992.

Sierra Berdecía, Fernando. *Esta noche juega el joker.* 3d ed. San Juan: Biblioteca de Autores Puertorriqueños, 1956.

Silén, Iván. *El pájaro loco.* Río Piedras, P.R.: Ediciones Librería Internacional, 1976.

—————. "The Citizens of a Phantom Country." In *Left Curve* 16 (1992): 45–58.

—————. *Los narcisos negros.* San Juan: Editorial de la Universidad de Puerto Rico, 1997a.

—————. *Los ciudadanos de la morgue.* Brooklyn, N.Y.: La Casa del Hada, 1997b.

—————. *Casandra & Yocasta, o, El libro de Tití.* San Juan: Instituto de Cultura Puertorriqueña, 2001.

—————. *La poesía como libertá.* San Juan: Instituto de Cultura Puertorriqueña, 1992.

—————, ed. *Los paraguas amarillos. Los poetas latinos en Nueva York.* Binghamton, N.Y.: Bilingual Review, 1984.

Silén, Juan Angel. *We, The Puerto Rican People: A Story of Oppression and Resistance.* New York: Monthly Review Press, 1971.

Sjostrom, Barbara R. Review of *Felita*, by Nicholasa Mohr. In *NABE Journal* 5.1 (1980): 113–14.

Sklodowska, Elzbieta. *Testimonio hispanoamericano: historia, teoría, poética.* New York: Peter Lang, 1992.

Sommer, Doris. "Rigoberta's Secrets." In *Latin American Perspectives. Voices of the Voiceless in Testimonial Literature,* part I, issue 70, 18, no. 3 (Summer 1991): 32–50.

Soto, Pedro Juan. *Spiks.* D.F., México: Presentes, 1956.

—————. *Ardiente Suelo, Fría Estación.* D.F., México: Editorial Veracruzana, 1961. Trans. *Hot Land, Cold Season.* New York: Dell, 1973.

—————. *Spiks.* New York: Monthly Review, 1973.

Soto-Crespo, Ramón. *Mainland Passage: The Cultural Anomaly of Puerto Rico*. Minneapolis: University of Minnesota Press, 2010.

Souchet, Clementina. *Clementina: Historia sin fin*. D.F., Mexico: Self-published, 1986.

Stanchich, Maritza. "'Borinkee' in Hawa'i: Rodney Morales Rides the Diaspora Wave in Transregional Imperial Struggle." In Padilla and Rivera, eds., 2008, 201–20.

Stavans, Ilan. *The Hispanic Condition: The Power of a People*. New York: Rayo, 2001.

Tashlic, Phyllis, ed. *Hispanic, Female, and Young*. Houston: Arte Público Press, 1995.

Taylor, Diana. *The Archive and the Repertoire: Performing Cultural Memory in the Americas*. Durham, N.C.: Duke University Press, 2003.

Thomas, Piri. *Down These Mean Streets*. New York: Knopf, 1968.

———. *Savior, Savior, Hold My Hand*. New York: Doubleday, 1972.

———. *Seven Long Times*. New York: Mentor, 1975; 2nd edition, Houston: Arte Público Press, 1994.

———. *Stories from El Barrio*. New York: Knopf, 1978.

Torre, Carlos Antonio, Hugo Rodríguez Vecchini, and William Burgos, eds. *The Commuter Nation: Perspectives on Puerto Rican Migration*. Río Piedras: University of Puerto Rico Press, 1994.

Torrecilla, Arturo. *La ansiedad de ser puertorriqueño. Ethnoespactáculo e hiperviolencia en la modernidad líquida*. San Juan: Ediciones Vértigo, 2004.

Torres, Edwin. *Carlito's Way*. New York: Saturday Review Press and Dutton, 1975; Dial Press, 1976.

———. *After Hours*. New York: Dial Press, 1976.

———. *Q and A*. New York: Dial Press, 1977.

Torres-Padilla, José L., "When 'I' Became Ethnic: Ethnogenesis and Three Early Puerto Rican Diaspora Writers." In Torres-Padilla and Rivera, eds., 2008, 81–104.

——— and Carmen Haydée Rivera. "Introduction: The Literature of the Puerto Rican Diaspora and Its Critical Practice." In Torres-Padilla and Rivera, eds., 2008, 1–28.

——— and Carmen Haydée Rivera, eds. *Writing off the Hyphen. New Perspectives on the Literature of the Puerto Rican Diaspora*. Seattle: University of Washington Press, 2008.

Turner, Faythe. *U.S. Puerto Rican Writers on the Mainland. The Neoricans*. Amherst: University of Massachusetts Press, 1978.

———, ed. *Puerto Rican Writers at Home in the U.S.* Seattle: Open Hand, 1991.

Umpierre, Luz María. "La ansiedad de la influencia en Sandra María Esteves y Marjorie Agosín." In *Revista Chicano-Riqueña* 11.3–4 (1983): 139–47.

———. *Y Otras Desgracias/And Other Misfortunes*. Bloomington, Ind.: Third Woman Press, 1985.

———. "When Sappho Suffers . . . : Marie-José Fortis Talks to Luzma Umpierre." In *Collage and Bricolages* 7 (1993): 55–61.

———. *For Christine: poems and one letter*. Chapel Hill, N.C.: Professional Press, 1995.

Valentín Escobar, Wilson. "'Nothing Connects Us All But Imagined Sounds': Performing Trans-Boricua Memories, Identities and Nationalisms Through the Death of Héctor Lavoe." In Laó-Montes and Dávila, eds., 2001, 207–34.

Vando, Gloria. *Promesas: Geography of the Impossible*. Houston: Arte Público Press, 1993.

———. *Shadows and Supposes*. Houston: Arte Público Press, 2001.

Varela, Frank. *Serpent Underfoot*. Chicago: MARCH/Abrazo Press, 1993.

———. *Bitter Coffee*. Chicago: MARCH/Abrazo Press, 2001.

———. *Caleb's Exile*. San Juan: Elf Creative Workshop, 2009.

Vásquez-Pacheco, Robert. "Brujo Time." In Manrique with Dorris, eds., 1999, 28–34.

Vázquez Paz, Johanny. *Poemas callejeros/Streetwise Poems*. Detroit: Mayapple Press, 2007.

Vega, Bernardo. *Memoirs of Bernardo Vega,* ed. Andreu César Iglesias. New York: Monthly Review, 1984.

Vega, Ed (Edgardo Vega Yunqué). *The Comeback*. Houston: Arte Público Press, 1985.

———. *Mendoza's Dreams*. Houston: Arte Público Press, 1987.

———. *Casualty Reports*. Houston: Arte Público Press, 1991.

———. *No matter how much you promise to cook or pay the rent you blew it cauze Bill Bailey ain't never coming home again*. New York: Farrar, Straus, and Giroux, 2003.

———. *The Lamentable Journey of Omaha Bigelow into the Impenetrable Losaida Jungle*. Woodstock, N.Y.: Overlook Press, 2004.

———. *Blood Fugues: A Novel*. New York: Rayo, 2005.

Vigil-Piñon, Evangelina, ed. *Women of Her Word: Hispanic Women Write*. Houston: Arte Público Press, 1987.

Waldron, John. "Tato Laviera's Parody of *La carreta*: Reworking a Tradition of Docility." In Torres-Padilla and Rivera, eds., 2008, 221–36.

Wallace, David William, ed. *Latin American Writers on Gay and Lesbian Themes: A Bio-Critical Sourcebook*. Westport, Conn.: Greenwood Press, 1994.

Wallenstein, Barry. "The Poet in NY: Víctor Hernández Cruz." In *Bilingual Review/Revista bilingüe* 1.3 (1974): 312–19.

Xavier, Emanuel. *Christ-Like*. New York: Painted Leaf Press, 1999.

———. *Americano*. San Francisco: Suspect Thoughts Press, 2002.

Yúdice, George. "Testimonio and Postmodernism." In *Voices of the Voiceless in Testimonial Literature, I*. Número especial de *Latin American Perspectives* 70, 18, no. 3. (Summer 1991): 15–31. Republished in Gugelberger, ed., 42–57.

Zavala, Iris. *Que nadie muera sin amar*. Madrid: Visor, 1982.

——— and Rafael Rodríguez, eds. *Libertad y crítica en el ensayo político puertorriqueño*. Río Piedras, P.R.: Ediciones Puerto Rico, 1975.

Zavala, Iris, and Rafael Rodríguez, eds. *The Intellectual Roots of Independence: An Anthology of Puerto Rican Political Essays*. New York: Monthly Review, 1980.

Zentella, Ana Celia. "Returned Migration, Language, and Identity: Puerto Rican Bilingual in *Dos Worlds/Two Mundos*." In *International Journal of the Sociology of Language* 84 (1990): 81–100.

Zimmerman, Marc. "A Meaty Slice of Life." Introduction to *Carnicería Rodríguez,* Act I. In *Ecos: A Latino Journal of People's Culture and Literature*. Chicago: University of Illinois Press, 1983, 28–29.

———. "Transplanting Roots and Taking Off: Latino Poetry in Illinois." In John E. Hallwas, ed., *Studies in Illinois Poetry*. Urbana, Ill.: Stormline Press, 1989, 77–116.

———. "Poetas puertorriqueños en Chicago." In Duchesne Winter, ed., 2009, 1003–36. Updated/revised Spanish-language version of "Defending their Own in the Cold: Puerto Rican Poets in Chicago," *Latino Studies Journal* 1, no. 3 (September 1990): 39–58.

———. *U.S. Latino Literature: An Essay and Annotated Bibliography*. Chicago: March/Abrazo, 1992.

Index

Boston, 18, 22, 63
botánica (type of store), 32
Bourgois, Philippe, 79, 86
boxing (boxeo), 5
Braga, Sonia, 11
Brando, Marlon, 8, 9
Brandón, Jorge, 54
Braschi, Giannina, 55, 73; The Empire of
    Dreams, 64; Yo-Yo Boing! 72
Braschi, Wilfredo, 150
brega, the (bregando). See Díaz Quiñones, Ar-
    cadio: El Arte de Bregar
Bricando el charco (film), 78
Bronx, the, 7, 10, 21, 22, 24, 70, 94
Brown Berets, 30
Bruce-Novoa, Juan, 142; Retro-Space, xiv, 6, 51
Buckingham, Jamie: Run, Baby, Run, 67
Buena Vista Social Club (film), 131
Burgos, Julia de, 54, 56, 76, 85, 126
Burgos, William, 151

Caballero, Luis: Puerto Rican Mambo (film),
    xiv, 78
Caballero, Pedro, Paca antillana, 65
Cadilla Martínez, María, 53
Caine Mutiny (film), 9
camouflage, xxii, 28
Campeche, José, 24, 85
Canary Islands, 21
Cañas, Dionisio: El Poeta y la Ciudad, 56
Cancel Miranda, Rafael, 9, 153, 154
Candelario, Sheila, xvi, 145
Cándido Tirado: "First Class," 75
Candy (film), 8
cantante, El (film), 7, 77
Capeman (play), 74, 142, 152
Capetillo, Luisa, xvii, 7, 53, 150; as anarchist,
    74; as feminist, 53 as writer, xvii, 7, 53, 74
capitalism, xx, 23, 30, 42, 79; capitulation
    to commercialism, 28
Capó, Bobby ("Bolero superstar"), 7, 136
"Caravan" (song), 8, 150
Cardenal, Ernesto, 126
Cárdenas, Brenda, 84
Cardona, Ed: Piragua Papa, 76
Caribbean, xxvii, 7, 14, 21, 24, 34–38, 50–58,
    61, 68, 79, 86, 87, 93, 94, 110, 137, 143,
    147, 148, 150; Caribbean-Harlem jazz fu-
sion, 114; identification with, 3; indirecto
    and, 130; literature, 126; performativity
    (Puerto Rican) and, xvi, xx, xxii, xxiii
Caribe Hilton, 114
Carlito's Way (film), 68, 77. See also Torres,
    Edwin
Carlos, Gil, 45, 147
Carnicería Rodríguez (play), 75, 82, 153
Carpentier, Alejo, 37
Carr, Vickie, 8
Carrasquillo, Pedro, 54
Carrero, Jaime: El hombre que no sudaba, 57;
    Jet Neorriqueño: Neo-Rican Jet Liner, 56; Los
    nombres, 57; Neorican, 21, 56, 57; and Rob-
    ert F. Muckley, xxi
Carrillo, Elpidia, 15
Casa de las Américas, 135, 140
Casals, Pablo, 85
Casiano, Américo, 59
Castellano, que bueno baila usted (song), 27
Castillo, Ana: 4, 155; and Sandra Cisneros, 80,
    81, 120, 127; Peel My Love Like an Onion, 4;
    Sapagonia, 4
Castillo Del Morro, El, 27
Castro regime, 130, 135
Casuso, Jorge, xix, 4, 75, 82, 142, 153n4; Car-
    nicería Rodríguez and, 75, 82, 153n4
Catholicism, folk, 32
Centro de Estudios Puertorriqueños (at Hunter
    College), 18, 84, 140, 154; Chicago issue of
    Bulletin of, 84
Certeau, Michel de: The Practice of Everyday
    Life, 3
cha-cha, the, 113, 140
Changing Education Through the Arts (CETA),
    43
Channing-Murray Foundation of the Unitarian-
    Universalist Campus Center, 156n2
Chávez, César, 16, 17
Chavez, Linda, 16, 18, 19, 78, 142
Chayanne (singer), 7, 17
Chicago, xv–xviii, 1–5, 22, 25, 27, 51, 64,
    75–102, 105–12, 115; crossovers and, 1, 4,
    7, 8, 11–17, 19, 146; Hispanic and Latino
    identity and, 4; Latinidad and, 2, 3, 19, 88,
    89, 128; as racist town, 101
Chicago Art Institute. See Art Institute of Chi-
    cago, School of the

Hernández, Rafael, 1, 7, 53
Hernández Cruz, Víctor, 55, 59, 61, 78, 151
Hickman, Trenton, 59, 151, 152
Hijuelos, Oscar, xix, 68, 134, 141, 142
hip-hop, xxiii, 14, 16, 18, 64
Hispanic Arts Association, 43
Hispaniola, 18
Hollywood, 1, 7, 8, 11, 12, 58, 111, 147
Holman, Bob, 152
Homar, Lorenzo, 25, 32
home altars, 32
homeopathicism (homeopathy), 47
Hostos, Eugenio María de, 52
House of Representatives, 153n5
housing, xix, 30, 50, 68, 91
Houston, xv, 19, 150
Huichol Indians, 37
Humboldt Park, 27, 75, 77, 85, 111, 155
Husband, Bertha: on Escobar, 48
Huyke, Juan Bernardo: *Vida escolar*, 65
hybrid identification, 71

Ichaso, León, 77
icons, 9, 22, 24, 28, 34, 39, 48, 49, 62, 153
identity xxii, xxiii, xxvi, 1–3, 5, 19, 21, 22,
   38, 61, 142, 144
Iglesias, Andreu César: *Memorias de Bernardo
   Vega*, 66, 76
I Like It Like That (film), 7, 77
Independendista (political movement), 11, 33,
   46, 57, 62, 63, 83, 84, 88, 130, 131, 136,
   138, 143
informal economy, 18, 53, 77, 149
Inter-American University, 36
Iowa Writers School, 115
Irizarry Rodríguez, José M., 150
isla del encanto, la, and Alice's Anglo wonderland, 108
island-oriented literature: vs. Nuyorican, 50
Italian, xx, 3–6, 11, 21, 69, 70, 113, 136,
   146
Italian-Americans, xx, 11, 113; Afro-Americans
   and, 5, 6, 136, 146
Izrizarry, Richard V. "Ariano," 75

Jackson, Jesse, 82, 117
Jaramillo, Juanita, 155
Jewish perspective, xiii–xv, xvii, xx, xxv, 74;

Jewish American plays on U.S. Puerto Ri-
   cans, 142, 144
jíbaros: *décimas*, 54; life of, 84
Jimenez, Cha Cha, 154
Jiménez, José (Bill Dana), 9
Johns, Jasper, 27, 31, 47
*Journal of the Centro de Estudios Puertorrique-
   ños:* special issue on Chicago, 154
Juárez, Benito, 8
Juliá, Raúl, 10
Jurado, Katy, 8

Kanellos, Nicolás, xviii, 4, 6, 51, 56, 65–70,
   74, 81, 150–53, 155
Keats, John: on negative capability, 98
Kutzinski, Vera, 151

Labarthe, Pedro Juan, 150n3, 150n5; *The Son
   of Two Nations*, 65
La Fountain-Stokes, Larry, 74, 145; *Blue Fingernails*, 152; *Queer Ricans*, 145
Laguerre, Enrique, 53; *El Laberinto*, 57
la India (singer), 17
Laó-Montes, Agustín, xxiii, 2, 142, 146, 150
Latin American, xiii, xix, xxvi, 1–3, 5, 8–10,
   13, 17, 21, 24, 44, 46, 50, 53, 57, 58, 69,
   78, 83, 104, 107, 116, 127, 139, 141, 154;
   identity, 3, 9, 121
Latin Kings (gang), 86, 88, 93
Latino identities, 1, 2, 31, 52, 110, 140; Latini-
   dad (Latinismo, Latinization), xiii, 2, 3, 19,
   88, 89, 128; as Latino and also American,
   116, 117; and mixed national origins, 146
Latino Institute of Chicago, 82
Latino literature, 80, 141, 151
Laviera, Tato, xx, 7, 59–62, 65, 78, 151
Lavoe, Héctor (La Voz), 77, 146, 152
Lazarillo de Tormes, 83
Lebrón, Lolita, 9, 33, 76, 153
Lee Tapia, Consuelo, 54
Left wing resistance, 53
Leguizamo, John, 77; *Mambo Mouth*, 78
Letras de Oro prize, 84
Levins Morales, Aurora, 72, 152; and Rosario
   Morales, xxiv, 62, 83; *Getting Home Alive*,
   62, 83
Lévi-Strauss, Claude, 37, 40
Lewis, Oscar, xv, xx, xxi, 6, 76, 79, 130–34,

Marc Zimmerman is professor emeritus of Latin American and Latino Studies at the University of Illinois and Hispanic Studies at the University of Houston. He is the author of *U.S. Latino Literature: An Essay and Annotated Biography* and has edited books and CDs on Chicago Mexican history and art.

Latinos in Chicago and the Midwest

The University of Illinois Press
is a founding member of the
Association of University Presses.
••

University of Illinois Press
1325 South Oak Street
Champaign, IL 61820-6903
www.press.uillinois.edu